STRANGERS IN THE BRONX

DiMaggio, Mantle, and the Changing of the Yankee Guard

Andrew O'Toole

TRIUMPH
BOOKS

This book is available in quantity at special discounts for your group or organization. For further information, contact:

Triumph Books LLC
814 North Franklin Street
Chicago, Illinois 60610
(312) 337–0747
www.triumphbooks.com

Printed in U.S.A.

ISBN: 978–1-62937-027-9

Design by Amy Carter

Photos courtesy of AP Images except where otherwise noted.

For Holly,
with love

CONTENTS

FOREWORD

MY FAVORITE STORY FROM 1951 INVOLVES THE "BOBBY THOMSON" game and one Yogi Berra.

The '51 season featured a terrific American League pennant race, and a similarly terrific one in the National League, where those other two New York teams—the Brooklyn Dodgers and New York Giants—needed a three-game playoff to decide a champion.

A number of New York Yankees players went to the third game at the Polo Grounds. Among them was Mr. "It ain't over til it's over" himself, Lawrence Peter Berra.

But it turned out that Yogi left the game early to beat traffic and missed the "Shot Heard 'round the World," the Thomson homer. Oh boy.

He didn't follow his own advice. It was one of the few times he got anything wrong.

Sometimes the baseball gods are especially good to us.

To show approval of the line of continuation that is part of the game we love, they will, from time to time, give us one immortal coming and one immortal going as teammates. So we see Ted Williams, circa 1939, in the same Fenway Park dugout with Lefty Grove. Tom Seaver with Roger Clemens in 1986. Phil Niekro as a Milwaukee teammate with Warren Spahn in 1964. Reggie Jackson with Mark McGwire in Oakland in '87. Or the Yankees' Don Mattingly and Derek Jeter passing in the night, in 1995.

Joe DiMaggio was a teammate of Lou Gehrig in his final seasons, and then Mickey Mantle was there in Joe's farewell season of 1951.

And that brings us to the events captured by Andrew O'Toole in this book. Because not only were Joe and Mickey "touching," as in Michelangelo's fresco of the creation of Adam, but baseball fans had a sense of what they were witnessing. This wasn't a random event. People knew that Mantle was something special, and they also knew that the magic that was Joe DiMaggio was fading. They just didn't know for sure that Joe was playing his last year of ball (his term for baseball.)

Mick was the proverbial "highly touted rookie," but the cliché barely does him justice. He wasn't on the roster when he went to Casey Stengel's instructional school and then spring training in 1951. He hadn't played Triple-A ball, and he was still a teenager. Yes, his was a name to "file away" for future reference.

But Casey saw it differently. He saw a raw talent, still without a position, who had such natural gifts that the temptation was there to give the kid a shot—right then. The Yankees were overloaded with outfield talent, but so what?

Casey got this one right.

Fans also knew that they were seeing them both at a very special time in Yankee history, as the team advanced to a third consecutive world championship. Casey may have arrived with the reputation of being a clown, but by 1951 that was all in the past. The winner of two straight titles was already a "genius" so far as baseball was concerned, and a master of maneuvering his players so that he seemed to be playing with a 35-man roster while everyone else had 25.

The Yankees were so loaded at this point in their history that by the end of the decade, almost every team in the league had a first-string catcher who came from the Yankee organization, and plenty of other players as well. There are a lot of "peaks" in Yankee history, years of such amazing dominance that many run together as one. But 1951, largely due to the crossing of Joe and Mickey, occupies a special standing among Yankee seasons.

Don't leave early on this story. There are plenty of twists and turns en route to glory.

Yogi would be well advised to read it all.

—Marty Appel

PREFACE
TO BE YOUNG AND A YANKEE

"TRUST THE ART, NOT THE ARTIST."

I first heard those words uttered years ago by a musician I admire a great deal. The sentiment struck me at the time and the refrain has replayed in my mind on many occasions since.

"Art" and "artist" may not necessarily translate to the world of sports, but public fascination with celebrity most certainly does.

As a child, one particular athlete captured my imagination. Indeed, the love an eight-year-old boy has for his favorite baseball player is a special relationship. In my case, my adoration was directed at a free-swinging, perpetually smiling Panamanian catcher: Manny Sanguillen. I took on Sangy's personality when playing sandlot ball, his mannerisms, his batting stance, as well as Manny's philosophy at the plate, which meant I swung at everything. A notorious bad-ball hitter, when asked why he swung at so many pitches out of the strike zone, Sangy replied, "Because it feels good!" Such an attitude frustrated my Little League coaches but did much to enhance my enjoyment of the game.

And then, on November 5, 1976, my hometown Pittsburgh Pirates traded Manny and cash to the Oakland A's for Chuck Tanner—*a manager!*

I was 10 years old, and upon learning that Sangy was no longer a Pirate, my innocence was forever lost. Nearly 20 years later I had the good fortune of meeting Sanguillen while working on my first book. The two of us sat behind the third-base dugout inside a virtually empty Pilot Field in Buffalo. Sangy put his arm around the back of my seat and graciously answered my questions. For the better part of an hour he was engaging and ebullient. I walked away from the interview gratified that my baseball idol did not disappoint.

Through the years I've done extensive study on sports history, and I have come to learn that not all idols were quite as affable as Sanguillen

I don't remember exactly how old I was the first time I read my brother's battered copy of *Ball Four*. But I was young, and I recall being enraptured with Jim Bouton's journal of the 1969 Seattle Pilots season. At the time of publication, *Ball Four* famously shocked the reading public with behind-the-scenes escapades and sundry stories of Bouton's current and past teammates. It was the tales which involved Bouton's former Yankee teammate Mickey Mantle that garnered the most attention. Bouton portrayed a Mantle whose nocturnal escapades flew in the face of his All-American image, as well as a baseball hero who occasionally displayed boorish behavior toward his fans.

Ball Four did not sour me on the game or the men who gloriously displayed their skills on the playing field. In fact, I came to appreciate the game even more. Bouton simply revealed a truth that needed to be explored; outside of their athletic ability, our sporting heroes are, in fact, not different than us. They endure the same struggles with mortality and suffer from the same bouts of insecurity as the fans cheering in the stands. Indeed, the sole trait that differentiates them from the rest of us is the ability to hum that pea across the plate or knock the piss out of a big league curveball. This reality helped me enjoy baseball all that much more.

Joe DiMaggio—It is one of the most mythic names, not only in the annals of baseball, but also in pop culture. Perhaps more than any other figure in sports history, DiMaggio isn't revered so much for what he accomplished on the field of play. Rather, we relish the *idea* of Joe DiMaggio. Reality can sometimes clash with our ideals. In the instance of DiMaggio, the imperfections of a prickly personality are obscured by the magnificence displayed on the emerald green fascinations of time and memory.

Mickey Mantle—He was the exemplar of what so many believed a ballplayer should look like: the golden hair, the Adonis physique, and talent bursting from his every pore. It's fair to say that no single player has ever been idolized and loved by his fans in quite the fashion Mantle enjoyed and endured. Certainly he had his detractors during his career, but those countless young boys who pledged their allegiance to the Mick in the 1950s and '60s remained unflinchingly loyal to their hero. Through the good and the bad, Mantle was their guy. He was the standard by which they measured all other athletes. And, long after the days of their youth had faded, they wept when Mickey passed away.

Mantle and DiMaggio were iconic figures who transcended their sport, and each found a place in American pop culture. While DiMaggio was admired, and to some extent, exalted,

Mantle was beloved. He was loved by his legions of fans despite his fatal flaws.

The 1951 New York Yankees...this book is a thumbnail sketch, a glimpse at a long-gone era; a time when four-man pitching rotations were the rule, St. Louis was baseball's western outpost, when each league consisted of eight teams, two-hour games were the norm, and, despite Jackie Robinson's arrival on the scene four years earlier, more than half of Major League Baseball teams remained lily-white, including the franchise at the center of this story.

This book recounts the waning days of an American hero and the birth of the next legend.

Inside these pages is the culmination of an idea I had years before putting word to paper. The 1951 New York Yankees— for that one year the paths of two great baseball icons converged. The nascence of Mickey Mantle's career poignantly coincided with Joe DiMaggio's struggle to reconcile that the Great DiMaggio was no more. This is the story of two men ill-equipped, emotionally and psychologically, to meet the fame and idolatry that came their way.

Baseball can be a cruel game, as I learned when Manny Sanguillen was dispatched across the country for a manager. But the game can also stir the soul. Close your eyes for a moment and there it is, a snapshot in time, memories etched in our consciousness: the elegant swing and graceful gait of DiMaggio, the boundless promise of a 19-year-old Mickey Mantle. For a moment we are all young again and the world is at our feet.

PROLOGUE
WE WANT YOU ON OUR SIDE

THESE DAYS IT WAS GETTING HARDER TO BE JOE DIMAGGIO... NOT that it was ever easy.

He was 36, and an old 36 at that. Since he had come back from the war in '46, Joe had been hampered by a bum left heel; for the remainder of the decade and the dawn of the next, the nagging injuries mounted. Here now, on an early February morning in the winter of 1951, Joe had finally come to a decision. He had spent much of the off-season loafing with his family in San Francisco, playing a few rounds, and procrastinating more than a little.

The Yankees had mailed Joe a contract for the coming season a few weeks back. The figure was the same as last year, $100,000. One hundred grand was the magic number and a couple of years earlier, Joe had been the first to reach the threshold. While he wanted the distinction of being at the top of baseball's pay scale, money wasn't the sole issue at the moment. In truth, Joe's vacillation was rooted in desire. He wasn't certain that he even wanted to play any longer. Sure, his body felt pretty good at the moment; then again it had been almost four months since he'd been on the field as his Yanks swept the Whiz Kids from Philadelphia in the '50 Series. The ensuing months had given his old bones some time to heal. Still the aches were sure to re-surface if he returned for another season. More than the money, and more than the pain that was certain to follow, was the lin-gering question: Would he still resemble Joe DiMaggio on the playing field?

Joe was a perfectionist. He was also vain.

By nearly every measure DiMaggio was considered the most popular athlete of the day, and the epochal summer a decade ear-lier had been the pinnacle of his brilliant career. That last sum-mer before the war came to America, those were the months of Joe's streak—56 consecutive games! The country watched, listened, and read, anxiously awaiting news: *Did Joe get a hit?*

The streak would become a part of baseball lore, but a closer examination of the numbers reveals just how spectacular Joe's season was. His batting average, an impressive .357, was aug-mented with 30 home runs and 125 runs batted in. But perhaps even more impressive, Joe struck out a mere 13 times. On the playing field, DiMaggio strived for perfection and at the apex of his sterling career, Joe nearly achieved his goal.

Even to the untrained eye, DiMaggio stood out on a baseball diamond. He possessed a hard to define quality, a regal elegance that magically drew attention his way; Joe simply carried him-self in a different manner. His play on the field certainly aided the magnetic aura, for DiMaggio was among the finest to ever play the game. At bat or effortlessly patrolling center field, Joe performed with a stylish grace. His fluid swing connecting for a home run, the loping gait carrying him from first to third, the innate ability to track down every ball hit his way. *Did Joe ever make a mistake on the field?* This is the DiMaggio the nation revered. His public image had been cultivated by a chorus of sportswriters who prized a night of DiMaggio's companionship at Toots Shor's or the 21 Club.

In truth, Joe was self-conscious away from the baseball diamond. He lacked eloquence; indeed, DiMaggio was a man with remarkably little to say. When interviewed, his responses were void of insight and thoughtfulness.

Still, in the melancholy residue of a remarkable career, the fame remained. His distinct features regularly greeted readers of daily newspapers and national magazines. The name "DiMaggio" still commanded headlines. If anything, Joe's celebrity was bigger than ever, rivaling any glossy Hollywood star or self-inflated politician.

A small cadre of New York sportswriters gathered in the office of Yankee general manager George Weiss. Red Patterson, the team's public relations director, had called the impromptu press conference to announce that Joe DiMaggio and the Yankees had come to a contractual agreement for the coming season. The terms of the deal were left unsaid, but the numbers were anything but a secret. One of Joe's biggest boosters was Yankee co-owner Dan Topping. All through the winter, Topping had repeatedly reminded Joe that he was welcome back to the club for the same $100,000 contract they'd agreed upon for the previous two seasons. DiMaggio's response in December was the same as January, a polite, "I'll think about it."

Two days after Christmas, Dan Topping phoned DiMaggio, who had just arrived home from a tour of the Far East. He was a bit tired following a trying season, a World Series, and then an exhibition excursion to Japan. Joe was certainly feeling his age like he never had before. The purpose of Topping's call wasn't to press Joe on a new contract. The sole reason for Topping's call was to tell DiMaggio, "Hello," and to wish him a "Happy New Year." This was the type of consideration that Joe appreciated, and it reinforced why he admired Topping.

On several occasions in the past, Joe had tested the allegiance of Yankee fans by insisting that he be paid more money than the Yankees were offering. Prior to the 1938 season, for instance, Joe held out for a handsome raise, a demand that enraged a large portion of the Yankee fan base. Even after Joe and the Yankees came to a mutually accepted contract, fans couldn't forgive and forget. For example, throughout the '38 season DiMaggio heard from spectators in the Stadium stands who rode him hard over his contractual demands. All he wanted, Joe insisted, was "what's fair." Whether the paying customer agreed with his worth mattered not at all to DiMaggio. He knew that he gave his employers a full effort every game. DiMaggio approached every game in the same manner—after all, the spectators deserved their money's worth, so did the men signing his paycheck, not to mention his teammates. Every game was played as if it may be his last. Perhaps, Joe thought, someone in the stands would only see him play this one time. His self-imposed standard of excellence would not allow him to give anything less than an all-out effort.

Now, in February 1951, with spring training fast approaching, Yankee brass was growing anxious for a decision. It was just in the last couple of days that DiMaggio, Weiss, and Topping had spoken on the phone. Given DiMaggio's relationship with Topping, the monetary details were easy to iron out. The difficult task lie in getting Joe to commit to one more season.

In actuality, Joe was ready. The end was near, certainly, but he was not yet prepared to walk away from the game that had given him fame, riches, and clarity.

With the formal announcement made, Patterson grabbed a phone and patched a call through to DiMaggio in San Francisco, where Joe was staying with his mother, Rosalie, who had been ill since the holidays. Moments earlier, Patterson explained to the writers the ground rules for the interview...there would be no exclusive with Joe. One pool reporter would be chosen to conduct the interview and be the spokesman for the group. That responsibility fell to Milton Gross of the *New York Post*.

Patterson handed the receiver to Gross as the operator announced that "San Francisco is ready with Joe DiMaggio."

"Joe, this is Milton Gross. Congratulations!"

"Why congratulations?" DiMaggio asked. "This isn't my first contract I've signed with the Yankees, even though it's the first time everything's been done by mail."

"Maybe this year won't be like the other years, Joe." Gross replied. "When the news got around that you signed for $100,000 again it wasn't like other years."

Gross then explained that his editor wanted to know how far Joe could go.

"Don't you believe in me?" DiMaggio asked, facetiously. "I've had a good winter. I'm up to 200 pounds. Usually I'm about 193 or 195. Nothing's bothering me now. The pain in my left knee is gone."

"What about your bum left heel?" asked Gross

"The heel? I've forgotten about it. I'm not thinking about it in terms of this one season or two or three. I'm going as far as my body will carry. Right now it feels no worse, maybe better than other years."

After a brief pause, DiMaggio continued. "They've been saying I'm through for the last few years...I know when to quit. Nobody'll have to remind me, I won't be *a drag on the club*."

The last sentence hung in the air; words that Gross would never have imagined being uttered by DiMaggio—*a drag on the club*.

The men who inhabited Yankee Stadium's press box weren't above hero worship. And the club's beat writers occasionally wrestled with objectivity when it came to Joe D. Sitting in the office of George Weiss, Milton Gross wasn't the only reporter in the room who admired DiMaggio. Gross had been covering the Yankees since '38, and Milton had seen plenty of Joe through the years, his prose extolling DiMaggio's exploits in the pages of the *Post*. The previous few years, however, Gross and his colleagues were witnessing a transformation in Joe. The inherently taciturn DiMaggio drew further inward as his physical abilities diminished. Following a hitless day at the plate, a much more frequent occurrence in recent seasons, DiMaggio sat silently in his locker stall, not allowing anyone, not a member of the press or even a teammate, to penetrate his hardened shell. The unbecoming behavior tarnished the carefully crafted image that Joe's friends had polished for years.

"Are you pleased with the terms of the agreement, Joe?" Gross asked.

"They wouldn't have given me that kind of contract if they hadn't been happy about it, so I'm happy too. I'll play for the Yankees as long as Stengel wants me and as long as this body holds out."

How long Joe's aging body could withstand the physical toll of a strenuous baseball season was a question on the mind of every working reporter gathered in Weiss' office. Gross then asked the natural follow up.

"How many games do you expect to play in 1951, Joe?"

"Just say I might play from five to 155 games next season." DiMaggio replied, allowing for the possibility of a one game playoff. "I intend [on] playing with the Yankees as long as I can."

———

TEN YEARS HAD PASSED.

It seemed like yesterday. It felt like a lifetime ago. The streak played out on fields of green under the warmth of the sun, when the widening conflict in Europe and the turmoil in the Pacific was on everyone's mind, when it seemed inevitable that the United States would be dragged into the hostilities. Still, for a few weeks that summer, those last months before the war touched American shores, Joe helped take the country's mind off the ominous dark cloud hovering.

During the streak, when the name "Joe DiMaggio" was on the lips and the minds of so many, some fella wrote a song about him. Les Brown and his Band of Renown played the tune that was put to the words of Alan Courtney.

"He's started baseball's famous streak
That's got us all aglow.
He's just a man and not a freak,
Joltin' Joe DiMaggio.
Joe, Joe DiMaggio
We want you on our side"

It was a helluva thing, trying to live up to the reputation of a legend. And now, at the age of 36, Joe DiMaggio had signed up for one more year of chasing immortality.

1   YOU CAN LOOK IT UP

IT WAS A DAY BUILT MORE FOR FOOTBALL THAN BASEBALL.

October 12, 1948. The weather in New York City was cloudy and rainy, but thankfully this event was held indoors at the 21 Club. The World Series had just concluded one day earlier, as the Cleveland Indians won the championship in six games over the Boston Braves.

Dan Topping, the co-owner of the New York Yankees, stepped before a phalanx of microphones, photographers, and cameras conveying the events to television viewers. Topping was there to welcome the new manager of the Yankees, one Charles Dillon Stengel, or as he was better known, Casey.

It was a mismatch for certain. What had Stengel ever done as a manager other than finish in the second division?

For those questioning the choice, Stengel didn't help matters when he rose from his seat to address the media in the room.

"I would like to thank Mr. Bob Topping for this opportunity." Stengel began.

"Cut!" the television people called out. Stengel needed to

start anew. "Bob" Topping wasn't the Yankee owner, but rather he was Dan's brother, who was then embroiled in highly publicized marital strife.

Nonplussed, Casey began anew. "This is a big job, fellows, and I barely have had time to study it. In fact, I scarcely know where I am."

Stengel then steered the discussion toward the Yankees. After a few generalizations about the state of the club, Casey said, "There'll likely be some changes, but it's a good club and I think we'll do all right. We'll go slow because you can wear a club down a lot quicker than you can build it up."

He chased the game wherever it was played and wherever they would pay him to participate. He played in nearly every port of call. Casey Stengel wore the uniform of the Brooklyn Dodgers, Pittsburgh Pirates, Philadelphia Phillies, New York Giants, and Boston Braves, and that was just the major leagues. Stengel also had stops in Kansas City, Kankakee, Shelbyville, and Montgomery in the bushes.

In fact, it was 25 years to the day that Stengel hit a home run in Yankee Stadium. His was the only run scored in the third game of the World Series which pitted Casey's Giants against Miller Huggins and the New York Yankees.

And then once he couldn't cut it on the field any longer following the 1925 season, Casey started calling the shots from the bench.

To assure the public, and more importantly the press, that the Yankees were in lockstep, Joe DiMaggio was placed on display right alongside his new manager. New York had finished in third place in the season that had just concluded, two-and-a-half games behind the Cleveland Indians. The 34-year-old DiMaggio had begun to exhibit the wear of age that season.

Never one to enjoy the give and take with the press, DiMaggio was present only out of friendship to Dan Topping. Joe's attendance was called upon to comfort those who may question the questionable decision to hire Casey Stengel.

Do you have any plans to manage the club, Joe?

"You know me, boys," DiMaggio answered. "I'm just a ballplayer with one ambition, and that is to give all I've got to help my ball club win. I've never played any other way."

Despite Joe's presence, Stengel was the focus of press attention.

He was comical, irreverent, and because he knew the moment demanded it, solemn.

"I didn't get this job through friendship," Stengel told the gathered press in a firm and even voice. "The Yankees represent an investment of millions of dollars. They don't hand out jobs because they like your company. I got the job because the people here think I can produce for them."

———

THE NEW YORK YANKEES HAD PREVIOUSLY SET UP CAMP IN A variety of locales. From Asbury Park and Atlantic City, to the more exotic settings of Bermuda, Cuba, Puerto Rico, Panama, and Venezuela, the Yankees had ventured to numerous Western Hemisphere outposts, but never the western states. Throughout the 1920s, the years of Babe Ruth's great reign, various promoters made lucrative invitations for the Yankees to train in California. Bringing the Babe out West was a surefire way to break the banks and fill the coffers. However, every entreaty was rejected out of hand by the team's owner, Jacob Ruppert. In fact, the Yankees had never trained west of the Mississippi, a tradition that was finally going by the wayside when the team set up their 1951 camp in Phoenix, Arizona.

Why Phoenix? Simple, Phoenix was the hometown of Yankee co-owner Del Webb, as well as the headquarters for his construction company. Webb envisioned a mass exodus of Northeasterners, tired of snow and congested cities; of Midwesterners exhausted by their never ending winter season, staking a claim of their own in the perpetually blissful climate of Phoenix, Arizona. And in this dream, the Del E. Webb Construction Company would help build the three new communities that would house these westward bound migrants. The New York Yankees would train under blue skies, when back in Gotham, New Yorkers read about their hometown heroes' spring exploits in sunny Arizona while mired in the residue of yet another endless winter. The publicity emanating from the idyllic clime of Phoenix would surely draw some new settlers to the land of sun and shine. Besides, Webb really liked the prospect of showing off his world champion Yankees in front of his well-heeled friends.

During the winter of '49, Webb approached Horace Stoneham, the owner of the New York Giants, with the proposal of swapping training spots for one spring. The Yankees had signed a 10-year contract to train in St. Petersburg, Florida, a pact that had seven years remaining. There was a contingency in the agreement that allowed the club to train elsewhere for three of these 10 years, so long as these expeditions did not come in consecutive seasons. The Yankees had their escape clause, and so too, did the Giants. Stoneham took Webb up on the offer and for the spring of 1951 the two clubs, whose home ballparks were separated by the Harlem River, agreed to swap training sites.

———

ALONG WITH HIS PARTNERS, DAN TOPPING AND LARRY MACPHAIL, Del Webb purchased the Yankees in January of 1945. The announcement of the $2.8 million acquisition was made at the 21 Club on West Fifty-Second Street before a bevy of reporters and photographers. Topping, a captain in the United States Marines, was not present because he was then stationed in the Pacific. For the headline-making sum, the trio bought not only the Yankee ball club, but also the team's extensive farm system, the ballparks that housed their Newark and Kansas City minor league teams, and also Yankee Stadium.

The agreement between the three men stipulated that MacPhail would have complete control and full say over all baseball matters. Under the terms of their contract, MacPhail was given this control for 10 years.

The 52-year-old Webb had long possessed a passion for the game. He also, in his younger days, enjoyed the ability to play baseball at a high level, though his playing days ended abruptly when he tore a knee ligament as he was sliding into home. This unfortunate injury in fact turned into a blessing of sorts as Webb set aside his athletic ambitions and instead focused on building a business empire. Not that it came easy. Throughout his abbreviated baseball career, Webb also worked as a carpenter. The tall, lean Webb took his penchant for carpentry one step further and formed The Del E. Webb Construction Company in 1928. The company grew rapidly into one of the largest contractors in the Southwest.

"He came to Phoenix without a dime," Webb's close friend Arthur Nehf said, "and parlayed a saw and a hammer into a million dollars."

During the war, Webb's company received numerous military contracts, including the construction of a Japanese/American internment camp in Poston, Arizona. The war was a boon for Del Webb Construction, but the post-war years were equally rewarding. In '46, Webb was contracted to build Las Vegas' first luxury casino, The Flamingo. One of his partners in this venture was the notorious and suave gangster Bugsy Siegel. Siegel's death at the hands of a mobster hit man proved advantageous for Webb. At the time he was taken out, Bugsy owed Webb a substantial amount of money. As payment for Siegel's debt, Webb was given part ownership in The Flamingo. His partners in the venture included a couple of characters known to comfortably walk on the dark side of the street: Gus Greenbaum and Meyer Lansky.

Beyond Siegel and his ilk, Webb enjoyed close relationships with a number of high-profile characters. He had befriended Howard Hughes, and often hit the links with his pals Bing Crosby and Bob Hope. Webb's close relationship with Crosby actually led to the speculation that the world-renowned crooner was a partner in the Yankee venture. Bing didn't invest in the purchase of the Yankees, but he would become a partner in the conglomerate that bought the Pittsburgh Pirates in 1946.

The bespectacled, soft-spoken Webb was too preoccupied with his business interests to spend much time with his newly purchased ball club. In the late '40s, his company began building large housing communities in Arizona. When he did visit New York, Webb liked to promote these quickly sprouting hamlets by distributing copies of *Arizona Highways* to the press covering the team. The visually intoxicating magazine was created to lure new comers to the Southwest. Now, with the Yankees in Phoenix for the first time, Webb had them in his own Garden of Eden in person; his world champions playing before his friends and associates.

2   PLAY BALL WITH THE YANKEES

YANKEE GENERAL MANAGER GEORGE WEISS AND THE TEAM'S scouting staff put together a list of 28 bonus babies and minor league prospects who would be invited to attend the club's training school.

This would be the team's second attempt at running such a clinic. One year earlier the Yankees sent 50 minor league prospects to Phoenix, the organization's initial foray out West.

"Our first coaching school last year was interrupted by Commissioner Chandler's order that Yankee players could not have worked out until March 1," Weiss explained to Dan Daniel of the *New York World Telegram*.

This initial foray was sniffed out by a nosy Branch Rickey, who brought the camp to the attention of Commissioner Happy Chandler. Rickey, in his first year as general manager of the Pittsburgh Pirates, alerted Chandler that the Yankees, Cubs, and Giants were "cutting corners." A request was made by Rickey that the Commissioner issue a clarification of the March 1 spring training parameter. Chandler acquiesced to the request.

"Spring training will officially start on March 1, 1950," the Commissioner stated in a press release. "No player shall be required to report for training until that date, nor shall players don uniforms or engage in practice with a bat, ball, or glove, at a club's spring training headquarters until March 1."

Though the Yankees believed they were well within the guidelines of Chandler's edict, the team sent home the nine players invited to Phoenix as "instructors."

"We are making no admission of guilt," Yankees press secretary Red Patterson told reporters. "We still maintain that we have interpreted the spring training rule correctly and that in assigning nine players we did not violate the March 1 rule."

The club insisted, "It was strictly a schooling, and not a training, session."

To aide Stengel and his coaching staff with the tutoring, the nine "instructors" also traveled to Arizona. Among the nine were infielders Fenton Mole and Billy Martin; outfielders Cliff Mapes, Hank Bauer, and Jackie Jensen; as well as pitchers Hugh Radcliffe, Dick Carr, Don Johnson, and Duane Pillette.

Despite the commissioner's curtailing of the organization's original plans, Weiss called the first training school an "unqualified success."

"Quite a few of the boys learned so much in the coaching school that we were able to jump them a classification, and bring them a year closer to the Stadium," Weiss continued.

The Yanks general manager was looking forward to the "second class" of the organization's training school.

"Among the farm boys will be such standouts as Mickey Mantle, from Joplin, who may be converted from a shortstop into an outfielder," Weiss explained, "Gil McDougald, second baseman from Beaumont, and a couple of college heroes, Bill Skowron and Kal Segrist."

Each member of the Yankee farm system was given a pamphlet produced by the club, the purpose of which was to welcome and introduce them to the organization. "Play Ball with the Yankees" explained in detail what these prospects could expect now that they were a part of the Yankee family, and the booklet also made sure to remind these youngsters that the organization was held to, and lived up to, a higher standard than the rest of major league baseball.

> "Joining the Yankee organization means you become a member of baseball's most progressive ensemble. You will be placed under 'teaching managers' on your way up to the majors. You will be watched, too, by a corps of highly efficient scouts who have brought to the big leagues some of the greatest stars of the game. And, as a Yankee you will, in the parlance of the dugout, 'go first class.' The Yankees patronize the country's leading hotels. While on the road, see to it that their players are offered the best in Pullman accommodations, food, and medical care at all times. The player's locker, lounge, and training rooms at the Yankee Stadium are unquestionably the finest in the country."

———

THE ROOKIE PROSPECTS WHO REACHED ARIZONA ON FEBRUARY 13 were greeted by an unusually cool, cloudy day. Phoenix mayor Nick Udall headed a party on hand to deliver a "Western" welcome to the core group of prospects when they arrived at 11:55 Wednesday morning. As he had done a year before, Casey Stengel asked several Yankee players to assist at the school as "instructors." Billy Martin, Jackie Jensen, and Gene Woodling, among others, would be helping the team's coaching staff teach the prospects the game's finer points. The rules which forbade major leaguers from coming to camp before March 1 hadn't been altered since Rickey challenged the legality of the "schools." To circumvent the rule, Stengel designated these young Yankees as "instructors."

The first member of the Yankee party to reach Phoenix on the 11th was Pete Previte, the team's assistant clubhouse man. Previte began preparing the dressing room and organizing the many trunks of equipment prior to the arrival of the school attendees. Four days later, Stengel flew in from San Francisco along with Del Webb.

Before 24 hours had passed, the loquacious Stengel was giving the local press an update on the coming prospect school.

"We'll have all our boys here today, and we might as well start tomorrow at the beginning," Casey explained. "If we had held our regular meetings today, we would have to go over it again tomorrow, so we'll just use today as a preliminary. That way, we'll get started all together.

"They tell me the experts already have made the Red Sox the pennant favorite and that the Yankees are picked to finish somewhere around Scranton," Stengel added with a chuckle.

There was nothing Ole Case liked more than being

underestimated. He was certain to surprise a few of these base-ball authorities.

The minor leaguers enjoyed the hospitality of mayor Udall, but once the pleasantries were over, the kids were put to work with little break from the well-choreographed daily regimen.

The daily drills began at 10:00 AM and were open to the public for no admission fee. Following a brief break at noon for sandwiches, the workouts continued through the afternoon. The "school" was a regimented day. Instruction was given on every phase of the game. Bill Dickey worked with the catchers, Neun with the first basemen, Frank Crosetti the infielders, and Jim Turner coached the pitchers. "Iron Mike," a mechanical pitching machine, handled most of the batting-practice duties. A series of four night classes were scheduled, during which the Yankee prospects would be tutored through film study and "skull" sessions with the coaches.

The temperature was a biting 48 degrees when they took the field for the first intra-squad game. One of the pitchers selected for the initial scrimmage was $40,000 bonus boy, Jackie Jensen. Just a couple of months earlier, Stengel shared the frustration he endured concerning this talented Californian.

"This Jensen kid is one of my biggest problems," Stengel said over the winter. "He lacks polish in the field, and I don't believe he ever will learn to hit the right-handed curveball. Maybe he would do better as a pitcher. We'll see at Phoenix."

A two-sport All-American at the University of California, Jensen made his Yankee debut the previous spring, appearing in 23 games in the outfield and another 22 as a pinch runner or hitter. In college, however, Jensen was also an effective pitcher. His arm played a significant part in the Bears' victory in 1947's inaugural College World Series. For a time the consensus in the press was that Jensen would replace DiMaggio in center when Joe hung them up. This belief was encouraged by both Stengel and Weiss. With a new season, however, came a new approach. Casey now was leaning toward Jensen taking to the mound full time. Jackie did not impress in his first outing of the season, however, tossing only a few curves and not putting full effort into his fastball.

"Jensen did some impressive pitching in winter league ball in California," Stengel said, "and I expected him to come here and to move right into the mound squad. However, he has done no such thing. I have said nothing to him and he has said nothing to me.

"If I had Jensen's curve and his overhand and underhand slider, I know what I would be doing right now. I'd be registered with Professor James Turner [the Yankees pitching coach] for his famous course on mound dynamics.

"Jackie seems to overlook that we are paying some of our pitchers pretty good salaries and that most often the path to success in the major leagues follows the line of least resistance.

"Jensen can run. He has a great arm. He learns fast. He might make it in left field. In right he is not at home. But while he is making the fight, I might run into a better looking outfield prospect, and then where will Jackie be? I dunno."

Following Casey's discourse, Dan Daniel then went to the Yankee dressing room for a comment from Jensen. The veteran reporter repeated to Jensen what his manager had said.

After listening to an echo of Stengel's lengthy monologue, Jensen replied, "I want to be an outfielder."

Three of Stengel's boys had yet to arrive in Arizona. One

of the absent boys was 19-year-old Mickey Charles Mantle. Mantle, Stengel had been assured, was en route.

In mid-January, a letter postmarked New York, New York, was delivered to Mickey Mantle's Commerce, Oklahoma, home. Inside the envelope was a note from Yankee farm director Lee MacPhail instructing Mantle to report to Phoenix in mid-February for a two-week training school. Over the ensuing four weeks, Mantle pulled out the letter, lightly fingered the pale-white paper, and gazed at the New York Yankee letterhead. Mickey had re-read the short message so many times that he surely could have recited the contents backward if need be. One issue absent from the letter, however, was a ticket to transport Mantle to Arizona, or information concerning expense money.

So Mickey just folded the letter and placed it back inside the envelope...and waited.

Mantle, in fact, attended the 1950 school. At the time, Mantle had only one year of professional experience, with Independence in the K-O-M League, where he hit .313. The '50 school was held several weeks earlier, in late January, and concluded on February 12. On the first morning of the camp, Mantle and fellow prospect Cal Neeman missed the team bus to the ballpark. Neeman and Mantle stood on the sidewalk outside the club's hotel, not sure what to do, when a taxi pulled up and the door swung open. Inside the cab was Casey Stengel, who invited the boys to jump in. This happenstance encounter was the initial meeting between Mantle and Stengel.

The Yankee manager wanted to know who he had picked up. With great hesitation, Mickey told him his name.

"Mantle," he said.

"Oh," Stengel replied with a sign of recognition. "You're the kid that's all mixed up. You're not supposed to be able to run like that and hit the ball so far."

Mantle kept a low profile at that first training school. In fact, few people had any idea he was even in attendance until Yankee coaches asked the prospects to line up for sprints down the first-base line. The stopwatch read 3.1 from the left handed batter's box; surely the clock was wrong. But the naked eye didn't lie. Nobody present had ever seen anyone kick up dust the way the Mantle kid did. And during the first intra-squad game, Mickey hit a ball a half mile down the road. Later in the same contest against a different pitcher, he switched sides of the plate and hit one even further than the first blast.

Yankee coach Bill Dickey was pitching batting practice one morning when Mantle's turn came. "He hit the first six balls nearly 500 feet," Dickey said in wonder. "He hit 'em over the fences right-handed and left handed, and he hit 'em over the right-field fence right handed, and the left-field fence left-handed."

Though Stengel and his coaches had read the glowing reports on Mantle, not even Hemingway's writing could do this kid's reality justice. Stengel knew he had something special on his hands

Commissioner Chandler may have cut short Mantle's spec-tacular debut, but Stengel could not chase from his mind what he had witnessed in the brief training school.

Following those couple of weeks in Phoenix, Mickey spent training camp with the Kansas City Blues. His Independence teammates barely recognized Mantle when he arrived at camp. Over the winter, Mickey had put on a substantial amount of muscle and increased his already impressive speed to the category of "stunningly fast." By the start of the 1950 season he had been promoted to Class C Joplin. He turned in a spectacular season at the plate for the Joplin Miners. With the added muscle, Mantle was measurably stronger and drove the ball harder with more power, which translated in a season batting line that read: .383 batting average, 26 home runs, 30 doubles, 12 triples, 199 hits, 136 runs batted in, and 141 runs scored. Mantle's eye-popping production earned him the MVP of the Western League.

The January 31, 1951, edition of *The Sporting News* introduced the country's fans to baseball's next marvel. In an article subtitled, "Jewel of the Mine Country," correspondent Paul Stubblefield wrote:

> "Nineteen-year-old Mickey Mantle, dubbed by some big-time scouts as the number one prospect in the nation, will be off for Phoenix in a few weeks to display the talents that won him such raves from talent hunters."

Ironically, Mantle was not slated to receive an invitation to the 1951 training school. Despite Mantle's presence at the previous year's school, George Weiss was against the idea. Weiss did not want to rush the 19-year-old. Pushing Mantle to do too much, too soon, might set his progress back. Others in the Yankee system did not agree with Weiss' opinion. Tom Greenwade, the scout who discovered Mantle, pressed MacPhail to bring the kid to Arizona. Casey Stengel, too, wanted to get another look at Mantle.

Following his successful season at Joplin in Class C ball, Mantle got a taste of the big leagues when he was invited to join the Yankees for a brief stay in September. He met up with the club in St. Louis on September 17 and was enthralled by nearly everything major league. Over the course of the next week and a half, Mickey was understandably in awe of his surroundings—the majestic ballpark, the blindingly white pinstripe jerseys, and most important, the men inside those iconic uniforms: Rizzuto, Berra, and most of all, DiMaggio. Mickey did not speak unless spoken to, and even then, his reply came out as inaudible mumbles. Overwhelmed, Mantle stood back in the shadows and tried to absorb the experience. Still, the week was mostly a blur to him. He'd gotten to know a few Yanks, fellow prospect Bill Skrowon seemed like a good fella, and there was Jerry Coleman, Bobby Brown, as well as a slick rookie left-hander named Whitey Ford, a good guy who Mickey hoped to team up with one day.

Mantle was just one of several minor leaguers brought up for the close of the regular season. The mornings for these prospects were filled with batting practice and fielding practice workouts. The kids would then retreat to the stands to watch to big leaguers play. Following the game, after the Stadium had emptied of fans, the prospects would once again go through another practice session led by the Yankee coaches Johnny Neun and Frank Crosetti. At the conclusion of their second session the boys were let loose on the city. Mantle's running partner was his roommate, the 19-year-old Skowron. The two teenagers had the run of the town. They would venture into Manhattan and take in the sights, hop on a subway train with no destination in mind, get lost, and then somehow find their way back to their room at the Concourse Plaza. Hanging out at Yankee Stadium and wandering around the boulevards of New York City; they were having the time of their young lives.

"In actual playing experience, it probably meant nothing to the kid," Stengel acknowledged, "but it got him used to being around big league ballparks. It let him get the feel for being a Yankee."

For the moment at least, the fun came to a close following the Yanks' 7–3 October 1 loss at Fenway Park to the Red Sox. While the American League pennant winners moved on to play Philadelphia's Whiz Kids in the Series, Mickey returned home to Oklahoma and looked forward to the day he would make the big league club. Hopefully, Mantle thought, he'd reach the Yankees in a couple of years. But for the moment, a winter in the ore mines for 35 bucks a week awaited Mickey.

———

ON JANUARY 9, AT THE REQUEST OF THE YANKEES, MANTLE FLEW TO New York for a physical examination. The team's physician, Dr. Sidney Gaynor, assessed the health of Mickey's left leg. The limb in question had been injured when Mickey was hurt while playing football for Commerce High.

Yankee general manager George Weiss told the press, "We are simply bringing in Mantle for a checkup. He definitely will be with the main squad when it reports for duty in Phoenix in March."

Mick's dad, Elvin, or "Mutt" as everyone 'round Commerce called him, never did want his son to try out for the school football team. Nothing good could come from playing that brutal game. Baseball was Mickey's sport, and that's where he should place his focus. Mutt's apprehension was realized when in the fall of 1946, just a couple of weeks before Mickey's 15th birthday, he was accidentally kicked by a teammate during practice. Mickey's left leg turned several shades of purple, but those present thought little else of the seemingly innocuous injury.

The following day, Mickey's leg had swollen and turned a frightening shade of red. After Mickey failed to appear at school, his concerned football coach came to the Mantle home. One glance at the state of the injured extremity, and Mickey's coach immediately transported the boy to the closest hospital, which was located in Picher. Mystified doctors struggled to find a remedy. Several therapies were tried before Mantle was treated with penicillin, which seemed to help the swelling, and following a two-week stay in the hospital, Mickey was released. However, just a couple of weeks later, on November 15th, Mickey again was admitted to the local hospital. Still, physicians attending to Mantle could not determine the explanation for his discomfort.

It wasn't until Mickey's third stay in the hospital, in the spring of '47, that a definitive diagnosis was given. Mantle was suffering from osteomyelitis, an infection of a bone, which could have terrible consequences, including amputation. During this third stay, doctors operated on the injured leg, opening an abscess and draining the damaged limb. A few months after correctly diagnosing the issue plaguing him, Mickey was treated at the Crippled Children's Hospital in Oklahoma City. Following weeks of frustration, the treatment of penicillin took hold. Nearly a year and a half after the initial injury, Mickey was apparently free from all complications. By the summer of '48 he began to fill out, putting on nearly 40 pounds of muscle. Now, instead of a scrawny teenager, Mickey began to look like an actual ballplayer. Still, despite his outward appearance, his health remained in jeopardy, as osteomyelitis was a chronic disease.

———

WHILE IN SEARCH OF HIS TARDY PROSPECT, LEE MACPHAIL REACHED out to the *Miami Daily News*. MacPhail did not have a telephone number to reach Mantle and so he hoped that the local paper might give him a lead on how to track down Mickey. MacPhail was patched through to a local sportswriter, who promised to deliver the message to Mantle. The writer hopped in his car and headed over to the mine looking for Mickey.

Once he tracked down Mickey, the *Daily News* reporter asked why he wasn't in Phoenix with the Yankees.

"They didn't send no ticket or nothing. Ain't no phone in the house. Besides," Mickey added, "Harry Craft knows I'm a miner down here. They should've checked."

The next morning, Yankee scout Tom Greenwade brought the ticket to Mantle.

Mickey packed his bag—a gray sport jacket, two pairs of jeans, and his favorite tie, which sported a painted peacock and his Marty Marion Playmaker glove. He got in his father's battered old pickup, and headed out for the first leg of the trip to Arizona.

Mutt Mantle pulled his truck up outside Oklahoma City's Union Station. The Mantles all got out and Mickey grabbed his modest luggage. As he prepared to say goodbye to his mother and father, Mickey, suffering from a case of cotton mouth, swallowed hard. Wearing a straw hat and gripping his four-dollar cardboard suitcase tightly, Mickey turned to his parents, barely choking back his tears as he uttered his goodbyes. He stepped aboard the Heartland Express bound for Phoenix; chasing a dream while abandoning all he'd ever known.

The train slowly pulled from the station. From his window seat Mickey took a last glance at his family waving from the platform. Try as he might, Mickey could not stifle the sobs that had been building.

———

ON THE 22ND, CASEY CONDUCTED HIS FIRST PRESS CONFERENCE OF the year from his well-appointed penthouse atop the Adams Hotel. With Stengel these affairs weren't burdened so much by Q&A, but rather consisted of stream-of-conscious meditations by the "Perfesser."

"Sure, we got problems, and a lot of them," Stengel admitted without any prompting. "I've been thinking about them all winter. We gotta find somebody to replace Ford and how long my old guys, Mize and DiMag, can keep going and if Page can come back. But those are for the future. Right now I'm thinking about a problem I've never really solved since I've been with the Yanks. That's third base. Yeah, we've won two flags with Johnson and Brown but I've always wondered if we couldn't do better. And this week with the cream of the Yankee farm kids at a pre-training school here, I've been looking around. So far I've had five of them at third. They all look pretty good.

Maybe one of them can go all the way this year. That's what I'd like to find out here."

There was one kid in the school who particularly enamored Stengel—Gil McDougald, who captured the Texas League Most Valuable Player in 1950. The tall, slender McDougald used an open stance from the right side of the plate to great effect. Despite his awkward build, McDougald was athletically versatile. McDougald spent the 1950 season with the Beaumont Roughnecks playing for Rogers Hornsby. The great Rajah concluded his Hall of Fame career with seven batting titles to his name.

"Hornsby knows all there is to hitting," Casey said. "I'll never forget the year I hit .368 and he beat me out for the batting title by almost 50 points with a mere .424. Well Raj says the kid is a natural hitter, and he looks it up there. And he's never hit under .336 in three years. He can run, too."

McDougald was precisely the type of player Stengel loved to have on his squad. Though McDougald had been an All-Star second baseman in the Texas League, Stengel noticed the strength of the kid's arm and thought third base might be a possible fit. Casey approached the baby-faced McDougald about giving third base a try. Without hesitation, McDougald jumped at the opportunity, anything that would help him make the club.

"They say he can't make the long throw, but that I gotta see when his arm gets strong," Stengel continued.

"Now mind you, I'm only thinking out loud. With Bobby Brown apparently stuck in that hospital job, we've got to do something. And I'm wondering about Jerry Coleman. I know for sure he'd be the best third baseman in the league. Now if this kid can do it at second and make the double plays like they say he can, maybe I'd be smart to try something. Sure, I know I got the best second baseman combination in baseball and probably I'd have rocks in my head breaking it up. Still, it might just be an idea."

Stengel's first impression of Mantle this spring wasn't too favorable. "He looks a little lazy out there," Casey admitted. "But I look at his record and I say to myself, 'Whoa, Case, he can't be too lazy.'"

"Funny thing about him," a bemused Stengel said of Mantle, "Weiss doesn't like him because he looks as if he's asleep on the field. Says maybe the kid isn't a hustler. I say to him, 'Look, George, you don't hit 30 doubles and 12 triples in any league unless you're trying.'"

Casey was asked if he had any promising arms ready to step up to the big team. Sure, Stengel replied with a grumble, there are a few players who somebody thought would be good someday or else they wouldn't be here.

"But," Stengel added, "if you mean who have I got that'll take Ford's place, the answer is 'nobody.'"

———

THE STORY THAT WAS DOMINATING THE SPORTS PAGES BACK IN New York was the point-shaving scandal involving the City College of New York's basketball squad. CCNY had a wildly successful basketball program, having won both the 1950 NCAA Tournament and the 1950 NIT tournament, when news of the scandal broke in early February. The scandal brought bold headlines in the boroughs, but the news wasn't confined to New York City. The story hit every major newspaper across the country, which prompted conversation in many walks of life.

Lefty O'Doul, former Yankee and current manager of the San Francisco Seals, was visiting the training school to get a look at the organization's young prospects. The CCNY episode reminded O'Doul of his playing days, when Miller Huggins lectured the 1919 edition of the Yankees on the evils of gambling and the dangers inherent in getting tangled up with the shady characters involved with bookmaking.

"I said to myself, who would be crazy enough to get mixed up in anything like that? O'Doul recalled. "However, it wasn't long before the Black Sox scandal broke and I discovered that there were a few daffy guys in this business."

O'Doul wasn't the only baseball man to read the dispatches detailing the ignominy at City College and recognized the possible implications for his game. Every spring Stengel made a point of addressing his team. The CCNY story motivated Casey to push up the timing of his speech. On the 22nd, days before the veterans arrived, Stengel spoke with the kids at the training school and afterward he explained what the talk entailed.

"Some time during the training session, I lock the clubhouse door and tell the boys the facts of life," Stengel explained.

"I told those Yank kids last week that they'd have to watch their company every step of the way," Casey told reporters, speaking of the CCNY scandal. "I'll tell the rest of them as they come in. It's our job to see that nothing like this creeps into baseball.

"I deliver my sermon not only on the subject of keeping honest, but of being a Yankee in all things. I tell them that as a member of the great baseball organization with a tremendous record of success they get more attention from the public than most ballplayers, and they should happily receive it.

"I also tell them, take care on and off the field. You cannot be a Yankee if you don't look like one."

Stengel continued, "You all want to be Yankees; well you gotta grow up and be Yankees. See these report cards? They tell me all about you. What you do off the field as well as on it. But you gotta do it off the field, too. Just remember that in order to be a Yankee, you gotta act like one.

"Remember to be a Yankee at all times. If you cannot do this, you are not wanted on this ball club…I warn the kids about the kind of company they keep in their social hours. Old stuff, but always important."

Stengel reminded his interviewers that before he became the Yankees' manager, the club had a private detective to shadow ballplayers after hours and report on any misdeeds that may have been committed.

"I do not believe in that kind of surveillance," Stengel said, "Sure, now and then a bad boy has to be watched, but he gives himself away on the field."

Surveillance away the field was off the table, but Stengel endorsed a scheme that the Yankee organization had begun to implement. An innovative theory for evaluating and measuring pitching prospects was being used in the team's farm system according to Burleigh Grimes, an organizational scout who won 270 games during his 19 years in the big leagues. Grimes revealed in a radio interview that he had been counting the number of pitches that a prospect threw during a game as part of his assessment of young arms. He wasn't the only member of the Yankee system who believed in the importance of a pitch count, Grimes told his interviewer.

"Jim Turner, the club's pitching coach, also counts the pitches each Yankee hurler throws during a game to get a line on how much work he is doing," Grimes explained.

Grimes and Turner were in agreement that ideally a pitcher should not throw more than 104 pitches in a game. If a pitcher threw 150 or more in a game, Turner's rule of thumb was to give an extra day of rest before sending him back to the mound.

Stengel's word was final, but he did value the opinions and ideas of his coaching staff. Counting pitches was certainly not conventional, but Casey listened to the arguments put forth by Grimes and Turner and their reasoning was sound. What would it hurt to keep track of the number of pitches his guys threw?

———

HE ARRIVED IN ARIZONA A FRESHLY SCRUBBED 19-YEAR-OLD, A physical marvel whose talent appeared to be limitless. And though he looked as if he had just come off the farm, in reality Mantle had left the ore mines to come to Yankee training camp. With his closely cropped blonde hair, inviting grey eyes, and a full, bright smile, Mickey had an undeniable boyish handsomeness. Besides his stereotypical All-American looks, Mantle's blend of blinding speed and raw power left spectators, teammates, and opposing players captivated. Who was this kid and where did he come from? Certainly, some knew Mantle was the top prospect in the Yankee farm system, but this specimen before them was otherworldly.

Casey Stengel, who always had an entertaining quip in his back pocket, noted the exceptional speed of his fledgling outfielder. "This kid runs so fast in the outfield, he doesn't bend a blade of grass," Casey said.

Though he was spending nearly all his time in the field playing short or third, Stengel envisioned a different course for Mantle in the long term.

"Mantle would probably develop into as great a player as the big guy in center field," Stengel told Ben Epstein of the *Mirror*. "I wouldn't be at all surprised if he wound up there either. With his tremendous speed and arm, it should be a cinch."

Epstein asked Stengel if he should infer that the kid wasn't going to be farmed out then?

Stengel mumbled his response to the *Mirror* reporter: "All I hope is that they don't take him away from me. Somebody might mishandle him."

———

WHEN HE FIRST LAID EYES ON MANTLE, YANKEE SCOUT TOM Greenwade thought to himself, "I know now how Paul Krichell felt when he first saw Lou Gehrig."

He may have thought he was seeing baseball's next sensation, but Greenwade downplayed his discovery. Greenwade had previously scouted for the Browns and after that, the Dodgers. He was with Brooklyn's organization when Larry MacPhail enticed Greenwade to join the Yankees. The scout had his eye on Mantle for a couple of years before procuring Mickey's name on a contract. Greenwade had to wait anxiously until Mantle graduated from high school before making an offer. In the meantime, Greenwade attended a handful a Mickey's games, but not too many to draw attention to his presence, and thus undue attention on Mantle. Greenwade wanted Mantle all to himself and he did a few unsavory things to ensure that other scouts would not "find" Mickey. He also played down Mickey's potential when speaking with Mutt, dismissing the kid's chances to make it as a shortstop, and referred to him as a "marginal prospect."

In addition to being disingenuous to Mutt Mantle, Greenwade had Commerce High principal A.B. Baker aiding his cause. Baker chased off Cleveland scout Hugh Alexander by offering disinformation. The football injury Mickey incurred left the boy with damaged legs, Baker told Alexander, and besides, Commerce High doesn't even have a baseball team. Why A.B. Baker helped Greenwade and the Yankees is open to speculation, but Greenwade's careful plotting and deception paid off when he was the only scout present on Mickey's graduation day.

Mantle skipped out on his commencement ceremony and instead played a game with his semi-pro Ban Johnson League team. Following the game, Greenwade approached the Mantle family car. Mickey's mother, Lovell, his father, Mutt, and Mickey were all present when the scout offered a signing bonus of $1,150. Greenwade felt no compunction about making such a lowball offer. Other, less promising prospects had been given 30, 40, even 50 times the amount he placed before Mickey, but Greenwade also knew he was the only scout in town, having chased all others off the scent. As for Mickey, sure, he could probably make more down in the mines with his father, but this was professional baseball and the New York Yankees. Without a second's hesitation, Mickey placed his name on the document. He was now the property of the Yankees and slated for Independence, Missouri.

———

ELVIN COULD PLAY SOME BALL HIMSELF IN HIS YOUNGER DAYS. HE was a hard-throwing right-hander off the mound, but luck and fortune skirted him. Instead of baseball glory, Elvin was bound for the mines. He staked out a life and began a family with his bride, Lovell. Mickey Charles was born to the couple on October 20, 1931. The "Mickey" came from Elvin's favorite player, the great catcher with the Philadelphia Athletics, Mickey Cochrane. It was as if the boy was pre-ordained for greatness on the diamond. He was raised to be a ballplayer, and Mickey was tutored in the game's finer points. From his paternal grandfather, Charley Mantle, a southpaw, Mickey learned to bat right-handed. And it was his righty tossing father, Elvin, who tutored Mickey on batting from the opposite side of the plate. To some observers in the spring of '51, Mickey seemed to possess a talent gifted by the touch of God. But it was countless hours of practice and schooling that formed Mickey into the player he had become.

Standing aside watching Mantle taking swings in Phoenix, Casey Stengel was properly impressed at the fine instruction Mantle had received at home.

"If that's how the kid learned to hit curve-ball pitching, maybe I ought to talk to George Weiss about signing the old man as a coach," Casey mused.

While taking balls at short, Mantle didn't particularly impress. His speed didn't show, his footwork was poor, and Mickey's arm was erratic, to put it kindly.

"We'll try Mantle at third awhile," Stengel said, "and see how he does. Later we'll decide whether he's a shortstop, third baseman, or outfielder."

While Mantle had been a pleasant surprise in the first few

days of training school, Stengel was agitated with Jackie Jensen, who he'd hoped would replace Whitey Ford in the rotation. Jensen possessed four good pitches: a curve, fastball, slider, and a screwball. But his heart wasn't into pitching. Stubbornly, Jensen insisted that the outfield was a better spot for him, and the University of California product rebuffed pressure to pigeonhole him as a pitcher.

"I know that Casey and the coaches think I could become a good pitcher," Jensen told Joe Trimble of the *Daily News*, "but they are saying so because they don't think I'm a good enough hitter to be an outfielder. Well, I think I am, and I intend to prove it in exhibition games."

"Gorgeous George," as Jensen was called by his teammates in reference to his golden locks, envisioned making the big league squad as a solid hitting outfielder, and he wasn't buying into all the talk that he could make the team as a pitcher.

"If I switch to pitching, they'll insist on sending me to the minors for a year to get experience," Jensen explained. "They never would let me pitch in the majors, particularly in the kind of pennant races we've had the last two years. Every game is too important to gamble on."

Despite hitting only .171 in 70 at-bats during his time with the Yankees the previous season, the supremely confident Jensen believed he could push aside Gene Woodling, Hank Bauer, or even DiMaggio from the starting outfield.

"I think I can nudge someone out of there, and I mean this year," Jensen said.

Stengel, however, wasn't committing to anything. "If Jensen can hit enough, he's an outfielder," he said, "and if not he's a pitcher. He's got the natural ability to make anything."

———

AS THE VETERAN MEMBERS OF THE TEAM BEGAN ARRIVING IN
Phoenix, there remained three holdouts: Tommy Byrne, Billy
Johnson, and Yogi Berra. Byrne and Johnson were nearly after-
thoughts by members of the media; it was the status of Berra's
contract talks that had everyone in camp buzzing. Even Casey
wanted more news as he kept hitting reporters up for information concerning Yogi's negotiations. Given his numbers for
the 1950 season: 124 runs batted in, 28 home runs, and an average of .322, Berra believed that he was vastly underpaid. The
Yankees original offer of $22,000 was dismissed out of hand by
Berra. The St. Louis born backstop was pushing for a contract
in the range of $35,000, which club officials thought was an
outlandish request.

Speaking for his bosses, Red Patterson condemned the demands and ultimatums the 25-year-old Berra was placing on
the Yankees.

"Berra's demands are so far out of line, that there is no basis
for reasonable negotiations," Patterson told reporters. "What
he wants approaches twice as much as any other catcher in
baseball."

DiMaggio may have been the biggest name on the club,
Rizzuto may have been named the league MVP last year, and
Mantle may have been the newest phenom, but Yogi Berra was
arguably the best player the Yankees possessed.

Berra had done his part during the war while serving in the
Navy. He volunteered for deployment on the dangerous "rocket
ships." It was aboard one of these small boats that Berra landed
on the beach in Normandy on June 6, 1944. Weeks later, during

another invasion, this one in the south of France, Berra was hit by a German bullet. The wound earned Berra a Purple Heart, though he never filled out the paper work for the actual medal. There were other commendations, indeed, like so many other young American men; Berra was a war-time hero. His experience during the hostilities, however, is something Yogi rarely mentioned. After all, he was just doing his duty like a whole lot of fellas.

The first time Larry MacPhail met Berra, Yogi was dressed in his blue Navy uniform and sailor's hat. Heaven help the soul who looked worse in this getup than Berra, and the then general manager of the Yankees was none too impressed with the specimen before him.

"He looks like the bottom man of an unemployed acrobatic team," MacPhail thought to himself.

Indeed, his looks weren't necessarily Berra's strong suit. Smart aleck writers described Berra as resembling a "pro wrestler more than a baseball player." These same reporters were playing on the same stereotypes propagated by their colleagues. What they missed in the evaluation of Berra's looks was a great baseball player with a remarkable baseball mind. Indeed, Berra served as Stengel's on-field manager. And boy, could he hit the baseball.

Despite his remarkable 1950 season, Berra hadn't won the American League MVP, but he had been given a distinguished honor when he was named one of the "most stimulating faces in America," by the National Association of Women. The distinction could be perceived as a backhanded compliment, or perhaps no compliment at all given the press release issued by the association.

"Yogi has the most down-to-earth face in America," the statement read. "It stimulates women's subconscious yearning for the Neanderthal man."

Shortly after the first of the year, the Yankees' offer for the coming season arrived in the mail: $22,000, or $4,000 above the previous season. Yogi returned the contract along with a note that explained why he was worth more than the 22 grand on the table. Included in the letter was a recap of Berra's spectacular 1950 season. The bartering went back and forth. George Weiss upped the Yankees' offer by $3,000, which Yogi politely declined. And then Roy Hamey paid a visit to Berra in Yogi's hometown of St. Louis in January. Hamey, an assistant to Weiss, made the trip as a follow-up to an unanswered contract offer. He found Berra at a local restaurant, where Yogi served as a celebrity greeter of sorts.

"Are you pleased with the offer Weiss sent to you?" Hamey asked Berra.

"I can give you a good seat alone, or would you rather be with three customers who will talk baseball?" Berra told Hamey.

"But I'm not here for a meal," Hamey explained. "I'm here to discuss your contract."

"The steak is good. The spaghetti is marvelous. You can't go wrong here," Berra said, ending all contract talk and sending Hamey on his way back to New York.

Up until June of 1950, Phil Rizzuto and Berra were roommates when the Yankees were on the road. The early summer call-up of Billy Martin and Whitey Ford broke up the tandem because Stengel did not like rooming rookies together.

"Put two kids together, and what will they learn," Stengel repeated when asked about his unwritten rule.

Whoever shared a room with Berra was sure to remember

the experience, and come away from it more educated in the game of baseball.

"Berra was anything but an uninteresting roomie," Rizzuto acknowledged.

The two would discuss that afternoon's contest. Berra was indefatigable breaking down every aspect of a game. Rizzuto preferred to hash out victories, but Yogi especially liked to dissect a defeat, to examine what went wrong and where strategy went astray. His was a brilliant baseball mind, Rizzuto said of Berra. Outsiders have no idea how much Stengel relied on Yogi's council.

He was something of a baseball savant, Rizzuto explained, but Berra loved to read comics and pulp detective paperbacks.

"Once he gets interested in a book, he will not lay it down," Rizzuto said. "I like lights out and sleep at 11:30.... I would chase Berra into the bathroom, switch off the lights, and fall asleep. The next morning he would tell me all about it."

When the Yanks visited St. Louis, Berra would invite Rizzuto to his home on "The Hill." There they would enjoy a nice home-cooked Italian meal, and play bocce.

"Boy, they really eat on The Hill," Rizzuto gushed. "They cut out a whole loaf the long way; throw in anchovies, salami and cheese, and go to work."

For his part, Yogi envied Phil. At least he admired Rizzuto's sense of style.

"He dresses like I'd like to dress and I can't," Berra said. "On him, collars and ties look good. Phil tried to wean me away from those comic books. I know they ain't good literature. But they relax me."

On the 26th, George Weiss finally addressed the status of the three holdouts.

"There will be no ultimatums," Weiss assured an office full of reporters. "We do not operate that way. In fact, although we do not want holdouts in this camp, if any of the three asked to come here and discuss his contract, I would roll out the welcome mat."

Weiss admitted that he'd even removed himself from the talks lest the ballplayers felt that there was personal animus on his part. The general manager stepped aside and allowed Hamey to take over the negotiations. Weiss then went into a discourse discussing the merit of each individual holdout. Saving Berra for last, Weiss argued, "Few players in the major leagues have enjoyed the remarkable financial progress, which has been Yogi's since 1947.

"Every player who becomes involved in a salary argument with the front office has an idea that he was responsible for most of the club's success the previous season."

Berra, reached at his St. Louis home didn't know about any of that. What he did know was his demands were not out of line. He was one of, if not the best, receiver in the game, and he handled the Yankee pitching staff to near perfection. That's not even taking in to account his impressive numbers at the plate.

"It's not like I'm being stubborn," Berra said via the telephone. "I came down a little bit, but they haven't come up a buck."

He would hold out until "doomsday," Berra vowed, in order to receive, "what's coming to me."

Not everyone was upset that Berra was sitting on a lounge chair in his living room.

From Lakeland, Florida, a telegram was sent to Berra: "As far as we are concerned, you can stay out all year and make us very happy indeed." Signed: "The Detroit Tigers pitching staff."

3   THIS MIGHT BE
MY LAST YEAR

JOE ARRIVED IN CAMP ON WEDNESDAY MARCH 1, JUST AS THE rookie school was breaking up. He was greeted at the team's headquarters, the Adams Hotel, by a handful of fans and a couple of reporters. As usual, he didn't have much to say.

"I feel great," DiMag told the small crowd. "I am out to surprise those who believe I am finishing up my career. Everything was fine this winter, except my mother is really bad."

Now here he was, about to embark on his 13th major league season, more certain than ever that this would be his last.

Joe had always been wary of the press, and lately he had grown even more tired of those bums. His problem wasn't so much with the fellas who covered the club, but rather columnists who made a living by printing the private business of people in the public spotlight, and in recent weeks Joe's name had not been restricted to the sports section. The gossip pages were filled with titillating reports declaring that Joe and his ex-wife,

Dorothy, were once again an item. These rumormongers irked Joe to no end. He and Dorothy weren't getting back together, they had been seen together lately only because of Joe Jr.'s activities, DiMaggio insisted. But the truth was beside the point; his private affairs were just that, private. Now here were some hacks putting his personal business in the papers. More than ever before, Joe thought, this fame stuff was for the birds.

Whether he was getting ready to hang 'em up or not, Joe didn't want to be pushed out the door. He had heard of Stengel's prognostication of this new kid, Mickey Mantle; that he would one day take over center field in Yankee Stadium. Joe reluctantly acknowledged that time waits for no one, but he didn't appreciate Stengel naming his replacement before he was gone.

Two nights into his Arizona stay, DiMaggio invited three writers to come sit with him in his room: Dan Daniel, Hugh Bradley, and Ben Epstein. Absent from the group was Joe's favorite reporter, Jimmy Cannon of the *Post*. Had Cannon followed the Yankees out west, he may have had an exclusive. Instead, Cannon chose to cover the Dodgers and Giants training in Florida.

All in all, the baseball press had been kind to Joe. This kindness had little to do with Joe's accessibility, but owed much to myth building. A postgame interview with DiMaggio was a painful experience, for the interviewer as well as the subject. Indeed, for all the confidence he displayed on the field, Joe was extraordinarily self-conscious off. DiMaggio wasn't the most articulate fella and he feared coming off as an uneducated rube. When confronted by a reporter, DiMaggio kept his answers short and to the point. The writers could expand on his words if they wished, as long as they made him sound good.

The *Journal American*'s representative, Hugh Bradley, threw a rather innocuous question at DiMaggio; asking Joe what his future baseball prospects would be. Joe paused for a moment, he was always deliberate when responding to press queries and on this night at the Adams, DiMaggio uttered the words that he surely knew would cause a sensation.

"This might be my last year," he told the writers gathered around his smoke-filled room. "I would like to have a good year and then hang them up."

Yeah, Joe admitted, over the winter he'd thought about not coming back for one more year, "What I'm telling you is only my viewpoint now," he said. "I'd like to quit on top rather than fade out."

DiMaggio had strongly hinted about possibly retiring previously, and so his words didn't shock the men seated before him. After all, these veteran reporters knew Joe to be his own harshest critic and they each understood that DiMaggio had noticeably slowed in recent years as he labored through numerous injuries. In addition, spring training had become a chore, and the travel had long since become arduous. No, Joe's words wouldn't be classified as a bombshell, but still, this was headline-making material. 1951 would be the Clipper's final season.

Joe, who was suffering from a bit of a head cold, sat back in his chair and gave each writer the chance to toss a few questions his way.

Daniel preferred to take the nostalgic path. "When you reported to Joe McCarthy at St. Petersburg in March 1936, did you figure you would last this long."

"I never gave the duration of my career any thought then, because I was intent on making good."

He certainly wasn't the sentimental type, but he did stop for a moment and think about the impact Bill Essick had on his career—indeed, his life.

"He and he alone scouted me," Joe said of Essick. "He was the only major league agent who had the sense to take me to a surgeon and find out about my knee, which all the others were so sure would disqualify me from a major career."

What would he do when it was all over? Joe refused to commit to anything. But managing or front office work was definitely not in his plans.

"I have enough headaches, handling my own business and managing myself, much less taking on a club."

What about television? Radio?

"I do not know," DiMaggio insisted. "I have a lot of propositions, and I am in no hurry to make a decision. After all, I still have another season before me.

"I doubtless could go right on playing ball for some years to come," he said. "I am not, as some writers have insisted, a brittle ballplayer. I never have been. I am a good, tough-boned guy.

"They said a year ago that I would not be able to play 100 games. Now they are writing the same thing."

Joe paused for a moment and chuckled softly. "Who knows? I might run into a bad season and not be able to buy a base hit. But that brittle stuff is bull.

"I put my whole heart into the game always. During the season I lead a pretty lonely life. I don't mind that. I concentrate on baseball. Maybe I take it too seriously. I like to win, and I guess that's where some people get the idea I'm anti-social. In the winter when there's no game to be played every day, I like mingling with folks just like everybody else."

No, Joe confessed, he hadn't informed his manager or Yankee brass about his decision, but "I think they probably have a pretty good notion about it…. We've all got to quit some time and in fact, it could be I might have something happen which would keep me from playing a game or getting a base hit this year."

The franchise won't suffer from his absence, Joe insisted, whenever that day comes. "Nobody is likely to stop the Yankees though, I think they'll be winning for many years to come."

———

THE HEADLINES OF THE NEW YORK PAPERS HADN'T YET REACHED Phoenix when Casey sat down for his breakfast of ham and eggs the next morning. Joe Trimble approached Casey's table. The *Daily News* beat writer asked Stengel what he thought of Joe's retirement announcement. Ol' Case looked up from his plate for a moment, startled by the question. With DiMag seated just one table away, Trimble explained to Stengel what had transpired the night before.

Casey failed to disguise his ire. "Well, what can you do?" he barked at Trimble, "You can't stop a man from doing what he wants. What am I supposed to do, get a gun and make him play? If he wants to quit it's his own business, not mine. If he wants to play it's up to him, and still none of my business. I can't get a gun and keep him working. Besides, the club owns him, not me. I am just the manager and such matters are not in my department, so you have to take the matter up with the owners and George Weiss.

"What his plans are, are his own. I don't govern those things. Its two people, the fellow himself and who owns him.

"I can't say, 'you play' or 'you don't' or 'I'll suspend you for five years.' I don't have that job. It's open but they haven't opened it to me," Stengel said, referring to the recent removal of Happy Chandler as the game's commissioner.

A reporter caught up with George Weiss and requested a statement concerning DiMaggio's retirement quotes. Before replying, Weiss asked for a few minutes to speak with Dan Topping. He returned after a few moments and then he said. "Joe DiMaggio hasn't discussed this angle with any club official. We regret to hear anything like this. We hope he will have the sort of season which will cause him to change his mind."

The day after Joe's comments made the rounds, a Yankee was questioned about Joe's comments. "Don't quote me, but when you get into the thirties and you have to start training for another season you often want to give up and try some other enterprise. But when your muscles get limbered up and the season's underway you forget all such ideas."

———

JOE WAS BORN GIUSEPPE PAULO DIMAGGIO ON NOVEMBER 25, 1914, in Martinez, a quaint village 35 miles northeast of San Francisco, to Giuseppe and Rosalia DiMaggio. Like generations of DiMaggios before him, the senior Giuseppe was a fisherman by trade. He came to America in 1898, leaving his young expectant bride behind. Giuseppe had learned from a relative that a man could earn a living from fishing the waters off the coast of California. He came and staked out his trade, and Giuseppe sent for his wife and first-born daughter before a year had passed. Indeed, one could make a life in America with a little hard work.

With the exception of Sundays, Giuseppe would rise each morning at 4:00 and board his modest boat that he'd christened the *Rosalie D*, and set sail for that day's catch. When Joe was one year old, Giuseppe relocated his family to San Francisco, where the fishing opportunities were more abundant. For a time the older boys, Tom and Mike, gave hope to Giuseppe's dream of continuing the lineage, of keeping the family name in the fishing trade. A whole fleet of DiMaggio-manned fishing vessels patrolling he sea.

Though fishing may have been in his bloodlines, Joe wanted nothing to do with the profession. He hated going out on his father's boat; even the shortest venture into the San Francisco Bay turned Joe's stomach. And what's more, he despised the aroma of dead fish. Such proclivities did not bode well for a life on the sea. To Giuseppe these traits were a betrayal; his son was nothing but a lazy boy. And to exasperate the disparity between father and son, Joe began playing baseball, a game that to Giuseppe was nothing but an indefensible waste of time. Baseball! This wasn't the work a man would do. It was a *game!* Played with a *ball!* Eventually, Giuseppe would take pride in the accomplishments of his baseball playing sons, of seeing the family name prominently displayed in the newspaper. He couldn't read the accompanied stories, but Giuseppe recognized the name *DiMaggio*. And like much of the country, he got caught up in the hysteria surrounding Joe's hitting streak in the summer of '41. Giuseppe, too, could barely contain himself while waiting for word to reach the coast if Joe had a hit that day.

In actuality, Joe stumbled into his eventual vocation. It was his older brother Vince who introduced Joe to the possibilities the game offered. Vince, the third-born son to Giuseppe and Rosalie, broke the hold his father had on his sons. Against Giuseppe's will, Vince lied about his age and signed a contract to play pro ball in Northern California. Vince's obstinacy emboldened his younger brothers. They, too, could chase a dream far from the San Francisco Bay and the fetid smell of fish. Joe watched with envy as Vince went from the Lumber Leagues of Northern California to the Tucson Lizards, where he played briefly before returning to San Francisco to perform with the hometown San Francisco Seals.

Early on, Joe proved quite adept at playing baseball. Still, he had no particular passion for the game. He had played several years of semi-pro ball when his exceptional skill earned Joe a spot on the Seals of the Pacific Coast League, where he made his professional debut on October 1, 1932. The following season, DiMaggio collected at least one base hit in an astounding 61 consecutive games. Before this hitting streak, Joe played the game for a payday, as a way to avoid laboring in an actual job. Something changed in him during the streak that ran from May 27 to July 25, though. Baseball got in his blood like fishing never would. From that moment on, DiMaggio was singly focused on improving his game in any and every manner. Refining his swing, adjusting his batting stance, strengthening his throwing arm, or polishing his base-running skills... DiMaggio pursued excellence on the baseball diamond.

Following a doubleheader at Seals Stadium one evening in late May 1934, Joe was running late for a dinner at his sister's house. When he arrived, the jitney pulled up to the curb before his sister's home and Joe jumped from the cab. Immediately Joe felt something pop in his knee when his foot hit the ground.

When Joe tried to stand, his legs buckled, and the cab driver assisted him into the house, while an ambulance was called.

The moment Joe took that misstep out of that taxi, interest from big league teams vanished. Yankee scout Bill Essick, however, had a hunch that DiMaggio's knee would heal. And after Joe was released from the hospital, Essick followed Joe and the San Francisco Seals up and down the coast. Once Essick had seen enough to convince him that Joe's knee was fine, he called the George Weiss, then the Yankees' minor league director.

"Buy DiMaggio," Essick implored Weiss.

Weiss took the information to Ed Barrow, the Yankee general manager, who questioned his scout and the soundness of DiMaggio's bum knee. Because of Barrow's faith in Essick, he came around. Once Bill vouched for a kid that was that was good enough for Barrow. The deal for DiMaggio was consummated on November 21, 1934: $50,000 and five Yankee farm hands for the rights to DiMaggio with one caveat—the Seals retained the rights to Joe for the 1935 season, a year in which he hit an eye-popping .398.

In the spring of 1936, Joe traveled across the country with Yankee veterans and fellow San Franciscans Frank Crosetti and Tony Lazzeri to his initial major league training camp. This was the first trip of any duration DiMaggio had ever embarked on. The lengthy four-day trip was made all that much longer thanks to the reticence of the three innately quiet occupants. The interminable silence was broken when the group made a brief stop in Texas.

"It's your turn to drive," DiMaggio was told by the veteran Yanks. With a degree of embarrassment, Joe told his car mates that he'd never been behind the wheel of an automobile. The journey to Florida continued, Joe alone in the back seat. Silence again filled the air.

When he arrived in St. Petersburg at the far end of the cross-country journey, Joe was met with much ballyhoo. Those who had been in and around the game for years could not recall such a build-up for a rookie. Anticipation among fans and the press was enormous: could the 21-year-old DiMaggio replicate his San Francisco heroics in the major leagues?

One of the first to greet Joe in camp was Ed Barrow, who had a big stake in the success of DiMaggio. Barrow was a long-time baseball veteran, and he had ample experience at nearly every phase of the game, having been a manager and a team president (an early version of what would become the position of general manager). Hell, Barrow even sold concessions at one point early in his career. Indeed, Barrow had seen much in the game and he could anticipate what was coming for DiMaggio. Few players, if any, had the type of buildup Joe had received before playing his first major league game. The press was sure to scrutinize every move made by DiMaggio. Barrow wanted to prepare Joe for the overwhelming barrage of publicity sure to come. He pulled the twenty-one year old aside.

There will be a lot of pressure placed on you, Joe, Barrow told DiMaggio. I'd hate for it to make you overanxious.

Joe listened quietly to the advice and politely responded, "Don't worry. I don't get excited."

And he didn't. Not then as an impressionable rookie. Not though all the years, all the tight spots, the big games; Joe never lost his cool. His demeanor was impenetrable.

The closest he ever came to displaying emotion on the field came in Game 6 of the '47 Series. In the sixth inning, Joe stepped in against Dodger left-hander Joe Hatten. With two men on and Brooklyn holding an 8–5 lead, DiMaggio smacked a line drive destined for the Dodger bullpen. Left fielder Al Gionfriddo, making a mad dash toward the ball, reached his glove out at the last instant. Gionfriddo's arm was extended over the chain link fence as the ball landed inexplicably in his glove.

Typically, Joe was running all out from the crack of the bat. He was bearing down on second base when the ball found Gionfriddo's glove. At that moment Joe lashed his foot at the infield dirt, kicking up dust as well as the eyebrows of those who witnessed the momentary loss of composure. The next day's papers were full of reports detailing Joe's "tantrum" in full.

Growing up in North Beach, San Francisco, Joe never gave pause to being Italian. In his neighborhood everyone was of Italian descent. Upon joining the Yankees, however, Joe was met with the reality of stereotypes and bigotry. To their Yankee teammates, Lazzeri was "Big Dago" and Crosetti was "Little Dago." Now, with Joe aboard, he became simply "Dago." These nicknames were part and parcel of life in pro ball. Often a player's ethnicity was used to bestow a sobriquet. And, frequently, a player's heritage was used to harangue and disparage. Some of it came with the territory; opponents would do anything to rattle a batter. Indeed, "Dago" didn't carry the same connotation that "Guinea" or "Wop" did, but these were but two of the epithets tossed DiMaggio's way from opposing dugouts. Bench jockeying or catcalls from the stands, these things Joe came to expect. Even a *Life* magazine portrayal used an unfortunate description in a profile of DiMaggio:

"Instead of olive oil or smelly bear grease he keeps his hair

slick with water. He never reeks of garlic and prefers chicken to spaghetti."

Through it all, Joe never batted an eye. Not at the ribbing, the insults, or the xenophobic writings. Baseball writers sometimes referred to DiMaggio in print as "the Yankee Clipper," or simply the "Clipper." Occasionally, "Joltin' Joe" was used, but those terms were media creations. In the Yankee clubhouse Joe remained, "Dago" or "Daig." Whatever the original intent, by 1951 Joe's nickname of Dago had morphed into a term of respect, even affection, among his teammates.

Being the game's most well-known—as well as the best—Italian ballplayer was a privilege that Joe never took for granted. DiMaggio took great pride in his ethnicity, but he felt obligations to a much wider following. With the fame of being his generation's finest player came the burden of expectation. In this his final summer on the playing field, Joe hoped against all practically to turn back the clock, that he might deliver for his fans and teammates as he did in his prime. But as his 36-year-old bones assured him, Joe knew that there was no rewinding time. All Joe could promise was to give the game all he had right up to the moment he hung up his spikes for the last time.

4 THIS KID AIN'T LOGICAL

AS HE DID EACH SPRING, STENGEL ADDRESSED THE ENTIRE TEAM before sending his players on the field for the first time. Attendance was perfect at this season's opening talk with the exception of Berra, who had accepted the Yankees' contract offer the night before but had not yet arrived in Phoenix from St. Louis. However, Yogi did come ambling into the clubhouse just as his teammates were headed out.

A couple of reporters grabbed Berra, who looked fit and trim, and asked the catcher how things had worked out for him contract-wise.

"Let me say that I got what I wanted," Berra replied. "George Weiss made out like he was fighting me hard, but when it came down to the showdown he was very kind to me and my family."

Reportedly, Berra received a $12,000 raise over his 1950 salary of $18,000.

"I plan to stick around with the Yankees for a long time, Berra said, "I am a young man. Won't be 26 until May 12. If I behave myself and keep in shape, what's to prevent me being with the Yankees for another 10 years?"

Yogi did have one complaint. In Arizona it was near impossible to find the reading material of his choice. Comic sellers, it seems, were hard to come by in Phoenix. "It is tough to find them out here," Yogi lamented. "In St. Louis and New York, I know where to get the latest. But around here it is tough."

Though he rarely kept such things to himself, Stengel did not share the contents of the closed-door talk with reporters, though he did let the writers know that he informed his players that they could play golf while in Arizona.

"I am not a golf player," Stengel admitted, "so I don't know whether it hurts our game or helps it. All I told them is that they were to do their work on the field for me, and they could play as much golf as they wanted."

———

FOR WEEKS, DEL WEBB HAD BEEN PREOCCUPIED WITH HIS obsession of driving Happy Chandler, baseball's commissioner, from office. Ironically, just a little more than five years earlier, Webb had played a significant role in the naming of Chandler to replace Kenesaw Mountain Landis. What happened in just a few short years to sour the relationship was open to speculation. Most observers pointed to Chandler's suspension of Dodger manager Leo Durocher for the entirety of the 1947 season. Chandler cited Durocher's comfortable familiarity with known gambling figures as justification for the banishment. Through his construction company, Webb too had close contact with a number of unsavory characters, including his notorious partners back in Vegas. There was talk around the press box that due to the Yankee co-owner's shady business associations, Chandler was having Webb investigated. This alone was enough to turn Webb against the commissioner, but there was also the Congressional committee that was scheduled to hold a hearing later in the summer, the focus of which would be the reserve clause. To many within the game, the reserve clause was the glue that held the sport together. "The Clause," a stipulation in every standard player contract, bound a player to his team perpetually, or until the club traded or released him.

Congressional hearings! If Chandler had been doing his job none of this would have come about, Webb believed. Part of the reason that Chandler was selected as commissioner was his contacts in government, and now this.

For the moment, though, Webb was putting aside that aspect of the business. His team was arriving in Phoenix and Webb wasn't going to miss this for nothing. This day had been marked on Webb's calendar all winter. All his plans and preparations had gone into making this come to fruition...Webb's Yankees were in Phoenix and he was there to welcome his ballplayers to his home state. The Giants and Yankees announced their plan to swap training camps in the winter of '49, and immediately interest in Arizona was robust. Even at that early date, more than two years before the Yankees would come west, tickets had begun to swiftly sell.

Webb initiated his team to the ways of the West by purchasing beige cowboy hats for every member of the Yankees' traveling party. Some players were flattered by the style. Berra, however, drew howls of laughter when he modeled his size-too-small cowboy hat.

The 10-gallon hats were handed out to players, front office personnel, even writers. The only person who looked natural was Webb, who wore his while playing catch in a business suit.

A glance under the brim of the hat exposed the haberdashery from which Webb purchased the Western wear. The transaction was not made in Arizona, nor in any other part out west, but rather Dobbs, on the western side of 5th Avenue in Manhattan

Webb was present at the field the next afternoon, a particularly cold day. Phoenix had endured a hailstorm and some light snow, enough snow to blanket the countryside a sparkling white. A number of people teased Webb about the unseasonably cold temperatures. Stengel even made a production of greeting and shaking hands with Webb while wearing wool gloves.

Webb took the jokes and ribbing in good nature and put on his best face. The weather would surely break and the typical climes would return to the desert.

———

THE TRAINING SCHOOL CLOSED UP ON WEDNESDAY, THE 28TH. Casey declared the camp to be "very good," evidenced by the participants being moved to higher classifications throughout the farm system thanks to their experience at the school. Stengel and Weiss selected six kids to remain in the big league camp and continue working out in Phoenix: Morgan, Wiesler, McDougald, Robertson, Casey, and Mantle.

"Don't read too much into this decision," Stengel said.

"We'll find out more about them," he explained. "We'll find out where they play best and where they'll be assigned. They'll play some games here and get some more experience.

"It's easier for them to switch to new positions when they're young."

Left unsaid for the moment was the decision to permanently shift Mantle to the outfield. The move was acknowledged within a couple of days by both Weiss and Stengel. Before the teaching school had concluded Casey had seen enough of Mantle at short. Indeed, the manager had surmised more than a year earlier at the first prospect camp, that Mickey was best suited for the outfield, and what he'd seen this spring in Arizona just confirmed those beliefs.

Mantle was a raw talent when playing shortstop. His strong arm was terribly erratic, and each ball hit to him at shortstop became an adventure for spectators seated behind first base. Given his natural gifts, had the Yankees chosen, Mantle could have eventually mastered third base if not shortstop, but the club had a backlog of talent at the infield positions. Rizzuto, Bobby Brown. Jerry Coleman, Billy Martin, and Gil McDougald were all vying for three positions already.

Stengel added his perspective on moving Mantle. "Well, as far as his hitting, he's a big league outfielder right now," Casey said. "He can run the bases, and his speed kind of keeps you on edge. His speed is so big that maybe he can use it in the outfield. His arm is so strong that he won't have to think out there. All he'll have to do is throw the ball in."

"The best way for Mickey to become a first-grade outfielder would be to play that position every day in our chain," Weiss explained.

He would do what was asked of him, but Mantle admitted that the switch wasn't easy.

"It's tough," Mickey conceded. "There's a lot more to playing the outfield than most people think. But the first day out there, I knew I was going to like it better than the infield. I can run a lot more out there and that's something I always like to do."

Tommy Henrich was completely invested in helping Mantle convert into an outfielder. The expanse of grass beyond the infield dirt was foreign territory to Mantle. He lacked the instinct to perform even the most rudimentary acts of an outfielder. He needed to learn to extend his right arm all the way through a throw. As a shortstop, Mickey's natural inclination was to "short-arm" his throws. Even more difficult to digest and apply was the seemingly simple motion of positioning himself to catch and throw with men on base. Before Henrich's tutoring took hold, Mickey would catch the ball before planting and throwing. Patiently, Henrich coached Mantle to time the catch with the planting of his right foot, which would propel his momentum forward in a hop/skip motion.

Even the untrained eye could see there was something special about Mantle. The Yankees' public relations man, Red Patterson sensed that there would be a lot of questions about Mantle's background and numerous requests for Mickey's time. Patterson sat Mantle down and began poring over the teenager's brief biography. The questions were neither penetrating nor especially illuminating, just basic queries to feed the press about who Mickey was and where he'd come from.

"Who was your favorite ballplayer growing up?" Patterson asked.

"Stan Musial," Mantle replied without hesitation.

"No, it was Joe DiMaggio," Red dictated.

That Stan Musial was Mickey's favorite player growing up was no great surprise. The Cardinals were the Mantle's "home" team, and after all, Musial was the finest player on that club. A couple of times each summer Mutt and Mick would climb into the family car and make the trek to Sportsman's Park. The 310 mile trip seemed all that much longer thanks to Mutt's deliberate driving pace. The lengthy car ride, though, was cherished by Mickey. Father and son bonded during the course of the outing. Whether over a comfortable silence, or, on the trip back home, dissecting every aspect of the game they'd just absorbed, Mickey and Mutt soaked up every moment of the day.

Regardless of Mantle's affinity for Musial, Patterson had a job to do—sell the Yankees. DiMaggio made a better story line and played better in the New York papers, so DiMaggio it would be.

Patterson became the major leagues' first full-time publicity director when Larry MacPhail brought him to the Yankees in 1946. Before Patterson took over the role, what little publicity emanated from teams was usually dispatched by the road secretary. When MacPhail approached Patterson, Red was working in the National League office under Ford Frick, a position he held for one year. Prior to that, Patterson had been a reporter who covered baseball for the *Herald Tribune*. Given his pedigree, writers who worked for the many New York dailies optimistically anticipated cooperation from Patterson as they went about their jobs of distilling information on the Yankees. At the annual New York baseball writers' dinner, Red often joined in the fun. Patterson was particular pleased with one skit in which he portrayed both Hitler and Larry MacPhail in the same bit, a rendering that was met with delight from both himself and the audience. This side of Patterson was rarely on display at the park, though. Too often writers were stymied in pursuit of a story or information from the club. The frustration many reporters felt was expressed in colorful fashion by Jimmy Cannon of the *New York Post*.

"Patterson," Cannon wrote, "was a dog editor before he became a censor. The company of animals appeals to Mr. Patterson, who flatters the squatters in the press box by treating them as though they were aristocratic contestants in the Westminster Kennel Club show."

———

YANKEE REGULARS PLAYED THEIR FIRST INTRA-SQUAD GAME ON March 6 against rookies and backups. Mickey played outfield in a game for the first time ever. Batting left handed against Wally Hood, Mantle hit a triple in the first and a home run in the second inning. The following afternoon Mantle made his debut in center field against the Indians. Mickey was wearing flip-down sunglasses, a contraption he was struggling to master. When Cleveland third baseman Ray Boone hit a line drive directly at Mantle, the fledgling center fielder took a couple of steps forward, fumbled with his sunglasses, and then was promptly smacked in the forehead with the ball.

Mantle's lack of dexterity when handling his sunglasses was one of his only failures all spring. Baseball writers following the Yankees were stumbling over one another trying to extol the rookie's many virtues. They also tried to outdo one another in bestowing nicknames on the Oklahoma wunderkind:

"The Oakie Dokie"

"Oklahoma Whiz Kid"

"Muscles"

"The Commerce Comet"

"Wonder Boy"

"The Sweet Switcher"

The sobriquets were coming at a faster pace than Mantle's home runs.

The Yankees concluded their initial stretch of games in Arizona on the 14th, with a 16–14 barnburner against the Indians. The high scoring affair was played before 5,431 at Municipal Stadium, with an overflow crowd standing behind a rope in the outfield. To date, DiMaggio was limited to just three pinch hitting appearances. While others openly wondered about Joe's lack of playing time, DiMaggio's manager was not concerned.

"Except for a cold, which he now had shaken off, DiMaggio has looked swell ever since he came here two weeks ago," Stengel said.

The morning of the 15th the Yanks played an eight-inning, intra-squad game before most members of the traveling party participated in a pro-am tournament at the Phoenix Country Club. Following the golf outing the team caught a flight to Los Angeles for the start of their highly publicized and much anticipated 11-day tour of California.

——

MARCH 16TH WAS DECLARED "YANKEE DAY" IN LOS ANGELES BY THE city's mayor, Fletcher Bowron. Gilmore Stadium was brimming with celebrities, such as Groucho Marx, Danny Kaye, Joe E. Brown, George Jessel, Pat O'Brien, and George Raft in anticipation of the Yankees' exhibition against the Hollywood Stars.

"It's like coming back to my old stomping grounds," DiMaggio said, while peering over the top of the dugout at the star-studded crowd of 7,359.

"You know, it's a good feeling to come back to this part of the country and see your old friends. Of course, I'm from up higher in San Francisco, but there will be a lot of people I know here."

Seemingly in high spirits, Joe eased back into the dugout for a moment and reminisced.

"Things have changed some since I played here back in 1935. Hollywood never played its games here at Gilmore Stadium. The team played at Wrigley Field in Los Angeles, alternating with the Angels."

During the game, Joe flew out twice in his two at-bats and then took the rest of the afternoon off. The Yanks won their first contest in California 5–1 before heading across town for the next day's game at Wrigley Field. With an overflow crowd of fans standing behind ropes stretched across the outfield, Mantle came up in the 7th inning against right-hander Bob Spicer. Mantle pounced on a Spicer delivery and belted a 410-foot home run to dead-center. The blast landed in the seats of the outer reaches of Wrigley Field and with one bounce landed on Avalon Blvd. DiMaggio also homered, his first of the spring, against the Angels' Ralph Hamner.

Mickey and fellow rookie Bob Wiesler took advantage of the club's stay in Hollywood. Both Mantle and Wiesler enjoyed the movies and the chance to visit a film studio was too much to pass up. For their effort, Mickey and Bob had the opportunity to see such stars as Debbie Reynolds, Red Skelton, and Esther Williams. Mantle also made the short trip to the Santa Monica Pier, where he saw the Pacific Ocean for the first time.

The tour continued with another game in Los Angeles and one more in Hollywood before the Yankees headed north. On the 21st, Casey was given a day in his honor by his hometown of Glendale. Prior to the contest against the White Sox a brief ceremony was held. The city's mayor, George Wickham, started things off by presenting Stengel with a plaque in honor of Casey being the initial inductee into Glendale's baseball hall of fame. Wickham was followed by a series of speeches. Stepping to the microphone were Dan Topping, Del Webb, and White Sox general manager Frank Lane. The most memorable of all the short speeches came from Casey's bride, Edna.

The press loved to play up Stengel as the clown, the carnival broker with juxtaposed quips and mangled syntax, but Edna hated these portrayals. How much of Casey's act was put on, who really knew?

Well, Edna knew but she wasn't talking.

The Charles she knew was smart. No, brilliant. Beyond his obvious genius as a baseball tactician, Edna's husband had a gift for financial acumen. Back in the '30s, Casey invested in some oil wells that paid off handsomely, in addition to a number of other lucrative investments.

She was a tall and handsome woman who accented her good looks by dressing fabulously. Mrs. Stengel frequently traveled with the Yankees, and in the off-season Casey and Edna journeyed the world together. She decorated their home with items purchased on their travels. Their house in Glendale had a Chinese room as well as a room dedicated to Japanese décor. Years earlier, Edna appeared in silent movies. Occasionally when addressing his team, Casey would conclude the talk by glancing at Edna and saying to her, "Tell them about the time you played with Hoot Gibson."

The citizens of Glendale came out in force for "Casey Stengel Day." And besides a rather mundane exhibition contest, Casey and Edna thoroughly enjoyed the quaint festivities. A group of Marion fighter pilots, squadron VMF 232, sat near the Yankee bench. The squad was comprised of several native New Yorkers, and fittingly they wore Yankee caps provided to them by ex-Marine Dan Topping.

The game itself was rather forgettable from a Yankee standpoint. It was a sloppily played, three-and-a-half-hour affair. The Yankees looked particularly bad as they scattered a measly four hits against a couple of White Sox rookies, Skinny Brown and Marvin Rotblatt.

Following the game a dinner was held for Stengel. Thankfully, the Yankees' poor performance didn't dampen the spirit of the evening. Mayor Wickham played along with Casey's old friend and partner in mirth, Carl Zamloch.

"It was the damnedest celebration over losing a four-hit shut-out I ever saw," one reporter present noted.

The next day, DiMaggio made a visit to the California State Assembly along with Joe Page and Phil Rizzuto. The senate recessed briefly, relinquishing the floor to DiMaggio. The honor of addressing the assembly fell flat on Joe. He reluctantly approached the dais and mumbled a few words of thanks before awkwardly telling the state senators that they "were in better shape than some ballplayers he'd come across."

The Yanks corrected their three-game skid against the Sacramento Salons, 11–0 in front of a crowd in excess of 10,000. Mantle, who had homered against the Salons, which brought his spring totals to 13 hits in 26 at-bats. Among the dignitaries present were Governor Earl Warren and Pittsburgh Pirate general manager Branch Rickey, long considered one of baseball's great talent evaluators. Warren's impression of the game went unrecorded, but Rickey, who was sitting with Dan Topping, marveled at Mantle's every move. His abilities were otherworldly, but maybe more impressive than Mickey's power, speed, and arm, was his technique. Everything he did was fluid, there was no wasted motion; the boy was a textbook perfect ballplayer. During the game, Rickey slipped a blank check to Topping. "You can fill in any figure you wish for the boy," Rickey advised Topping, "But please be reasonable."

Topping replied that Mantle could be had for Ralph Kiner and $500,000.

A chagrined Rickey changed the subject.

A handful of writers from the Oakland and San Francisco papers made the trek to Sacramento to interview DiMaggio prior to the Yanks' Bay Area visit.

The first question was predictable enough. "Will this definitely be your last year, Joe?"

DiMag reiterated what he said at each stop during the club's training camp tour. "Print it if you want to—the old geezer will be getting out.

"It's going to be tough giving this up. Baseball's been fun. I loved every minute of it, but now...well, why kid myself? I can't go on forever."

Prescott Sullivan of the *San Francisco Examiner* was with the paper back when Joe was taking the field for the Seals. "You don't look like you're through," Prescott said, "You look swell."

"And I feel swell, too," Joe admitted. "Never better, in fact.

I'm not worried about my condition or my ability to play the game. It's just possible that I'll have one of my best seasons this time.

"That isn't it, however. The big thing is that I can't do the things I used to do anymore without getting tired. Things that used to be fun are now more like work. All this traveling from one overnight to another—for instance. It was exciting once. Now it gets me down. Guess what I need are a pair of slippers and a big easy chair."

"You've only had two hits in 18 times up, are you concerned with the slow start?"

"Nothing's wrong with me," Joe stated. "It's just that I'm pacing myself. When I was a kid, I knocked myself out trying to peak too fast. Nothing like this, this time. If this is my last season as I am saying it's going to be, I want it to be a good one.

"I seem to have trouble getting my timing adjusted. That happens to me often early in the year. I manage to get a piece of the ball but not enough of it. That's really all I know."

Playing in his hometown of San Francisco might snap him out of the slump, DiMaggio hoped.

"I used to hit in this town long before I became a Yankee," Joe said. "And it's likely to be good luck for me still."

The evening before DiMaggio's homecoming at Seals Stadium, Joe hosted a party at the family restaurant, Joe DiMaggio's Grotto. During the night's festivities, someone inadvisably questioned Joe about the chances of him moving over to left field to clear the way for Mantle in center.

"There's nobody taking center from me until I give it up," Joe responded with a hint of conceit.

The game itself had received more buildup than anyone in

San Francisco could recall. Would the hype and promotion register in paid attendance, though? Unfortunately, the turnout at Seals Stadium was more than 9,000 below capacity. The disappointing turnout could be attributed to the imprudent decision by Seals management to predict a sellout for the past three months. These repeated pronouncements surely scared off a number of potential patrons from the park, not to mention that the game was played on Good Friday.

Indeed, "the religious significance of the day, and the fear of no seats were available to late comers probably kept the place from bulging," a member of the Seals front office admitted. Still, the lack of a sellout did not diminish the enthusiasm of the 20,181 present inside the ballpark. In the stands were Joe's brother and a collection of nephews and nieces. The oldest of the DiMaggio brothers was busy running the family restaurant, and sister Marie remained home with their ill mother, Rosalie.

The flag hung limp on Seals Stadium's center-field pole. A warm early spring evening sparkled with the light of a star-filled sky. The atmosphere blended; a perfect fusion for the festive night at hand. More than an hour before the first pitch, a third of the park's seats were already filled. DiMag first stepped on the field at 7:07. A number of early birds had already taken their seats and instantly recognized Joe's distinct gait as he headed toward the batting cage.

"I never played on such a warm night in my three years I was here with the Seals." Joe told Johnny Mize and Yogi Berra, who were both lingering outside the cage. DiMaggio's appearance triggered the large number of reporters milling about, and a swarm of writers immediately enveloped Joe.

"Are you feeling nostalgic?" a local correspondent asked.

"Nope, no sadness, just gladness." he replied. "I am proud to come home before my people with such a great ball club. I hope I don't disappoint."

He then stepped in to take a few practice swings, but the pack of writers surrounding the cage prevented fans from enjoying an unfettered view of the hometown hero.

"Get out of the way you guys, so we can see Joe..." a voice called from the stands.

The reporters politely complied.

What Joe hadn't mentioned to the writers he spoke with was the strained left knee that was bothering him. Normally he would have taken the day off, but Joe didn't want to disappoint his hometown crowd. And though he wouldn't admit it, this evening was pretty special to him, too. Joe didn't hit any out of the park with his practice swings but Mantle hit a couple over the wall, including a blast that left the park in right near the light tower and onto 16th street.

The crowd let out a thunderous roar when DiMaggio's name was announced in the top of the first. With a line-out to right field Joe did not deliver with that at-bat, nor did he get a hit in his other two chances. Regardless, DiMaggio's failure at the plate did not diminish the experience for the hometown fans who left Seals Stadium having finally seen their Joe in a Yankee uniform, plus Mantle hit yet another home run, this one traveled more than 400 feet over the left-field bleachers into the parking lot.

A trip across the bay for a game against Stengel's old team, the Oakland Oaks, came the next day. And then, on Easter Sunday, the Yankees played a morning/night doubleheader. The first game in Oakland and then later in the day a return to Seals

Stadium. The last stop on the Yankees' swing through California was a return to Los Angeles. Hugh Bradley of the *Journal-American* was speaking with Mantle before the Yankees took the field against the Trojans of USC. While conversing, Mickey innocently let slip that he was playing without a contract.

"They offered me a contract with Binghamton. I mailed it back," Mantle said. "Since then, nobody's said anything to me about money and I haven't said anything to them.

"I'd like to get married before the start of the season. If you've got $5,000 or maybe more in prospects, a fellow could do that and live pretty comfortably, don't you think?"

The game that was played following the interview was the stuff from which legends are born. The headline in the next day's *Los Angeles Times* read: "One For The Mantle: Yankees Dismantle Troy 15–1."

USC's Bovard Field was crammed to capacity and then some. Temporary seating was slapped together, and the outfield was roped off to increase the standing-room-only crowd itching to see the Yankees. Interest in the game was so high that KWKW broadcast the game for the many fans shut out from purchasing tickets.

Mantle hit two home runs, knocked seven runs across the plate, and added a single as an afterthought. True, Mantle's heroics came against a collegiate squad, but the visuals surpassed the most spectacular Independence Day fireworks.

The estimates varied: 400 feet, 500 feet, half a mile…one thing every soul in attendance could agree on, they had never seen a ball hit *that* far. The ball traveled far enough to send a postcard back to home plate. The journey sent the ball well beyond the right-field fence and into the USC football team's practice field. The ball invaded the Trojans' huddle, hitting running back Frank Gifford on the foot before continuing on its merry way.

The reaction in the Yankee dugout was very un-Yankee-like. The normally staid, all-business demeanor of the New York club broke character. They hollered, whistled, and yelled their appreciation for the mammoth blast. When Mantle reached the bench he was bludgeoned with congratulatory pats on the back.

Mickey hit a second home run in the sixth that came to rest on the front porch of a home situated beyond the left-field fence. This homer, though a little less ostentatious than the first, traveled an estimated 500 feet. One inning later, with the bases loaded, Mantle hit a triple into deep center field.

At game's end, Mickey couldn't make his way to the team's clubhouse due to the mob of USC students who surrounded him. He was besieged by dozens of kids who wanted an autograph, or simply to touch his powerful arms. Yes, he had been under a deluge of attention and praise, but this was something else altogether. Mickey was humbled by the attention, certainly, but he was also frightened by it at the same time.

The tour of California was a rousing success. Twelve games in 11 days brought out 133,328 fans to see the Yankees play some of the Pacific Coast League's best clubs. The boost in attendance not only bolstered the Yankees' coffers, but also did a great deal for the PCL teams they played along the way, teams that greatly appreciated the added revenue. The Los Angeles Angels cleared $19,000 and the Hollywood Stars $14,000. Indeed, the influx of revenue was welcomed by all. The Oakland club was able to pay off all their training expenses and came away with more than $7,000 to spare.

The only drawback: the Yankee players were exhausted at the conclusion of the whirlwind tour.

"There's no question that it tired the players," a team official admitted. "It means that we must double up the remaining days we have in Phoenix."

———

STENGEL USUALLY DIDN'T SIT FOR FORMAL INTERVIEWS. QUESTIONS rarely needed to be asked. If Casey had something to say, which was the norm, the words and thoughts just flowed forth.

"All I know is that he has me terribly confused and he's getting me more so every day," Stengel told a group of reporters following the game at Seals Stadium. "I know that he's not a big league outfielder yet and that he should have a year of Triple A ball under his belt. That's the only logical thing. But this kid ain't logical. He's a big league hitter and base runner right now. You writers have blowed him up so much that I have to take him to New York. Don't get me wrong. I'm not blaming you. He's been everything you say he is…. But it doesn't figure that he's ready. Then again nothing he does figures. He's too good. It's very confusing."

Before a couple of days had passed, Stengel denied making any such proclamation. Nonsense, Casey declared. "I never said it," Stengel emphatically said. "I am not letting the newspapers run the club, and I know the writers have no desire to do so. I am no less enthusiastic over Mantle than any of the writers covering the Yankees. The kid is the kind of player a manager runs into about once in his career, if he is lucky. To jump from Joplin Class C all the way to the majors would be a tremendous feat for Mickey. He may be able to do it.

"We have got to be very careful with Mantle. Not that he is the kind of boy whose head would be turned by success. You have seen him around, and you know that. He is quiet and shy.

"However, the kid is just about that—a kid. And we should not place on his shoulders responsibilities which he could not carry."

Mantle's exploits spread well beyond the world of baseball diehards. Even the nationally syndicated columnist Walter Winchell, who peddled in the gossip market, took note of the Mantle phenomenon. In his March 25 column, Winchell noted: "The way Yankee rookie Mickey Mantle is hogging sport page headlines, they'll be calling him 'another DiMaggio.' Time will tell, time will tell."

Stengel stood gazing out on the practice field, admiring Mantle's every move. "Can you imagine what McGraw would say if he saw this kid?" Casey asked a journalist standing nearby.

John McGraw was Stengel's template. In Casey's mind he was the greatest manager the game had known, and Stengel savored the time he played for McGraw, absorbing the wealth of baseball knowledge and strategy the Giants' manager demonstrated.

McGraw was in his mid-fifties when Mel Ott was dropped in his lap. Ott was just 16, but displayed enormous potential to be one of the all-time greats. He also possessed an unorthodox swing. The left-handed Ott lifted his right foot high in the air as he prepared to swing. And though the common move would be to send Ott to the minor leagues for seasoning—a chance to mature physically and mentally—McGraw feared some inept minor league manager would change Ott's natural swing. Stengel remembered how McGraw handled his prodigy, and he was quick to remind listeners of the similarities between Ott and Mantle.

"I keep remembering how John McGraw kept Mel Ott right by his side, and he was only 16 when he first appeared at the Polo Grounds. And I know this kid has the finest teacher right here in Tommy Henrich. On the other hand, it doesn't seem right to keep a kid like that on the bench. He should be playing every day. It's a tough one all right."

This Mantle, Casey thought, *will be my Ott.*

The McGraw/Ott comparison was explained to Mantle, who took a moment to digest the implications of such an analogy.

"I'd rather play anywhere than sit it out, even in a big league dugout," Mantle confessed. "I realize you could pick up a lot of pointers just by traveling with the Yankees, but give me action every day. I believe it will do me the most good."

"I'm not a big league fielder and I hope I'm sent out to Kansas City. It's only a little over 100 miles from Commerce."

———

AS THE MONTH OF MARCH CAME TO A CLOSE, MICKEY WAS OUT OF the lineup for a couple of days because of a sharp pain in his wrist. Though the team feared the possibility of a broken bone, X-rays revealed a sprain. He was back in the lineup April 1 for the Yankees last game at their spring home in Phoenix. Against nearly any measurement, Del Webb's Arizona excursion was a booming success. The Yankees drew 40,423 at Memorial Stadium in nine dates against major league opponents, 11,000 fans more than the Giants a year earlier. Against the Pirates in the Phoenix finale, Mantle had three hits in four at-bats, bringing his spring average up to .443.

"Mickey Mantle is here to stay," Arch Murray declared in

the *Post*. "They aren't going to get the kid out of his Yankee monkey suit and it's almost for sure that he'll be in the Yankee lineup opening day at Washington.

"The Mick has been sensational all spring," Murray continued. "He's been too wonderful to be true."

Murray wasn't just relying on his own beliefs as an eyewitness to Mantle's prodigious camp. He spoke to several Yankee coaches who, to a man, gushed about Mantle's abilities.

"He is just the greatest I ever saw," Jim Turner said. "Just the greatest. Why, you could pitch to Stan Musial when he first came up. But you can't to this kid."

The usually reserved Frank Crosetti was in agreement. "I've never seen a better looking younger hitter, and I've seen some great ones."

Bill Dickey added, "Somebody suggested I tell him something about hitting, I'd rather he tell me."

And, try as he might, Stengel could not contain his enthusiasm for the blonde prodigy. Just days after chastising reporters for trying to force his hand concerning Mantle, Casey was gushing with superlatives about the kid to Joe Trimble.

"He's the greatest switch hitter who has ever played baseball. I've seen them all for the past 30 years and there hasn't been anything like him. Frank Frisch was the best two-way hitter, but he lacked power from the right side…when he batted right handed, he looked awkward. This kid looks the same from either side."

That Mantle took swings from both sides of the plate was an exotic curiosity. The last effective Yankee switch hitter that the old timers in the press box could recall was Mark Koenig, and he played for the club more than two decades earlier, in the late '20s.

Stengel continued, "You know, that kid has me changing my mind like a chorus girl changing costumes. One day I think he's got more power from the left. The next day, I swear it's from the right. I really don't know. But I'll say one thing. He's got more natural power from both sides than anybody I ever saw."

In recent days, Stengel had been moving Mantle between all three outfield spots. The reasoning for this was simple, Casey explained, "Get him used to all positions."

Still, despite the superlatives and the manager's evident preparation in molding Mantle into a versatile piece of the big league team, Stengel refused to confirm that the kid had made the club.

For all his unabashed gushing over Mantle, Stengel was growing increasingly impatient with his team. Their training habits were sorely lacking, and many players were flaunting their disregard for the team's 12:00 curfew. Before the Yankees packed up their belongings in Phoenix, Stengel held a closed-door meeting with his players. That this was the second time during training camp that he had to address these same issues angered Stengel all the more.

This would the last meeting of this nature, Stengel told the clubhouse full of players. They were testing his leniency when it came to rules and regulations, Casey said, and the effort on the field was deficient. The Yankees' 15–9 record in the spring was irrelevant; they were here to prepare for the season. Stengel did not single out any individual culprits, but his stern message was delivered. From here on out even the most minor rules infractions would be dealt with.

When asked by a reporter afterward what the meeting was about, Stengel demurred. Instead of addressing the question, Casey discussed his plans for the coming journey through Texas.

"I want the club to be in shape by the time we reach Dallas next Monday," he explained. "That's a week from the start of the season. I want that much time to get used to playing my regulars regularly."

The club played one final game in Arizona, on April 3 in Tucson, before the start of their 10-day trip home to the Stadium; a trek that would carry the Yankees through Texas and brief stops in Kansas City and Pittsburgh before heading to New York.

The first town on the Yankees' tour of Texas was El Paso. From his room in that west Texas town, Mantle made his regular call home. His dad had some upsetting news: a notice had arrived in the mail. Mickey was to report to his local draft board in Miami, Oklahoma, at 7:00 AM on April 11.

The news wasn't a complete surprise. This fawning attention came with a price; how could this healthy, 19-year-old be deemed not physically fit to serve his country while so many boys his own age were fighting and dying half a world away on the Korean peninsula? Mantle had already been classified 4-F by his local draft board due to the chronic disease osteomyelitis he endured. A number of displeased people wrote "poison pen" letters to Mantle's draft board, the Yankees, and to Mickey himself.

After speaking with his parents, Mickey reported to Dudley Stadium and informed his manager of the turn of events.

"I don't know if I am to be re-examined or questioned, or what," Mantle told Stengel.

Just hours later, before an overflow crowd of 6,743, Mickey helped lift the Yankees to a 16–10 victory over the Diablos, with three hits, including a single, a double, and his sixth home run of the spring.

This wouldn't be the first time the Army examined Mantle's fitness to serve. A year and a half earlier, in the fall of 1949, Mickey was working as an electrician's helper for the motor crew at the Eagle-Picher mines, driving a pick-up and delivering equipment. One afternoon, Mantle explained, "My dad came by and handed me a postcard." The card advised Mickey that he was due to appear before the Ottawa County draft board.

Mantle was given a typical examination, including X-rays of his left leg. The X-rays confirmed that Mantle was suffering from osteomyelitis.

"I drove down to the draft board with a set of X-rays of my leg," Mantle explained. "They ushered me into this cubicle of a room containing a Toledo scale, examination table, an eye chart, and a kindly old doctor. He gave me the once over with his stethoscope, then probed at the scar of my left shinbone."

In early December of '49, Mickey received notification that he had been classified 4-F.

And now, 15 months later, who was behind the decision to re-examine Mantle? Dan Daniel believed he had the answer when he reported that the request came from George Weiss. Reportedly Weiss didn't want Mantle burdened by vicious letters or harassed by hecklers. Daniel's *World Telegram* piece drew immediate response from Weiss as well as Del Webb, who both vehemently denied that anyone in the Yankee organization asked for an official clarification of Mantle's 4-F status.

"Could be that the New York baseball writers have written marvelous Mickey Mantle smack dab into the Army," Bob Considine of the *Journal American* wondered in his "On the Line" column. "These are not days and nights when parents of lads of Mickey's age are surrendering their sons to UNC's latest crusade. Some of those draftees are being nailed even though their feet are as flat as a minute steak, their loins as rare as a keyboard, their vision roughly comparable to London fog.... They reason that war is a muscular business, and if their lads are tossed in the man-pool what's 4-F-ish about Mantle. And besides, what's osteomyelitis got to do with it, they wonder. There must be a UN rule against kicking in war."

In fact, Mickey had been examined by Sidney Gaynor in New York on the 16th of January. Following the exam, Red Patterson spoke with a few interested reporters.

"Mickey's locomotion is hampered only slightly, but we can't tell now what effect this condition will have on his baseball future."

Oklahoma Selective Service director Colonel Clive Murray explained that nothing should be read into the state's request.

"I just want to know one thing," Murray explained, "is the boy acceptable for military service? The only place to find out for sure is the examination station."

On the April 7, Casey met with the few writers traveling with the club through Texas in Beaumont.

"On arrival in New York Friday I will name the Yankee roster, which will go into the race in Washington a week from Monday," Stengel explained.

One of the reporters badgered Casey about the status of Mantle. Was he going up to the Yanks, or was he being sent down for seasoning?

"You are trying to get me to say that Mantle will be signed to a Yankee contract this coming week, aren't you? Well, I refuse to talk about Mickey at all. Let us proceed to McDougald.

Since our stay in San Francisco, he has come along fast. He appears to be our replacement for Bobby Brown."

Stengel had intended to play DiMaggio every day during the Yankees' six-day journey through Texas as well as their stop in Kansas City, where they had a date with the St. Louis Browns. Joe's bat had finally begun to come around of late. He'd had at least one hit in eight consecutive days and lifted his spring average up to .378.

"I am getting into great shape," DiMaggio said. "I used to rush my conditioning because I wanted to have reserve if I got hurt. This time I decided to take it easy."

Joe was pleased with the progress he'd made with his new conditioning regimen, though he wasn't happy with his weight.

"I weigh only 191," he explained. "I wish it were at least 198."

On the Yankees last day in Texas, Joe was asked his thoughts on the upcoming pennant race.

"There will be four clubs in the fight," DiMaggio replied. "New York, Boston, Cleveland, and Detroit."

Joe went on to break down the strengths and weaknesses of the four clubs he viewed as the favorites, but, he concluded, "We will win again because of our reserve strength. We will have some of it on the field all the way, and some in our minor league chain.

"One thing I would like to impress on the fans in New York: I will do my part. They need not worry about me."

The short jog through Texas concluded, the Yankees pressed on to Kansas City. When the exhibition expedition reached the city of Stengel's birth, Casey needed emergency dental surgery. He remained behind in Kansas City while the rest of the Yankee troupe moved on to New York. Stengel intended on joining his team in Pittsburgh, but poor flying conditions prevented Casey from meeting his club. Stengel's presence in Pittsburgh was unnecessary as the game against the Pirates at Forbes Field was rained out.

———

AS MANTLE'S TEAMMATES CONCLUDED THE LAST LEG OF THEIR trip back to New York for Opening Day, Mickey's parents made the 130-mile drive to pick their son up and bring him back home for his appointment with the draft board. Mutt and Lovell watched the game from the stands, and then made the return trip to Commerce.

The next morning, Mickey and nine other selectees boarded a bus in Miami bound for Tulsa. On hand to greet the bus as it pulled into the Tulsa station was a reporter peppering Mantle with questions. Mickey paused briefly before boarding the Army truck waiting to transport the group on the last leg of the excursion to the pre-induction station.

"Anybody would be a fool not to want to play major league baseball," he said. "But I'm ready to serve in the Army if the doctors think I'm fit. It's strictly up to the doctors."

Three days later, Joe Payton, a member of the Oklahoma Draft Board, disclosed the results of Mantle's physical. A notice had been mailed to Mantle declaring that he had been found "unacceptable," Payton explained.

The foundation for Mantle's rejection was not revealed by the board, Payton clarified, because Selective Service regulations forbid such disclosure.

Before the U.S. Post Office could deliver the official documents, the news reached Mantle via a reporter who was at his parents' home.

"I don't know how I feel about it, Mickey said. "It is kind of a relief to know one way or another."

For the first time in more than a week, Mickey could focus on baseball. But first he had to catch up with his teammates. Later that day he flew from Joplin to Kansas City, where he would board a flight very early in the morning, April 14, for New York.

———

DESPITE HIS FABULOUS SPRING AND A SUITCASE FULL OF FLATTERING clippings, Mantle still hadn't made the club. Not officially at least.

His plane landed at 8:30 AM and Mickey immediately hopped in a cab and headed to Ebbets Field. Later that Saturday afternoon the Yankees and Dodgers were to meet in the second contest of their annual three-game inter-borough series. Prior to the game at the Dodgers' 38-year-old park, Casey took Mantle to the right-field wall and began tutoring the kid on the idiosyncrasies of the concrete wall.

"Now when I played out here…" Casey began.

A dumbfounded Mantle looked at Stengel and asked in amazement, "You played here?"

Following the tutorial, Casey came back to the dugout, where a few writers were gathered.

"Boy never saw concrete before. I told him not to worry about it, that I never had no trouble with it and I played that wall for six years. He don't believe what I'm telling him. I guess he thinks I was born 60 years old. They never believe we done anything before they did."

Stengel had no intention of placing Mantle's name on the lineup card for that afternoon's exhibition. The kid had been in an airplane all night, Casey told the press an hour before game time. But, "I asked him if he wanted to play and he said, 'Yes,' so he's gonna play," Stengel explained. "Said to him, 'You couldn't have got much sleep last night,' and he said, 'What difference does it make?' Maybe at 19 it doesn't."

To prove that he was well rested, Mickey blasted Tommy Henrich's deliveries all over—and out of—Ebbets Field during batting practice. More than a few Dodger players stood at rapt attention, watching as Mantle slashed line drives all around and out of their home park. After witnessing the hitting clinic, Stengel relented and placed Mantle's name in the starting lineup. Besides, the New York audience had been clamoring to see the rookie they'd been reading about for the last six weeks.

"But don't expect too much from the kid," Stengel pleaded with newsmen after he announced the lineup change. "Remember, it's the first time he's ever played with a concrete wall in back of him, and those balls coming off there will give him trouble."

Stengel's audience was populated by a number of reporters who hadn't yet seen Mantle in the flesh. All the information they'd received on the rookie sensation had come from the dispatches sent from Arizona and California by their peers.

"They see him a few times, and they ask me what am I going to do with him." Stengel said as he began a rambling discourse summing up the eventful spring. "Well, he is a shortstop but we ain't going to get that fellow out of there. So I try him in the outfield. I put him in right field but he misjudges fly balls and one of them sticks on top of his head. I try him in left field. I think he can play there, being an infielder, and he's used to going back on fly balls. And he's right-handed. But he has trouble with fly balls too, and he throws like an infielder. Well, we try him in right field again but the curves bother him. I mean the curves on those line drives. He is turning this way and the ball goes that way.

"'They ask me, 'Is he a major leaguer?' 'How do I know?' I say, 'He is in Joplin last year. Joplin, it's a long jump from Joplin up to here, He is a shortstop in Joplin last year and how do I know whether he can play the outfield up here?'

"But he can fly. He hits a ball and he rounds first base. Looks like he's pulling up. Then he sees a chance for an extra base and…" at that moment Casey smacked his hands together. "Like this. Run? I'll say he can run. He don't run. He flies.… They get him out sometimes, but he scares the hell out of those pitchers. He hit a couple back to the pitchers and he damned near ruined them with fright. They shook all over."

With that kind of buildup, it would be difficult for Mantle not to disappoint. During Saturday afternoon's game, Mantle gathered one hit with his first swing and threw a runner out at the plate from right field. But it was the next day, the final rehearsal before Opening Day, that Mickey offered New York City a glimpse of his immense promise. Joe Hatten struck him out the first time Mickey stepped to the plate, but then Mantle delivered three consecutive singles before lifting a monstrous home run out of Ebbets Field.

As Mickey rounded the bases, Red Patterson announced in the press box, "That's number nine for Mantle." To which a writer responded, "How many does that put him ahead of Babe Ruth?"

There may have been one skeptic jaded by the hyperbole surrounding Mantle's spring adventures, but he was in the distinct minority. Sitting in the Ebbets Field press box were a number of local writers who hadn't made the trek out west for training camp. For these men, this was their introduction to the Oklahoma Sensation. Mantle's debut weekend drew the expected praise in the sports pages of the city's numerous daily newspapers. Few writers were as smitten as the *Mirror*'s Dan Parker, who penned a laudatory column after catching his first glimpse of Mantle.

"If Mickey himself isn't fake, he is going to cause the greatest revision of the dictionary since Samuel Johnson's time, as all the superlatives now listed will be word weaklings that should be discarded as too anemic to allow a baseball writer properly to pay homage in printers ink to such a prodigy."

Following the Saturday afternoon game at Ebbets Field, Stengel encouraged his team to attend Whitey Ford's wedding reception.

Ford, a left-handed pitcher, joined the Yankees as a rookie in July of 1950. Earlier in the spring a couple of Yankee pitchers were overheard lamenting the loss of Ford to the Army. "We're sure going to miss him," Vic Raschi said of Ford. "He was a life saver down the stretch last fall."

Tom Ferrick nodded in agreement. "You're not kidding," Ferrick replied. "He had the most moxie of any rookie I ever saw."

Ford won nine straight contests after being called up by the Yanks, and he added one more against the Phillies in the Series. Following the season, Eddie Ford, as his mother named him, was called into the service.

A bus full of Yankees pulled up to Donahue's, an establishment in Astoria. The bus emptied and the team joined the reception for a few hours of revelry and relaxation. The entire ball club, that is, with the exception of Mantle, who remained on the bus. The kid was too shy and uncomfortable to step into the unfamiliar social situation.

Earlier that day, just prior to the Ford wedding, the Yankees purchased the contracts of Gil McDougald and Tom Morgan from the Kansas City Blues. Morgan, a 20-year-old who hadn't been on the club's winter roster, had blossomed into a spring surprise. Weiss and Stengel had just one day before Opening Day. Just 24 hours to finalize the Yankees' roster. The GM and manager had diametrically opposing points of view. Stengel wanted the kid on the club; Casey wanted him nearby so no one could mess with Mantle's swing. Conversely, Weiss believed Mantle needed more seasoning. The kid would have the opportunity to develop out of the spotlight, Weiss argued.

Stengel persisted, though. He argued his point incessantly with the general manager, and whether he finally convinced Weiss or simply wore him down, Casey got his way. With 41 hits in 102 at-bats, nine home runs, and 32 runs batted in for the spring, how could Weiss deny Mantle a place on the Yankee roster? But if he were to make the Opening Day roster, Mantle needed to play. There was no sense in placing Mickey on the club and then sitting him on the bench. On this point both Stengel and Weiss agreed.

5   IT JUST ISN'T TRUE

FOLLOWING THE FINAL EXHIBITION GAME AT EBBETS FIELD, THE Yankees boarded a train and headed south to Washington for their season opener against the Senators. During the trip, Mantle sat with Topping, Webb, and Weiss in a drawing room aboard the Pullman and signed his first major league contract. Opening Day hoopla was a tradition celebrated across the big leagues. Washington, however, had the special privilege of having the President baptize the season by tossing out the first pitch. Despite the recent and highly controversial decision to fire General Douglas MacArthur, Harry Truman happily agreed to kick off the Senators' 1951 season.

The Yankees spent the night at the Shoreham Hotel and awoke the morning of the 16th to gray skies covering the capital. By noon a steady drizzle began to fall, and 70 minutes before the three o'clock game time the rain had not let up. Roughly 1,000 of the expected 33,000 spectators coming to Griffith Stadium had reached the park when the postponement was announced. The President was among the many

Senator fans who decided to remain at home rather than venture to the ball yard.

A couple of writers met with Stengel after the "no game" placards went up around Griffith Stadium.

"Well we haven't lost any ground to the Red Sox yet," Casey said. "Those Bostons were supposed to win the pennant last year, and the year before that, and got all fouled up. Maybe the Yankees will get lucky again this season."

He was a fan of Mantle, Stengel acknowledged, "and if he doesn't become a good big leaguer, I'll always think he should have made it.

"In the first place, Gene Woodling came down with the miseries and that left me short. Then Mantle started acting as if he belonged in there and the more I saw of him the more I had to like him. My first idea was to farm him out to Kansas City for a few weeks and let him learn how to play the outfield and then call him in. But Tommy Henrich did such a job on the boy he began to look ready. You have to believe what you see the kid do."

There was another factor Stengel confessed. "Mantle gave the newspapermen so much to write about, switch hitter and all of that. All the publicity can't wear off for a few weeks even if the kid doesn't make it. The club figures to make some money with him and I want to give George Weiss that break, too."

The postponement washed out what was only a one-game series, and the Yankees immediately jumped back on the rails and returned to New York for their re-scheduled season launch against the Red Sox at the Stadium.

———

RUTH, GEHRIG, DIMAGGIO.... IT SEEMED NATURAL, IF NOT presumptuous, that the kid, the next in line for Yankee greatness, should continue the lineage. Pete Sheehy had been the Yankees' clubhouse man for years; he went back to the days of the Babe and Gehrig, the wearers of the fabled numbers 3 and 4. In the ensuing years, of course, DiMaggio had made his own number 5 as iconic as the Babe and Gehrig had their numbers. And now Sheehy quietly decreed that the kid from Oklahoma would carry on the Yankee lore. Sheehy assigned Mantle jersey number 6, while placing him next to DiMaggio in the locker room.

Sitting in the home team's clubhouse prior to his first major league game, Mickey was asked to contemplate the improbable jump he had made in just two years, from high school to the world champion New York Yankees.

"How do you feel about all this?" a reporter asked Mick.

"It seems as if I hadn't ought to be here. I have been reading about these great ballplayers for years. Now I am a teammate of some and about to play against others.

"If I make good there is one thing I will not get, and that is a swelled head. I would not be able to go back home. They don't like swelled heads in Oklahoma," the kid replied. "This has all been so fast. I'm not sure I'm a major leaguer yet.

"It just isn't true, that's all."

Across the room, Stengel was holding court with his own group of writers. Casey speculated that the Red Sox would try to repeat the success they'd had in recent seasons by sending a steady diet of left-handers to the mound against his club.

"It sure looks like those fellas are gonna try an left-hand us to death from the start of this season," Stengel said. "Well, we may fool 'em. We may do pretty good against the crooked arms this time."

When speaking to a cognizant audience, Casey rarely used names. Keeping up with Stengel's game analysis required attentiveness and interpretive skills acquired only through practice. The uninitiated, however, looked hopelessly around for a translator. Stengel continued with his unique breakdown of his starting eight, and the proficiency of each man against southpaws.

"The guy in left who hit 'em last year has been takin' treatments and seems ready to go, but if he can't, why the young fella got a triple and a homer off a left-hander in Brooklyn Sunday and he might cut the mustard. The little-bitty fellow always hit 'em well, of course, and the kid in right doesn't know whether a left-hander or right-hander is pitchin'. The big guy murders 'em, of course, specially when they wear that Boston uniform. My first baseman hits 'em good and so does my catcher. The old guy on third hits 'em good, and my second baseman is a right-handed hitter who hurts 'em too."

As game time approached, Stengel moved out to the dugout and the group of writers trailed the Yankee manager's footsteps, sure that wherever Casey went, a good quote was sure to follow. With the first pitch still 90 minutes away, Stengel surveyed the field. Mantle came jogging by and Stengel noticed that the sole of one of his shoes was flapping loose. Casey stepped on the field, spoke briefly with Mantle, then returned to the bench.

"He doesn't care much about the big leagues does he?" Stengel rhetorically asked his friends from the press box. "He's gonna play in them shoes."

"Who is he?" a reporter asked.

"Why, that kid of mine," Casey replied.

"That's Mantle?"

"Yeah," Stengel confirmed. "I asked him, didn't he have any better shoes, and he said he had a new pair, but they're a little too big."

With all the buildup surrounding Mantle, the writers' demand on DiMaggio's time had lessened considerably. Speaking to reporters had never been pleasurable for Joe, so not being pestered as much was okay with him. Irritating to him, though, were the incessant questions concerning Mantle. Joe politely answered such queries, but the responses were brief and to the point.

What's Mantle's biggest weakness, Joe?

"His throws from the outfield," DiMaggio replied. "He still has to lengthen them out, but that will come. After all, he's got an infielder's arm, you know. But it's a good one, and he'll learn how to stretch that throw and still make it good."

Joe on Mickey—"He's the greatest prospect I can remember."

A writer quizzed Joe. Who does Mantle reminded you of?

"Well, there just haven't been any like him since I've been around. He's a big league hitter right now. Maybe he has something to learn about catching a fly ball, but that is all."

Do you resent the kid, a reporter asked?

"Resent him?" Joe scoffed. "Hell no, why should I resent him? He's great. I haven't helped him much; Henrich takes care of that, but if there's anything I can do to help him, I'm only willing."

Exhausting his questions about Mantle, the writer finally turned the subject to DiMaggio.

How are you feeling physically, Joe?

"Not strong yet," he said. "I reported to Phoenix weighing 200 and then for no reason started to lose weight. Went down to 195 and then got hit by the virus bug and went to 190. The balls I hit don't travel as far as they did.

"It's probably my fault, though. The doctor put me on that aureomycin and I stayed on those pills too long before asking when I should quit. They cured my virus all right, but now I have to recover from the cure, I guess."

———

THE STADIUM GATES OPENED AT 11:00 AND A LITANY OF PREGAME ceremonies began at 1:50. The temperature hovered in the low 50s as the Yankees took the field under partly cloudy skies. The Stadium was decorated with bunting and an impressive display of banners commemorating the many Yankee pennants that dated back to 1921. Casey looked around at the flags and cracked, "But for a couple of homers by a guy named Stengel for the Giants, there would be another championship flag up there," he said with a chuckle, referring to his heroics in the '23 Series.

Thanks to the meticulous planning of Red Patterson, the lengthy program went off without a hitch in a mere 22 minutes. Happy Chandler was slated to hand out World Series rings to the 1950 champs, however, the lame-duck baseball Commissioner canceled at the last minute. The Commissioner's absence was fine by Webb, who stepped in for Chandler and awarded his players their well-earned rings.

Chandler may have skipped out, but American League president Will Harridge was there to present Phil Rizzuto with the league's Most Valuable Player award. Other prizes and plaques included the league's best executive to George Weiss, and the

Babe Ruth Award, which was given to Jerry Coleman from the New York Chapter of the Baseball Writers Association for the top performer of the 1950 World Series. Even Mel Allen, the Yanks' radio voice, was anointed the game's finest broadcaster by *The Sporting News*.

Before Lucy Monroe continued her tradition of singing the National Anthem, the 1950 championship pennant was raised to the top of the center-field flagpole. The honor of hoisting the ceremonial flag was given to Casey Stengel. A hitch in the ritual arose, however, when Stengel managed to tangle himself up in the ropes, and the banner refused to budge.

An onlooker shouted to Red Sox manager Steve O'Neill, who was standing nearby, "Give him a hand, Steve!"

"Nuts to you, Case," O'Neill snapped. "I'm not helping you with any pennant."

That the Red Sox and Yankees were meeting on this day was fitting. The two clubs battled down to the wire in '49, and though the 1950 race was not as tightly contested, New York and Boston remained the circuit's elite clubs. And most of the preseason prognosticators were picking the Red Sox to take the pennant in '51.

As players milled around the field prior to the game, a group of photographers asked an awestruck Mantle to pose with DiMaggio and Red Sox slugger Ted Williams. With trepidation, Mickey walked over toward the two star players, who were in the midst of greeting one another.

"Hello Joe," Williams said in his booming voice.

"Hello Ted," DiMaggio replied as the two rivals shook hands. An awestruck Mantle stood silently by, nervously shuffling his feet.

Williams waited a few moments for DiMaggio to introduce the rookie before taking the initiative himself. A large smile creased Ted's handsome face as he stuck out his hand. "You must be Mick," Williams said.

Seeing the group huddled around the batting cage, Red Sox center fielder Dom DiMaggio strolled over and tapped his older brother on the shoulder.

"Hi DiMag."

Joe casually turned around and returned the greeting. "Hi DiMag."

Dominic was the youngest of the nine DiMaggio siblings, and like his brothers Vince and Joe, he started his professional career with the San Francisco Seals before reaching the major leagues. While Vince was toiling around the National League with a variety of clubs, playing a good center field but striking out far too much, Dom was joining the Boston Red Sox in 1940. Over the next decade, Joe and Dom's teams clashed repeatedly while battling for the American League pennant. The rivalry often extended beyond the playing field and into the bleachers where hecklers reminded Dom who his big brother was.

"You'd never been in the bigs if it weren't for Joe."

"You're not half the player your brother is."

The youngest DiMaggio certainly didn't possess the stereotypical guise of a major league ballplayer. Dom's slight frame—he was a full five inches shorter than brother Joe and a good 25 pounds lighter—added to the verbal taunts.

"Hey Dominic, shouldn't you be playing with some school kids?"

He was handsome, in a bookish way. His wire-rim glasses presented a studious appearance, far different than the grizzled, hardened look worn by so many of his contemporaries. Despite his unlikely mien, Dom could play the game and he could play it very well. Truth was, he'd become one of the finest center fielders in the league, Joe included. Dom was everything that Joe was not. He was easygoing, lively, and made friends effortlessly. To watch Dom and Ted goof around shagging flies before a game you'd think they were brothers.

Off the field it seemed as if nothing came easy to Joe, even relating to his brother.

———

MANTLE WASN'T THE ONLY MEMBER OF THE YANKEE FAMILY making his debut on this day. Bob Sheppard, the team's new public address announcer, began the proceedings in his clear and distinct voice by introducing newlywed Ed Ford, who stepped on the pitching rubber to deliver the season's first pitch. With Stengel and O'Neill standing on, Ford, dressed in his Army uniform, tossed a waist-high strike to Berra. Ford then took a few steps toward the plate, where he met Yogi and retrieved the ball. With the baseball in hand, Ford proceeded toward the box seats behind the Yankees dugout, where he presented the ball to his bride.

Despite all the pregame hoopla, the contest itself was a rather uneventful 5–0 Yankee victory. Mantle did collect his first hit, RBI, and run scored; most importantly, he made no glaring rookie mistakes in his initial big league game. On a fair, though chilly afternoon, Tommy Henrich was the only Yankee in the team's dugout not wearing a jacket. Henrich endured the cold to better be seen by Mantle as he signaled the rookie on how to play each hitter.

In the locker room afterward, reporters reminded Stengel that he had been concerned about having to use "so many green peas." But his kids more than held their own. Jackie Jensen hit a home run in the third and added a double in the sixth.

"Yes, they did all right," Casey acknowledged before swiftly turning the topic to the performance of the veteran DiMaggio. "That young fellow in center field did all right too. In the first inning, they could have given us a lot of trouble. But he caught the ball." You couldn't blame the young fellow on first base. After all, the ball looks like it's in there and if I was him, I would run too. Just like he did. But he catches the ball. If he don't, it can be a different ball game."

Following the game, reporters were more anxious to ask DiMaggio about Mantle rather than Joe's own performance.

DiMaggio admitted that yes, he gave Mantle a few pointers during the contest, but "It was tough hollering to the boy; because the 45,000 fans made so much noise.... He did okay."

A couple of hours earlier, Jimmy Cannon slipped into the Yankee dugout prior to the game and found a seat next to DiMaggio. Having skipped out on the trip to Arizona, Cannon was unfamiliar with the game's new sensation.

"Which one is Mantle? Cannon asked Joe.

"He's hitting now," DiMaggio replied.

As those words came out of Joe's mouth, Mantle hit a ball into the right-field bleachers.

"This is the next great ballplayer," DiMaggio flatly stated. "He's the Yankees' next center fielder."

The following morning, Cannon could not suppress his enthusiasm.

"Here it was, Opening Day at the Stadium and the people yelling his name before he had been in a big league game. I'm going along. This is the merchandise, original and immense. It is the first time I've ever jumped overboard on a minor leaguer. I'm cautious. I dog it. I like to be sure. The last one I rode the bandwagon with was Joe DiMaggio. I feel just as sure about Mickey Mantle.

"I've seen Mickey Mantle play one ball game. I put in with the boosters. This may not be Ruth or Cobb or DiMaggio or Speaker or Musial. But it's positively Mickey Mantle. This one's a hanger. I know Mantle is as sure as gambling dice. This is a wrap up.

"I'm all out of breath hollering it up for this kid."

DiMaggio, though, wasn't as taken by the rookie. Yes, he grudgingly acknowledged the bright future that awaited Mantle, but there was a palpable tension between the two in the locker room and on the field. There were layers to DiMaggio's coolness toward the kid. Joe never had taken to people easy, and Mantle was no exception. An innate resentment existed toward the guy who Joe knew would one day take his spot in center. The end was near, but Joe felt no inclination to befriend his replacement. To top it off, there was the Stengel angle. There was no love lost between Casey and Joe, and then throughout the spring Stengel had been practically cooing over Mantle. Add it all up and Joe barely acknowledged the kid's existence.

For his part, Mantle could not help but feel DiMaggio's frosty demeanor as he sat in his locker stall just a few feet away from the legend.

———

ON THE MORNING OF APRIL 11, THE NATION AWOKE TO BOLD headlines. The newsprint varied slightly in each city's newspaper, but the report in every town was the same: TRUMAN FIRES MacARTHUR!

General Douglas MacArthur had been serving as the commander of United Nation forces in Korea. His dismissal came after MacArthur threatened to escalate the war by expanding the conflict into China, in clear defiance of Truman's attempt to open peace talks with the Chinese. The President's decision to fire MacArthur was not done without deliberation and great contemplation. Truman understood that the political fallout would be severe, and the public backlash brutal. He was not wrong on either count. Reaction to the sacking of MacArthur was frenzied and harsh. More than a few called for the impeachment of the President, several even hinted that a Communist cabal was at the helm of the American government. And across the country dozens of protests took place, including more than 2,000 longshoremen walking off the job, citing their objection to Truman as the cause for the strike. Gallup quickly released a poll that reported 69 percent of American's were on MacArthur's side of the debate.

Through it all, Truman remained silent. The President had met with reporters on the 18th, but he refused to answer any questions concerning the MacArthur affair. When the Senators opener was postponed, Truman's appearance was also washed out. And now, nine days after shocking his nation by removing the popular MacArthur from his command, Harry Truman was making his first public appearance since the beginning of the controversy. The opener was rescheduled as the afternoon half of a day/night doubleheader; and the President was still set to sanctify the earlier game with the first pitch. Truman was a veteran of such Opening Day ceremonies, though the Nats had lost both previous contests baptized by this particular president. In '47, Washington fell to the Yankees 7–0, and the following year came a 12–4 defeat. His Senators may have lost these contests but Bucky Harris liked what he saw in Truman's delivery.

"In '48," Harris recounted, "Truman threw one ball right-handed and another left-handed. I thought he showed more promise as a left-hander."

Stengel sat in Griffith Stadium's visiting dugout before the game, entertaining a corps of reporters with random thoughts and obscure memories. Glancing out at the Senators starting pitcher, the 5'11", 140-pound Sandy Consuergra, who was loosening up on the field, Stengel harkened back to his playing days in Brooklyn and his manager with the Dodgers, Wilbert Robinson.

"I played under Uncle Robbie," Casey reminisced, "and if there was anything that burned him up it was being beaten by a little guy. I remember how he blew his top when Dick Randolph of the Braves would beat the Dodgers.

"Uncle Robbie used to burn when Randolph, who was a young guy, took off his cap. 'There's a bald-headed high school kid who's no bigger than a minute, and you guys can't hit him,' Robbie would bellow at us.

"I couldn't hit Randolph," Stengel admitted. "Neither could Dauber and the good Brooklyn hitters. It used to kill Robbie. He always used to say, 'I don't mind getting beat by six-footers, but when my club can't beat midgets, I'm finished.'"

One of Stengel's dugout guests mentioned to Casey that protocol called for the managers of each team pay their respects to the President.

This news seemed to surprise Stengel.

"How do you address a President?" he asked John Drebinger of the *New York Times*. "Is it Mr. Truman or Mr. President?"

"You say, 'It's a pleasure, Mr. President," Drebinger informed Stengel. "Haven't you ever met a president before?"

With a wink and a smile, Casey replied, "Not many."

Another reporter standing nearby chimed in, "Harry'll get booed worse than Hoover in 1931 at the World Series in Philadelphia." This writer recalled that at that time, deep in the depths of Prohibition, Athletics' fans serenading Herbert Hoover with the chants of, "We want beer!"

A couple of days earlier, on April 17, MacArthur returned to the country. An estimated 10,000 supporters greeted the embroiled general at San Francisco's airport. The city's streets were so thick with well-wishers that it took MacArthur's motorcade two hours to travel from the airport to the general's hotel. Once he'd made his way through San Francisco's crowded roadways, MacArthur greeted his devotees.

"The only politics I have," MacArthur told the crowd, "is in the simple phrase known to all of you—God bless America."

And now, in Washington, The President and his party climbed a ramp inside Griffith Stadium to their seats. Some scattered applause and cheers greeted Truman from the fans seated nearby the Presidential box. Then, off toward the third base line, boos began to swell. The Air Force Band quickly struck up "Ruffles and Flourishes" followed by "Hail to the Chief," to help drown out the chorus of jeers. The booing only increased a few moments later when Truman, surrounded by dignitaries, stood before the sold-out crowd. The President, a left-hander, had to adjust a right-hander's mitt, and with a broad, confident, smile fixed on his face Truman lofted a ball from his box seat. The toss sailed into a group of Senators and Yankees where it was gloved by Allie Reynolds. Reynolds then took the ball to the railing and asked the President for his signature.

The frosty reception did nothing to deter Truman from enjoying the game. A couple of hot dogs and a cup of hot chocolate, combined with a 5–3 hometown victory, provided a slight remedy to the turmoil of the previous few days.

The heckling returned in the eighth inning when the public address announcer asked all fans to remain in their seats until the President and his party left the park. The announcement brought on the most boisterous boos heard all afternoon. On his way out of the park, President Truman stopped for a moment to extend his greetings to Senators owner Clark Griffith. As he spoke to Griffith a woman called out to Truman, "Where's MacArthur?"

It was, "the coldest reception ever given a chief executive at an opening ball game," according to the *Washington Evening Star*.

The Yankees had arrived in the capital a perfect 2–0 thanks to their sweep of Boston, but by the end of the day their record had evened out after dropping both ends of the doubleheader to Washington. Though the Yanks salvaged the last game of the series to the Senators, one week into the season, Stengel wasn't pleased with his team's performance. It wasn't just their middling 3–2 record, the club's approach at the plate desired attention.

"I did not like the looks on our batting in Washington, so I ordered everybody to report for a morning workout and that meant no exceptions," Stengel explained. "I took Mantle in hand, and told him that he was not getting the most out of his exceptional speed. I pointed out that he had been holding the bat wrong for bunts, and had been tapping the ball mostly to the pitcher.

"I told Mickey that a lad with his speed ought never to have a hitless game."

He also moved Mantle from the third spot in the lineup to leadoff.

"I'd been thinking it would be more fair to the kid to get him out of there. It looks better, that way, with Berra and DiMaggio batting three and four and the kid on top. I had to figure I was putting him under too much pressure hitting third where the real good ones belong. Breaking him in on top is the smart move, I figure."

Casey was beginning to come around on Jensen. Only a few weeks had passed since Stengel declared that Jackie would have to convert to pitching if he were going to contribute to the Yanks.

"That's right, I said that, and you know, funny thing, I can be wrong sometimes. Now I want Jensen as one of my outfielders."

Hank Bauer was suffering from tightness in his right leg. Bauer was a war hero who, while with the Carlson raiders, took a bullet through the thigh on the 14th day at Okinawa.

"There's another feller who will help us soon as he gets his leg fixed up," Stengel said of Bauer. "We're lucky to have him, and he's lucky to be alive.

"Y'know, his outfit had 110 percent casualties, and as I figure it, he should be buried on one of those islands, but there must be something wrong in my reckoning. I know he's with us because I've sent him up to pinch hit this year and he's driven in a run each time."

Prior to the Yankees 3–0 victory over the Athletics on the 24th, Stengel suffered from nausea and "belly pain" in his hotel room before heading to the Stadium. Initially, Stengel thought little of the twinge, but a second attack caused painful "knots in my belly," Casey explained.

At that moment, Stengel saw Bobby Brown in the locker room. Brown had recently taken a leave from his internship from Southern Pacific Hospital, and returned to active duty with the Yankees. He wanted to play ball as long as he could, Brown reasoned, before the inevitable call up from the armed services.

"You're the fella I'm looking for," Casey said. "My stomach's giving me hell."

Brown gave his manager a quick once over and directed Stengel to the hospital, where Casey was diagnosed with kidney stones.

Jim Turner and Frank Crosetti managed the club for the two games that Casey missed while laid up at Lenox Hill Hospital. When Stengel returned to the bench following his brief absence, he didn't pencil Mantle's name in the lineup for the first time in the young season.

"The big right field here, plays in the sun, might be a little too much for sonny boy," the manager explained. Mickey was utilized in the ninth inning as a pinch-hitter, though he struck out, capping a 13–7 New York defeat.

April concluded with the Yankees holding a respectable 8–4 record. The team certainly didn't seem to be firing on all cylinders, and on May 1 the club embarked on their first lengthy road trip of the season. The schedule had the Yanks slated for two games in Chicago, three in St. Louis, three in Detroit, and a pair in Cleveland before returning to New York. Stengel had slightly more than two weeks to decide how he and Weiss were going to trim the roster from the current 29 to the required 25 by May 17. The western swing would serve as a good trial for what Joe Trimble termed, "The Stengel Youth Movement."

"I'd like to keep Mantle because I think he's got the stuff to be a real big leaguer," Casey explained. "But Jensen has forced himself into the picture, too. Both are too young to sit on my bench. They play every day either for me or in Triple A ball. Same goes for McDougald. I hope the kids show me a wonderful Western trip. With their speed, they'll make my team better."

———

BEFORE HE STEPPED ON THE FIELD FOR THE FIRST GAME IN Chicago, DiMaggio felt a pain in the left side of his neck. The discomfort was so much that Joe took himself to nearby Mercy Hospital for X-rays. DiMaggio's pain was diagnosed by Dr. John Claridge as, "nothing serious, only a muscular spasm in the neck." It was DiMaggio's second trip to a hospital in four days. The previous Saturday an exam of Joe's shoulder disclosed a strained ligament in his shoulder. The next morning he felt a twinge in his neck while entering a taxi while on his way to the Stadium. DiMaggio then went 0-for-4 that afternoon against the Senators.

The frustration of being out of the lineup was eased a little for Joe by the presence of Dorothy, who accompanied the team to Chicago. What didn't please DiMaggio were the rumors circulating among the gossiping type that the two had secretly re-married.

Joe loved Dorothy. He always had, and she him. They had met in the fall of '37 during the filming of *Manhattan Merry-Go Round.* Joe had a small speaking part in the flick, while Dorothy had no lines. When they were married on November 18, 1939, at Joe's home parish in San Francisco, a huge throng of 10,000 people packed the streets and sat in the trees outside Saint Peter and Paul. In the days before Joe Jr. had come along, Dorothy and Joe were New York's glamorous couple. They'd be seen out at some of the city's hottest night spots: The Copacabana, El Morocco, and though less enchanting, Joe's favorite place, Toots Shor's. Wherever they went, the DiMaggios would turn heads—he, the baseball hero, she, the movie starlet. Together they were a stunningly attractive couple and they seemed to have it all.

But Joe could be impossibly hard to live with. Too often he would sit stone silent while Dorothy tried desperately to engage him. Try as she might, Dorothy couldn't reach him at these moments. These dark moods would last hours. Sometimes days would pass before Joe would emerge. There were places Joe went, places in his mind where he wouldn't permit *anyone* to reach him. In those moments he was a man alone with his private burdens, his own dark thoughts.

More than anything else, it was these all-too-frequent black moods that drove a once happy marriage apart. Dorothy filed for divorce in the fall of '43, citing "cruel indifference," but in truth the union had been unraveling for some time before that. Following the birth of Joe Jr., Joe continued to lead the same lifestyle as he always enjoyed. The difference was, while Joe went to Toots Shor's, Dorothy now stayed at home, tending to the baby.

After their divorce, Dorothy had remarried in 1946 to a stockbroker, a fella named George Schuster. DiMaggio was not pleased with Joe Jr. having another "father" around, but there wasn't much he could do about the situation. When Dorothy and Schuster split up late in 1950, Joe was hardly upset. Now he was taking every chance he could to be around Dorothy.

———

MAY 1, A BEAUTIFUL, SUNNY SKY SHONE DOWN ON CHICAGO when Mantle came to bat in the sixth inning against Randy Gumpert during the first game of the western trip. Mickey stepped in the left side of the box against the right-handed White Sox hurler, and moments later he crushed a Gumpert delivery deep over Comiskey Park's center-field wall, some 440 feet away, for Mantle's first big league home run.

Red Patterson quickly took off for the center-field bleachers in search of the home run ball, believing it would make a swell souvenir for Mantle.

The Yankee's P.R. man reached the center-field stands and found the lucky recipient six rows up from the outfield wall. Patterson wasn't the first to try and pry the ball from the fan. Members of the Yankee bullpen crew had already been attempting to barter for the ball to no avail. Patterson's initial entreaty was shut down straightaway.

"Go 'way," the fan told Red, "I came here to enjoy the ballgame. You bother me."

"Look," pleaded Patterson, "I'll give you five dollars for the ball. All right, 10 dollars."

"Listen," answered the fan, "I'll pay you a couple of dollars to go away and stop bothering me."

Patterson finally gave up after getting the fellow's promise to maybe see Mantle himself after the game. When he left the boys in the bullpen renewed their argument, not stopping until the Yanks had finished off the Chisox 8–3. It didn't look as though they made any progress, but when Mantle came out of the clubhouse 39 minutes later the fan was waiting for him with the ball. A deal was made. Mickey got the ball and in exchange the fan received a dozen new ones, including an official American League ball autographed by every member of the Yankees.

In Detroit a couple of days later the *Mirror*'s beat writer Ben Epstein put a clock on Mantle running to first. From bat on ball to spikes hitting the bag, Mantle was timed at three-and-three-fifths seconds from the left side and a second longer from the right. More than any other aspect of his physical abilities, Mantle's speed enamored veteran players, writers, and especially his manager.

During the May 6 game at Briggs Stadium, Mantle stood on first following a base hit when Phil Rizzuto laid down a sacrifice bunt. Tiger second baseman Jerry Priddy, covering first base, caught the putout of Rizzuto and momentarily held the ball as he looked up and saw Mantle streaking past second base. Though startled, Priddy fired the ball to George Kell at third, but Mantle beat the tag easily.

As his green pea slid safely into third, Stengel erupted from his seat on the bench.

"He went from first to third on a bunt!" an excited Stengel exclaimed. Casey repeated the words to everyone in the Yankee dugout as if to assure himself and the rest of the club that what they'd just witnessed wasn't a mirage. Stengel exhibited unbridled joy viewing Mantle's natural talent unfold before him.

"You ain't seen nothin' yet," Casey promised the horde of writers traveling with the Yankees. "This kid doesn't run, he flies. He's probably the fastest man on the bases I've ever seen."

The May 10 game in Cleveland was rained out. In fact, every game in the league was washed out, which presented a good opportunity to take stock of the standings. To this point the Yankees had played every team in the league and they had come away from this experience none too impressed with their competition. Their number one rival, the Red Sox, were just one game above .500 and spinning their wheels. And in Cleveland, the Indians' general manager Hank Greenberg was busily trying to plug significant gaps in their lineup. The only deals Greenberg could muster up were three middling trades with the Athletics in the previous two weeks. Yes it was early, very early, but Stengel liked where his fellas were situated at the moment at 15–6, two games ahead of the Senators.

MAY 10 STANDINGS

Team	Record	GB
New York	15–6	–
Washington	12–7	2.0
Cleveland	11–7	2.5
Chicago	10–8	3.5
Detroit	9–8	4.0
Boston	10–9	4.0
St. Louis	5–16	10.0
Philadelphia	5–16	10.0

———

THE LIST OF YANKEE CASUALTIES CONTINUED TO GROW AS THE season extended into May. There was DiMaggio's stiff neck, Mantle had strained his right hand, Charlie Silvera was suffering leg woes, not to mention the two fingers that Jerry Coleman smashed in a door while the team visited Chicago. Stengel had seen it all before. He advised his players, "Stay in your rooms as much as possible and keep out of drafts."

Stengel sat in the Yankees' dugout before their May 14 game against the Indians. Sitting with Casey was Arthur Daley of the *New York Times*. The conversation between the manager and the columnist began with a discussion about the sale of Billy Johnson from the Yankees to the St. Louis Cardinals. News of the transaction had just reached Stengel.

"Billy Johnson," Stengel softly murmured. "I thank him for all the hard work he did for me. He was a true Yankee and always played like one, hustlin' every minute and never giving anything but his best.… But that's baseball for you. I can't win a pennant with my old men. We've come to the stage where we have to rebuild and we'll stay one-two-three while we're rebuildin'. With two more pitchers I can win it. Howja like that, huh?"

That was Casey's plan, winning the pennant with his kids.

Stengel then nodded to the playing field in the direction of Mantle. Without using any names in his rambling narrative spoken in vintage Stengelese, Casey described for Daley a play from a few days earlier that demonstrated Mantle's striking speed.

"That feller out there," Stengel began, "the other day he's on first when the feller at bat hits a line single to left. The feller in left catches the ball on one bounce, hesitates, and—whoosh—my guy has gone all the way around third. My guy has run so fast that someone sez, 'He musta went through the pitcher's box.' How can you figger him out? One day on the road he's the damndest fielder you ever saw, and the next day he's chasin' the ball like a handball player off them concrete walls. He's just a green pea. That's what he is, a green pea."

Stengel's club had won 14 of 16, and during this stretch Casey used a half dozen different batting orders. Trying to discern the method to Stengel's madness was futile. He seemingly mixed things up for the hell of it...and Stengel's madness worked.

Beyond the success in the win column, Casey was pleased at the progress Mantle was making. Mickey excelled during the nine games out west, not only by batting a respectable .333 during the stretch, but also playing fine defense in three ballparks he was unfamiliar with. He'd also awed the people of St. Louis with a drive over the right-field pavilion in Sportsman's Park. The ball went across Grand Boulevard and came to a peaceful rest against a building across the avenue from the stadium. Among the 4,500 fans in attendance for the game were Mickey's girl, Merlyn, and the mothers of both kids, who made the trip up from Commerce.

Mickey and Merlyn met at a high school football game. She was a cheerleader with nearby Picher High, while Mick was starring for the Commerce 11. Once he laid eyes on her, Mickey was smitten. She was a cute redhead, her face sprinkled with freckles.

As the Yankees were making their way back east, Stengel held court with the reporters traveling with the club.

"We are in the midst of a lot of important and interesting experiments," Stengel said on the train ride bringing the team from Cleveland to Philadelphia for a series with the Athletics before returning to the Stadium for a 12-game homestand. "Taking them by and large, these experiments have produced more than gratifying results."

First on Casey's list was Gil McDougald—"McDougald looked promising at Phoenix, but he has exceeded my expectations," the Yankee manager admitted. "In short, he is a fine, fighting ballplayer."

The second player mentioned by Stengel was Jackie Jensen. Stengel was frustrated with Jensen's obstinacy in February as the youngster objected to Casey's wish that he give the mound a go. That Jensen was performing well in the outfield and at the plate resulted in a slight change of the narrative by Stengel.

"This spring I figured that Jensen might not be able to overcome batting weaknesses, and perhaps would do better as a pitcher," Stengel explained.

But Jensen balked at the taking the mound; he did not want to change positions. Jensen's insubordination did not rile Stengel. To the contrary, Casey now said he found Jensen's obstinacy admirable.

"He knew what he wanted, had confidence in himself, and was determined to get a full trial in the outfield," Stengel said.

"Jensen has succeeded beyond my fondest expectations," he continued. "That catch he made in St. Louis on the fourth, when he caught Ray Coleman's low liner, tumbled head over heels, and doubled Ken Wood, was our masterpiece so far this season."

"Now we come to Mickey Mantle," Stengel said. "I have put in a lot of work with that boy, and so has Tommy Henrich. Mantle is the fastest ballplayer in the major leagues. The main thing for him to learn is to get the most out of that speed. That means running harder for balls in the field. It means learning to bunt expertly. If he ever becomes a polished bunter, he will be really terrific.

"Mantle must also kill the impression that his arm is strong. But he doesn't put enough stuff on his throws. I want that kid to put on a show, no matter what he is doing. The boy is going to develop into one of the standout players of the decade."

Given the team's record and the development of several youngsters on the team, the trip to the league's western outposts was an overwhelming success. Still, DiMaggio's slowness to return to the lineup was concerning. The best Joe could muster was slipping on his uniform at Briggs Stadium and playing some soft toss, and the next day he took batting practice for the first time since last playing against the Senators on April 29. The neck stiffness spread to pain in his shoulder and what had been estimated to be a one-week recovery turned into an extended 15-day absence for DiMaggio. He missed every game of the trip, but Stengel believed Joe would be back in the lineup soon.

"DiMaggio was free and loose in practice Wednesday in Cleveland," Casey said. "He hit a few in the stands. It's up to him to decide when he'll play. He's the only one who knows how he feels."

With Bauer also out of the lineup nursing his bum leg, Stengel had few options at his disposal. Woodling, certainly. Jensen and Mantle shared the team lead with 17 runs batted in, but after that there wasn't much to choose from. Cliff Mapes? Johnny Hopp? Championship clubs are not made of Hopps and Mapes, Stengel need remind no one of this fact.

Mantle had gone hitless in his previous nine trips to the plate out west. Or, as Joe Trimble described it, "Mickey

Mantle has been wheezing more often than whizzing lately." Mickey snapped out of the slump when the Yankees reached Philadelphia, though, with three hits against the Athletics at Shibe Park.

As could be expected at this point in his career, Mickey was piling up a lot of "firsts." Once the team returned home, Mickey belted his first home run at the Stadium, which came off the Indians' Dick Rozek.

When the Yankees were at home, Stengel instructed Mantle to be on the field, ready for special instructions at 11:00 AM. Each day, Stengel, Henrich, and Dickey gave Mantle a special 90-minute tutorial.

"There is no reason why you should ever get a horse collar, daytime or under the lights, just so long as you retain the ability to run," Stengel told Mantle.

Casey also offered Mickey some showman's advice. "When you go after a ball in the field, run harder, put on a show," Stengel said. "You can out-run any player in the majors, but one would not get that impression watching you field. Put on a show, be more dramatic.

"When you throw you look as if you had a weak arm. Kick up a leg and haul off with the ball. Put more behind it. In short, be alive. And don't let yourself moan or get discouraged. Your average does not bother me too much.

"You mean you want me to kick up a leg and really haul off?" Mickey asked.

"Exactly," Casey said with a wink.

Stengel was finally able to pencil Joe's name into the lineup card when the Yankees returned home on the 14th following three games in Philly. DiMaggio received a warm reception from the crowd each time he came to the plate, and Joe obliged with two hits, one of them driving in a run in the seventh.

With the May 17 deadline for teams to reduce their rosters from 29 to 25 players just a couple of days away, Mantle was admittedly apprehensive. He believed he might be one of the casualties.

"Sure I'm concerned," Mickey acknowledged. "That date is getting awfully close. I still think I can hit as well right-handed as left-handed. I feel a lot better in the outfield now and I'm doing things easier out there; major league pitchers are awfully smart, smarter than I've ever seen. I noticed I've been getting mostly curveballs and slow stuff."

The day of reckoning came, and to Mickey's relief, his name wasn't on the list. Not so fortunate were pitchers Joe Page and Max Peterson. Page had been sold to Kansas City, and Peterson shipped to Toronto. Neither Page or Peterson had appeared in a game all season. The roster had been trimmed to the mandated 25—well actually, 26. Billy Martin had been dismissed from the Army and the club was permitted to carry him on the National Defense List.

Taking stock of his club, pitching was at the forefront of Stengel's concerns.

"You can't win a pennant with three pitchers," Casey said as he sat in office, futilely trying to wait out the May 19th rain delay against the White Sox. "I've got Lopat, Raschi, and Reynolds, all good men. But those two other fellows have to help out." Stengel's frustration was directed at Spec Shea and Tommy Byrne, neither of whom had lived up to the manager's expectations.

Tom Morgan was a possibility to step up. It was hoped that Morgan could be this year's Whitey Ford. He'd been given the nickname "Plowboy," and according to Joe Trimble, Morgan walked "with a Groucho Marx stoop, which makes it seem as though he is always going downhill." Despite his spring promise, to this point of the season Morgan had failed to deliver. Stengel hadn't given up on the right hander, though. At least, not yet.

———

ON MAY 21, GENERAL MACARTHUR AND HIS WIFE WERE THE guests of Dan Topping. Settled into their box seats alongside the Yankee dugout, the MacArthurs were presented to the crowd just prior to the first pitch. Handed a microphone by Red Patterson, MacArthur spoke for a few moments over the public address system, sharing with the fans in attendance the first time he saw Babe Ruth play—Ruth was pitching that day against the great Walter Johnson. The General also recalled seeing Gehrig before he was the Iron Horse, back when Lou was playing first base for Columbia.

"Unlike the old soldier of the ballad, these men never died," MacArthur said, "but in the memory of the American public they will never fade away."

Preceding the General's introduction, a series of competitions were conducted between players on the Browns and Yankees. The most entertaining was dubbed "a blind man's search for home." In this contest three men from the home team and three from the visiting squad were placed at second base, blindfolded, and then given a wheelbarrow. The closest to home plate would be declared the winner.

The smartest contestant, Bobby Brown, headed straight for first base before he took off down the base line toward home.

Brown's ingenious plan worked to perfection, he crossed directly over the plate. Unfortunately for Brown, he continued on until he came to a stop in the Browns dugout. The winner of the $50 prize was Allie Reynolds, whose route took him along the box seats near the St. Louis dugout and concluded in the right-handed batters box.

Though to some it was anti-climactic given the pregame festivities, Vic Raschi became the second pitcher in baseball that season to reach seven victories (the first being Eddie Lopat the day before) when he beat the eighth place Browns 2–0. This particular victory, which maintained the Yankees hold on first place, pleased Casey Stengel more than most. Five weeks into the season, he was beginning to believe his team was on the right track.

"Excuse me," Casey said to writers following the game, "but I hope I don't see any more like that this season. And I hope I don't see [Stubby] Overmire anymore, either. I wish there was some way I could get a National League club to buy him from the Browns so he wouldn't work against us any more.... We'll have to get some sort of medal for Yogi for knocking in both runs to beat that guy."

Overmire's repertoire of pitches included a slow curve, a slower curve, and a curve that stopped halfway before proceeding to the plate.

"When we beat a pitcher with a lot of stuff we're doing all right," Stengel continued. "But when we get beat by a nothin' ball pitcher like Overmire, why we're terrific."

General MacArthur continued his tour of New York City ballparks with his third stop in the five boroughs. MacArthur stopped by Ebbets Field for the Dodgers' May 26 game against the Braves. A Ladies Day crowd warmly received the returning hero who was dressed all in gray, down to his immaculate bow tie. The general accepted a lifetime gold pass to Ebbets Field from Dodger president Walter O'Malley before he addressed the crowd over the stadium's public address system.

"I've just been to see the Giants and Yankees," MacArthur began; a greeting that was met with a resounding chorus of boos in the home of the Dodgers. But MacArthur was a politician at heart, and he knew well how to pander to his audience.

"Somebody said to me, 'If you want to see a real game of baseball, go over to Ebbets Field.' So here I am."

Whether he was running for President or campaigning to replace Happy Chandler as the game's commissioner, no one knew for certain; one thing was undeniable, the general was campaigning for something.

———

TO MICKEY, IT WAS ALL JUST A DREAM.

After all, he was just a shy teenager trying to fit in while not ruffling any feathers. In short, he was overwhelmed. The attention coming Mantle's way both on and off the field was more than even a seasoned veteran could swallow. The playing field was the only place Mickey could find solace, and even there, every moment was a learning experience. Once off the diamond he was inundated by reporters asking this question and that. The sheer number of reporters in New York was astonishing. There were so many writers coming and going out of the dressing room, throwing absurd questions at him, Mickey couldn't even tell them apart. He politely answered what was asked of him, always with a whole lot of "Sirs" thrown in as punctuation. But this constant inquisition, this was something Mickey didn't believe he'd ever get used to.

Joe DiMaggio, too, was a heralded rookie one time long ago. He also came to the Yankees a reticent kid not ready for the hype and publicity.

"I can appreciate what he's going through," DiMaggio told a magazine reporter several weeks into the season. "I had played before large crowds in the Coast League before I came to the Yankees, but I was too shy and afraid to talk for fear I'd say the wrong thing and make a clown of myself."

Like so many young men, Mickey had often played out the scenes in his mind of making the big leagues. And now here he was performing side by side with the legendary Joe DiMaggio. At times life in New York City swallowed up the young Oklahoman, as should be expected. Too often Mickey trusted the wrong people. He was charmed by a nice suit, a well-spoken lie, and occasionally, sweet perfume.

Attention on the young slugger was magnified when Mantle began the season where he had left off in training camp. He was inundated with requests from radio, television, and countless business opportunities throughout the early weeks of the season. Mickey popped up on numerous radio programs, including the quiz show *Break the Bank* and among the television shows he appeared on was Ed Sullivan's *Toast of the Town*, and two stints on *We, the People*. Mickey's first appearance on this 30-minute talk show was April 20, when he was on the same bill as country singer Roy Acuff. A month later, Mantle was invited back to visit with the show's host, Dan Seymour. Mickey's act for these shows rarely strayed from his wheelhouse. He would walk on stage, display his oversized "aw shucks" smile, and tell the host how happy he was to be there, and how great it was to be a Yankee.

With so much coming at him so quickly, it was not surprising that Mantle entered into several ill-conceived business opportunities.

Earlier, during spring training, Yankee general manager George Weiss could see what lay ahead for Mickey and offered Mantle a bit of advice.

"Mickey," Weiss said, "we like to have our boys protected off the field as well as on. You'll get all kinds of propositions advanced to you. I would suggest that you avoid getting tied up with anybody. The club is at your service without cost."

Mantle listened politely, and then proceeded to make a few business deals on his own. He received $50 for endorsing a bat. The compensation for allowing his facsimile autograph to be printed on a glove? Mick was provided with two mitts. A brand of bubblegum paid Mantle off with a wristwatch for backing their product. And even though he didn't smoke, Mickey gave a plug to a brand of cigarette.

The naive 19-year-old Mantle was quite gullible when it came to the many business offers tossed his way.

"People up here have funny ideas," Mickey told a reporter. "Everybody's got a different way of making money up here. Down where we live, all we got is mining and a rubber company."

As April turned to May, Mantle found himself embroiled in a controversy of his own making. Mickey received a call at his room in the Concourse Plaza Hotel during his first week in the city. The exact date was April 15, and the voice on the other end of the line belonged to Allan Savitt, a sly lawyer equipped with a line of promises. He would, Savitt assured Mantle, deliver the young star to an agency, which would secure Mantle on a generous split of endorsement fortunes that were sure to come. All this, and Savitt guaranteed Mickey $50,000 a year. With Mick's okay, Savitt came to the Concourse to discuss the proposition in detail.

Without seeking advice from the Yankees or his parents, Mantle leapt at the "golden opportunity." Mickey had barely hung up the phone when he heard a rap on his door. Outside his room stood a small, stout man sporting wispy mustache and horned-rimmed glasses; Allan Savitt's personal appearance accurately resembled the huckster he played so well. Savitt brought with him to the Concourse a contract that bound Mantle to an agency for two years. The terms of the agreement provided 50 percent of the proceeds to Mantle with the agency receiving the other half.

If this impetuous decision wasn't foolhardy enough, less than two weeks later, Mantle signed a second contract which made Savitt Mickey's personal representative "in the field of radio, television, personal appearances, stories for books and magazines and all other fields, exclusive of playing baseball." From his Madison Avenue office, Mantle's new agent also set up a "Mickey Mantle Fan Club." For his work, Savitt was to receive 10 percent of Mickey's endorsements for 10 years.

Hank Bauer heard of the contractual mess that Mickey had got himself into and tried to help the rookie extricate himself from the onerous agreements. With the assistance of Bauer and the Yankee front office, Mantle did eventually get free of Savitt, but this divorce did not come easy or quickly.

Not surprisingly, Casey recognized Mantle's naiveté. He saw the hustlers pressuring the boy and felt certain that this green pea just might purchase the Brooklyn Bridge. The Yankee front office was in tune with Stengel's sentiment. Weiss believed the off-the-field frenzy would prove distracting. In early May, the front office asked their new sensation to decline all radio and television requests. Mickey listened and nodded his ascent to the command, and though he cut back on the extra-curricular activities, he did not completely stop all media appearances.

"This publicity isn't too much good for him," Casey said. "Here he is with all those interviews trying to enlighten other people about himself rather than tending to baseball business."

And then there was Miss Holly Brooke.

Though Mickey was engaged to be married to Merlyn, his girl back in Commerce, he became hypnotized by the affections of a showgirl named Holly Brooke. That this older woman was nothing but bad news in a fine dress mattered not at all to the impressionable Mantle. An attractive and cunning redhead, Brooke latched on to the guileless and testosterone-filled Mantle.

The two met through Savitt at Danny's Hideaway, a New York steakhouse. Savitt, in need of an infusion of cash, sold Brooke a quarter interest in Mantle's off-the-field earnings. Mickey was kept in the dark, however, and had no knowledge of the deal brokered between Brooke and Savitt when he met the striking showgirl at Danny's Hideaway. Mantle was immediately enamored. Before long the two were spending time together, running around the city. Often their rendezvous involved such innocent activities as golfing and taking some swings in a batting cage.

Though the press still played up Mantle's clean-cut all-American image, Mickey was stepping to the wild side with the desirable showgirl. Before Brooke, Mantle's beverage of choice might be a soda, or the all too predictable wholesome glass of milk. But through Brooke Mickey was introduced to, and developed a taste for, bourbon.

In time Mantle learned that Brooke had a financial interest in him, but that knowledge didn't bother Mickey at all. He was enjoying the education he was receiving from Brooke on the ways of the big city. Mickey even expressed aloud the wish that the two could get married. The thought had barely escaped his lips when he acknowledged the sophisticated Brooke could never be happy in Commerce. Perhaps marriage was out of the question, but Mantle was going to grab some fun while he could.

During the first weeks of the season Mickey called the Concourse Plaza Hotel home. The Concourse served as the home for a number of unmarried Yankees and also hosted most visiting teams coming to New York to play the Yanks. While the accommodations at the Concourse were nothing fancy, the hotel was just a short walk to the Stadium. The proximity made getting to the park for an afternoon game following a late night all that much easier.

And then there were the clothes he wore. Mickey's wardrobe was hardly befitting New York's latest sensation. His pants too short, his socks too white, his only tie too garish, and his shoes too country...Hank Bauer reached out to the unsophisticated and out-of-his-element rookie. Bauer took Mantle to Eisenberg and Eisenberg, where the veteran bought the kid a couple of sport coats. Bauer also introduced Mantle to a few variations of New York City cuisine. Mickey's taste testing of the many ethnic staples found in the city pushed his weight from 165 pounds to 190 pounds.

———

MICKEY'S THREE STRIKEOUTS ON MAY 24TH AGAINST THE TIGERS gave him 25 in 32 games, a pace of 115 over the course of a whole season. The American League record for whiffs was 120, which was set by Gus Williams of the 1914 Browns. The Yankees team mark of 105 was set by Frank Crosetti in '37.

The Yankees dropped to second place following a 3–2 loss to Boston coupled with a Chicago victory. New York batters were ineffectual while falling to the Red Sox and Mel Parnell. Mantle, dropped to sixth in the batting order, went 0-for-4; three of his four outs were weak comebackers to the mound. DiMaggio was nearly as feeble at the plate. Joe failed to hit the ball out of the infield all day, and only broke his 0-for-17 streak with a weak ground ball that he was able to beat out.

The Red Sox swept a three-game series in Boston that closed out the month of May for the Yankees. Mantle's frustration at the plate and on the field was prolonged at Fenway. He was hitless in nine at-bats, including five consecutive strikeouts in the Memorial Day doubleheader. The sting of failure was only exasperated by the biting commentary directed at Mantle by the Fenway bleacherites. During the nightcap of the twin-bill, Stengel replaced Mantle late in the game with Cliff Mapes. This wasn't the first time Casey removed Mantle in a late-inning situation, but there was no denying the kid had been out of sorts of late.

"Mickey has been striking out a lot, but mostly because he's pressing hard in his effort to live up to his notices," Stengel explained to reporters as he and his team prepared to depart for Detroit. "If I bench him against left-handers in Detroit it will be because I think Jensen might do better against them right now."

Stengel continued, "I believe that if Mantle were turned into a straight left handed batter, and did not hit against lefties, he would be more valuable to the club, and it would be a big break for the kid.

"I'm not disposed to quit on the boy. I just want to make his task easier. I was an outfielder myself, and I know what he is up against. Ty Cobb, like Mantle, [was] originally a shortstop, had a terrible time in his first season with the Tigers. Far more nerve wracking than Mantle's experiences. I keep telling this to the boy, and he is not inclined to accept comparisons. He merely says, 'That doesn't help me,' He is so upset, so inclined to blame himself. He's a great kid with a great future.

"Funny thing. I keep talking and he keeps shaking his noggin, so I said, 'Look, young man. I wasn't born at age 60 and thrown right into managing the Yankees. I went through all the anguish you are suffering, and you will be all the better for it.'"

Stengel refused to be bound to a set starting eight. He was debating on whether to platoon Woodling and Bauer in left and Mantle and Jensen in right.

"If Mantle can't hit southpaws, maybe Jackie Jensen can. If anybody else runs into trouble against certain types of hurling I believe we can rearrange our lineup to produce better results. The one thing we have to get away from is a feeling that our lineup is static. If Hank Bauer cannot hit right handers, perhaps Gene Woodling can do better."

Stengel refused to lay the blame for his team's four-game losing streak at the feet of his rookie Mantle.

"It's not all his fault," Stengel said. "Lots of ballplayers hit
slumps. I have to keep being glad the kid hit in 31 runs for me
before this. I'm over .500, ain't I? And didn't the kid play in all
those games that got me there?"

————

THAT HE WAS RULED INELIGIBLE TO SERVE IN THE ARMED FORCES
on two separate occasions didn't silence Mantle's critics. On
June 8, the Yankees visited Comiskey Park for a three day
weekend series with the White Sox. During the first game of
the set, Mantle was peppered with a barrage of catcalls from the
right-field bleachers.

"Draft dodger" and "commie" were some of the heck-
les heard by Mantle. But a few Comiskey Park patrons set
themselves apart by hurling firecrackers at the Yankees' right
fielder. During the June 10 game at Comiskey Park, Chicago
fans in the right-field stands threw nearly everything in their
possession at Mantle; beer bottles, flasks, straw hats, sandwiches, newspapers, and most frighteningly, firecrackers.
Before the incidents in Chicago a patron at Detroit's Briggs
Stadium threw rocks at Jackie Jensen. And in Cleveland someone tossed a black cat on Ed Lopat as he made his way to the
mound in the bottom of the first inning of the June 4 contest
at Municipal Stadium.

"In Briggs Stadium, my other young fellow, Jack Jensen, was
pelted with stones when he went after a fly ball," Stengel told
a group of reporters. "Foolish stunts like that might cut short

a man's career or even cost him his eyesight. "Something's got to be done to stop this carnival they're making out of the game. Why yesterday somebody threw a firecracker right behind my 19-year-old kid right fielder just before he had to catch a ball. If it doesn't stop, one of these games I'm just going to pull my team off the field. Suppose one of those firecrackers exploded right at Mantle's eye level? Or what if Jensen had gotten an eye knocked out by a stone? I guess they'd fine the guy $10 or $25, but that wouldn't restore a man's eyesight.

"If park management can't stop it, why don't they bring in the police to stop it?"

Stengel grumbled all the way home from Chicago. Some of his complaints were tongue in cheek, such as his gripe about White Sox reliever Marv Rotblatt.

"He throws grounders," Stengel said. "He might as well be bowling out there. Every pitch is around the shins and my men can't hit down there."

The actual source of concern to Casey was his relief corps. More than any other aspect of his ball club, Stengel's bullpen was giving him fits and he wanted his club to make a move. A month earlier the Tigers offered either Fred Hutchinson or Hal Newhouser for Tom Morgan and Jackie Jensen. Weiss wouldn't bite, though, because he believed in the promise of Morgan and Jensen. Stengel wasn't giving up on acquiring another arm, though. The man he had his eye on was Ned Garver of the Browns. While pitching for the cellar dwelling Brownies, Garver had already notched nine wins. Seemingly it was a perfect match. The Yankees were in the market for a pitcher, and the Browns, in the midst of an ownership change, were receptive to all offers. Though he wouldn't officially take over the club for several weeks, Bill Veeck was advising the Browns' operating officer, Bill DeWitt, behind the scenes. Veeck had already expressed the necessity for the St. Louis club to get younger. Being the club's most valuable asset, Garver was certainly the one player who would bring reasonable value in return. Still, despite the aligned needs, the Brown and Yankees made no headway in trade talks.

The Yankees' special Pullman arrived at Penn Station at 2 o'clock in the afternoon. Once back in the city Casey sought out Weiss to discuss his concerns. The two men, however, had differing philosophies on how the Yankees should proceed. Casey wanted to move a couple of the franchise's younger pitchers for Garver. Weiss, though, did not want to mortgage the future. The team's youthful arms were the key to the Yankees' future.

While Weiss and Stengel debated the team's most pressing needs, observers around the country saw the Yankees as an over-the-hill outfit with far too many youngsters on the roster to make a serious run for the pennant.

"Casey Stengel knows better than any man that the Yankees are no longer a great team, or even a good one," opined Bill Lee of the *Hartford Courant*. "He is constantly juggling the lineup and batting order...."

———

LELAND STANFORD MACPHAIL WAS ANYTHING BUT DULL. AN iconoclast, compulsive, emotional, genius, combative, and temperamental, MacPhail held all these traits and more. His biography included an adventurous escapade during the First World War, when on the evening of January 8, 1919, Captain MacPhail joined his commander and some other members of the 30th Division in an off-the-books mission to the Netherlands. It was there that this covert crew hoped to capture the Kaiser and bring him to trial for war crimes. The operation didn't turn up William II, but MacPhail, who answered to Larry rather than Leland, returned home with a great tale to share and an ashtray he filched from the Kaiser's hideaway.

Between the wars he became involved in baseball, first with the minor league Columbus Red Birds and then the Cincinnati Reds, where MacPhail brought night baseball to the major leagues, then to the Brooklyn Dodgers. He resigned his position as the Dodgers general manager on September 23, 1942, to accept a commission in the Army.

At the conclusion of the Second World War, MacPhail came back to baseball. This time he would have a stake in the club he joined as a part owner in the outfit.

They certainly seemed a mismatch. The staid Del Webb, the playboy Dan Topping, and the maddeningly unpredictable Larry MacPhail, but each needed the other to make this unlikely venture successful. The money, of course, came from Webb and Topping. And while MacPhail had to chip in his own share of cash, it was the immense baseball knowledge he held that made him such a valuable part of the group.

The announcement came on January 25, 1945, that the group of Webb, Topping, and MacPhail had purchased the storied New York Yankees from Ed Barrow and the heirs of Jacob Ruppert. The money guys were unknowns, but every reporter knew of MacPhail. How would the rambunctious MacPhail fit into an environment that had been conservative under Ruppert and then staunchly conservative under

Barrow? This was the question on the mind of many writers. Barrow looked down his nose at MacPhail's intemperate antics in general, and he couldn't stand the idea of night baseball specifically. Conservative forbearers or not, Topping and Weiss gave MacPhail *carte blanche* control when it came to baseball decisions. And during his brief, tumultuous tenure with the Yankees, no one could deny that MacPhail livened up the offices in Squibb Tower.

Dan Topping was not yet 39 years old when the 1951 season began. Tall, strong good looks, squared jaw, and dark hair, Topping appeared as if he'd just emerged from central casting. He achieved his wealth thanks to his paternal grandfather, John A. Topping, who was once the president of Republic Iron and Steel, and his maternal grandfather, Daniel Reid, who made a fortune in copper. Inherited or not, Topping's money still spent, and Dan enjoyed the little and big things his affluence provided. Along with the Yankees, Topping was the primary owner of two professional football teams, the Brooklyn Dodgers and later the New York Yankees of the All-America Football Conference.

While serving with the Marines, Topping had done his duty during the war, spending 26 months in the Pacific theater. During his time in the service, Topping had risen in rank from private to major. He'd returned home and picked up the playboy lifestyle he'd been living so well prior to the war. Like many men of leisure, Topping enjoyed a round of golf. In fact, it was a sport that he excelled at, having once reached the quarterfinals at the British Amateur, and on three occasions Topping qualified for the U.S. Amateur. He frequented Manhattan's trendiest spots, El Morocco and the Stork Club. Out on the town,

Topping would always have a striking date on his arm, the type of gal who recognized wealth.

To Joe DiMaggio, the change at the top in '45 was a mixed bag. Webb was okay in his book. But with Topping, DiMaggio had formed something of a friendship. MacPhail, well Joe had no use for him.

On a couple of occasions MacPhail tried to trade DiMaggio. Indeed, one deal was actually made with Red Sox owner Tom Yawkey, Joe for Ted Williams straight up. The next morning, however, MacPhail sobered up and canceled the transaction he had made under the influence. On another occasion, Larry tried to deal DiMaggio to the lowly Senators for Mickey Vernon, and Washington turned down the offer.

These attempted trades chafed Joe and stung his ego. They also reinforced the distaste he felt for MacPhail. General Manager or not, DiMaggio refused to show deference to MacPhail. At one point during his tenure with the Yankees, MacPhail was feuding with Toots Shor, as he was wont to do with any acquaintance. During their fallout, MacPhail barred all Yankee players from frequenting Shor's establishment. While this ban remained imposed, MacPhail asked DiMaggio to join him for dinner. "I'm sorry," Joe replied. "I have a previous engagement. I'm having dinner at Toots'."

Joe also had tired of MacPhail's endless promotions and had begun to blow off the dinners and events that Larry had lined up for the team to attend. The end for MacPhail came in spectacular fashion. Hours after the Yankees had defeated the Dodgers in Game 7 of the '47 Series, MacPhail got into a kerfuffle at a celebration dinner following the game. Larry punched someone, a player or a reporter, whoever it was; in the end it didn't matter. MacPhail's temper had caught up with him once again in fabulous style. Before his partners Topping and Webb could push him out, MacPhail jumped.

"That's it," MacPhail told the press that same evening. "That's my retirement. It's been tough and I've been in there trading punches all the time. Now I'm through."

———

GEORGE WEISS WAS EQUAL PARTS BRILLIANT, CALCULATING, AND cold. A social introvert, Weiss earned the nickname pinned on him by the New York press, "Lonesome George." And though most observers perceived Weiss to be aloof, the few people who penetrated his natural defenses found in Weiss a considerate, affable friend. Weiss was short, overweight, his face dominated by full jowls and a dour expression. He had no hobbies to speak of, seldom smiled, certainly never laughed, not that anyone remembered at least. Weiss was completely dedicated to the Yankees. In that, he was completely indefatigable.

His one true friend was his wife, Hazel. She was as outgoing as George was shy. A sculptress who learned to fly an airplane in 1926, Hazel brought to Weiss' life a spark that George couldn't, on his own, ignite. She was his social crutch. When Weiss was compelled to attend formal baseball functions or a soirée of any nature, George insisted that Hazel linger right by his side so as to stave off any uncomfortable small talk he may be forced to endure.

Weiss had been in and around baseball for decades, having worked at nearly every level of play the game offered. His lengthy career began while Weiss was studying at Yale in 1915.

At that time, Weiss became involved with the semi-pro New Haven Colonials. By "involved" that is to say, Weiss took over nearly every aspect of the Colonials operations, sans roaming center field. As a promoter, Weiss threw everything at the local professional team, the New Haven Murlins, which were a member of the Eastern League. Weiss regularly took advantage of local Blue Laws that restricted professional sports on Sundays. He filled the entertainment void on the Sabbath by bringing in an array of visiting nines. There were the Bloomer Girls Club, and an "all Chinese" team, among other unusual traveling outfits. The most popular attractions were the exhibitions that involved major league players.

Ty Cobb had served as a semi-regular opponent for the Colonials. When his Tigers had an off day in New York or Boston, Cobb would slap together a rag-tag team and perform for a New Haven audience. Providing, of course, Cobb received his $350 guarantee up front.

Cobb always drew a big crowd, but one of Weiss' best promotions came on October 15, 1916. Just three days after they defeated the Brooklyn Robins in the World Series, the Boston Red Sox came to town for a memorable exhibition. During that game, Wally Pipp of the Yankees played first base for the Colonials while Babe Ruth handled the same chore for the champions.

By 1919, the owners of the Murlins had raised a white flag; they were spent. Trying to compete with Weiss and his innovative promotions proved too taxing.

"You want to buy the club for $5,000?" one of the team's proprietors asked Weiss.

Though he had to borrow the whole amount, Weiss leapt at the opportunity.

For the next decade, Weiss directed the New Haven Weissmen, Indians, Profs...whatever the club was named that particular season. He continued to make his name known around baseball circles, and Weiss also cultivated many relationships that he maintained through the years.

The New Haven experience was followed by a three-year stint as the director of the International League Baltimore Orioles, where he succeeded Jack Dunn, who had suddenly passed away in the fall of 1928.

In 1932, the big leagues called. Colonel Jacob Ruppert extended to Weiss the offer to become the farm director of the New York Yankees. His early days with the organization were marred by strife as Weiss' direct supervisor, Ed Barrow, held a grudge that went back a ways. The origin of the rift dated to an exhibition appearance the Yankees made in New Haven years earlier. When Babe Ruth failed to appear with his teammates, Weiss withheld the Yankees' fee, a slight that Barrow, despite the passage of time, remembered well.

Weiss oversaw the Yankee farm system for 15 years, an era that produced numerous quality major league talent for the big league club. Miraculously, Weiss survived the tempestuous tenure of Larry MacPhail, though barely. Too often, MacPhail allowed his volatile temper to overtake his better judgment. In fits of rage, MacPhail was given to firing any subordinate within earshot. Often MacPhail recanted the next morning, and when he didn't it was left to Topping or Webb to smooth over Larry's fits and bursts of anger.

That he survived is not to say Weiss escaped the wrath of MacPhail. On that fateful evening in 1947, the night the Yankees captured the world championship, MacPhail imploded and Weiss was one of several targets. Drinks were drunk, tables turned over figuratively and MacPhail dismissed Weiss among others. The scorched-earth evening concluded with MacPhail tendering his resignation. Larry had given notice in the aftermath of previous tantrums, but this time was different. Topping and Webb accepted MacPhail's resignation the next morning and bought out his shares in the club. The new co-owners also reinstated Weiss and promoted him to general manager.

His first year in that role proved frustrating for Weiss. Though the Yankees finished in third place, just two-and-a-half games behind the pennant winning Indians, Weiss struggled to maintain control of the team's direction. Throughout the season he butted heads with Bucky Harris, as the manager refused to accommodate the organizational plan to blend younger players with the aging Yankee club. Simple conversations with Harris proved near impossible for Weiss as he could never reach his manager by phone. Calling Harris' room when the team was on the road drew the predictable response from the hotel operator—Mr. Harris was "out." Bucky was always "out." The inevitable change came at the conclusion of the season. Harris was ousted as Yankee manager, and to replace him Weiss selected an old acquaintance from his days in the Eastern League—Casey Stengel.

Given Casey's less than spectacular career as a major league manager, many commentators questioned the choice. Stengel was fresh off of winning a Pacific Coast League championship as the manager of the Oakland Oaks. For Weiss, hiring Stengel was a natural fit. Theirs was a professional, though genial, relationship. Casey was amiable and never at a loss for words. Not to be overlooked, Stengel's effervescent personality deflected attention from Weiss.

Every morning by rote, George Weiss emerged from his home in Greenwich, Connecticut, slipped into his car, and made the commute into the city. He arrived at the team's office and began a flurry of activity that included responding to mail, manning the phone, scouring farm reports on the minor league system, and scrutinizing every aspect of the Yankee financial report. No detail of the organization's business slipped by Weiss, down to the minutia of the profits taken in on each souvenir sold in the stadium. Weiss was exhaustingly meticulous.

If the team was on a homestand, Weiss would head uptown to Stadium at noon. Once there he would grab lunch before retreating to the ground floor where he would squeeze in some more work while waiting for the first pitch.

"Lonesome George, the friendless general manager of the New York Yankees, who glared at whoever comes his way as though expecting a touch from every passerby," Jimmy Cannon wrote. "Lonesome only makes briefly formal appearances rabble, as signs of his utterance to a hack, denounces any criticism as the barbaric challenge of an infidel, locates security in privacy and expects the community to support his firm as a civic service."

———

ROSALIE DIMAGGIO HAD BEEN SERIOUSLY ILL FOR MONTHS. It was around the holidays that Rosalie's family was informed that she had cancer. And since her diagnosis, Rosalie's health had steadily deteriorated. On June 17, Mrs. DiMaggio slipped into a coma—Joe was in the Yankees dugout when his brother Tom phoned with the news. He immediately left New York for the coast. The next morning, while surrounded by seven of her eight children, Rosalie DiMaggio passed away. Only Dominic was absent; he arrived from Boston just 30 minutes too late, having missed a connecting flight.

Born in Isola delle Femmine, an islet off the Sicilian coast, Rosalie died in the family home, not far from the San Francisco wharf, where she and her husband Giuseppe had staked their claim to their American dream.

During the war, Giuseppe and Rosalie were compelled to carry identification. The DiMaggios had not been forced to live in one of the internment camps built by the Webb Construction Company, but they weren't allowed to travel beyond a five-mile radius of their home and Giuseppe was not permitted to fish in the waters from which he'd earned a living for decades.

In eulogizing Rosalie, Milton Gross evoked "the miracle of America" as her lasting legacy; she and Giuseppe, two Italian immigrants coming to the land of opportunity and fortune raising a family that chased a dream of prosperity and autonomy. Three of her boys took to a game she never completely understood, and they reached the pinnacle of the sport.

The DiMaggio siblings laid their mother to rest in Holy Cross Cemetery next to Giuseppe, who had passed in 1949. The next day, Joe and Dom together boarded a flight back east with heavy hearts to reenter the battle for the American League pennant.

JUNE 27 STANDINGS

Team	Record	GB
Chicago	42–23	–
New York	40–23	1.0
Boston	39–26	3.0
Cleveland	34–30	7.5
Detroit	31–30	9.0
Washington	25–36	15.0
Philadelphia	24–41	18.0
St. Louis	19–45	22.5

————

ON JUNE 27, JOE WAS JOINING THE LINEUP FOR THE FIRST TIME in a week. DiMaggio summarized what he'd thought of his team while speaking with writers in the Yankee dressing room. "We're not smooth."

Stengel was fretting over the need for a fourth starter—Raschi, Reynolds, and Lopat weren't enough for Stengel.

The threat of the White Sox was real. "Until you catch 'em, you have to respect 'em. I didn't dream they'd be up there this long, but there they are, and they may take some catching. I'm trying to make up my mind whether the White Sox or the Red Sox are the team to beat."

"Not a name guy in the whole bunch of them," Casey said of the White Sox admiringly.

For the June 27 game, Stengel penciled in an all-veteran lineup.

"Include Reynolds among the men," Casey said before the game. "He'll bring this one home."

Mantle was placed on the bench by Stengel, a move that re-sulted in reuniting the championship-winning outfield from a year earlier of Woodling, DiMaggio, and Bauer. Jerry Coleman stepped in for Billy Martin at second base.

The Yankees' second run was scored with an assist by DiMaggio's glove. Joe D hit what appeared to be a line-drive single to center field, but the ball struck his glove, which was lying on the grass beyond second base. Once striking the mitt, the ball stopped dead, allowing DiMaggio to reach second base. Joe then scored on a Johnny Mize single, giving the Yanks a 2–0 lead they did not yield.

6   THE OL' PERFESSER
AND THE DAGO

"I AM A GUM CHEWER," JIMMY CANNON ADMITTED IN HIS JULY 5 column, "but I refuse to patronize the machines in the subway. It always astounds me when a guy inserts a penny and is rewarded with a stick. Many a time my mouth is dry and I yearn for a slice of spearmint. But I refuse to risk even an inflation penny because I believe it is useless to bribe the machine."

In his unique style, Cannon was taking his annual stock of the pennant races at the July 4 milepost. The columnist took a look around at the two leagues and sized up what had already played out in the season's initial three months. Obstinacy in others was a foolish trait, but as evidenced by his chewing gum machine anecdote, Cannon's own stubbornness was "an expression of faith." And this is how Cannon summarized the pennant races in mid-summer.

Brooklyn, they're in pretty good shape, thanks to their

pitching. The Giants weren't going anywhere near the Dodgers unless their staff turned perfect. The Cardinals were staying right where they were, stuck in a distant third.

In the other league, only a psychiatrist could explain the Red Sox, or why Cleveland couldn't turn a double play. The White Sox, though better than Boston, had a fatal flaw when it came to their pitching corps.

As for the Yankees, "Pitching gets the Yankees by," Cannon summarized. "They are a lucky ball club...for years this team was founded on Joe DiMaggio and Tommy Henrich. Henrich is gone. The years are catching up with DiMaggio. It was thought that Mickey Mantle might be the base hit they lost when Henrich turned to coaching. But Mantle isn't ready yet. It is a ball club that beats you because they have confidence in themselves. They seldom make mistakes. But all ball clubs eventually fall apart. DiMaggio can't hold them together forever."

As the season neared its midpoint, authorities from around the league took a look at the standings and shook their heads. The White Sox couldn't keep this up, was the consensus belief. Steve O'Neill, for one, thought Chicago batters were performing well above their abilities, and were due for a market correction.

Stengel, however, thought the opposite.

"The White Sox do not need any garters to keep them up," Casey said with a smirk. "They are going to be tough all the way."

The Yankee skipper liked what he saw from the Chicago pitching staff. And the club's defense, led by their double-play combo of Nellie Fox and Chico Carrasquel, was greatly improved over White Sox teams of the recent past.

No, Stengel was not going to dismiss the surprising Pale Hose, even if the rest of the league did.

On July 1, by virtue of New York's victory coupled with the White Sox loss in the back end of their doubleheader with the Browns the Yankees slipped into sole possession of first place for the first time since May 27. Fittingly, moments before Eddie Lopat took the field en route to capturing his 11th victory of the year, the redheaded hurler learned that he had been named to the American League All-Star team.

Despite Lopat's fine season, not to mention the contributions of Reynolds and Raschi, Casey still wasn't happy with his pitching situation. After a July 5 victory against the Senators, Stengel met with Del Webb. While sitting with the club's co-owner, Stengel made his case: the team needed a pitcher. Pony up the money, and we can get a decent arm from the Pacific Coast League, Stengel told Webb. There were a few fellows out there that could help the club, for a price.

Three days later the Yankees played their eighth double-header of the season. Of the 16 games played in these twin-bills, the Yanks won only three, and had yet to come out on top of a single night cap. More than a few observers looked at these results and attributed the Yankees poor showing to weariness. The remedy seemed obvious, the club needed to field younger, fresher bodies in the second half of doubleheaders.

————

HE WAS BORN CHARLES DILLON STENGEL, JULY 30, 1890. OR MAYBE it was 1889. Or perhaps 1891. Any good legend needs flexibility in the telling. His birthplace, Kansas City, inspired the nickname by which he would be forever known. Charles Dillon, he wasn't, Casey was a much better fit.

Stengel's natural presentation helped perpetuate the image that he had fostered with mangled syntax. His rubbery face, large floppy ears, and legs that buckled at odd angles served to accentuate Casey's comic ramblings.

Following high school, Stengel enrolled at Western Dental College in Kansas City. Casey pursued his dentistry degree for two-and-a-half years, but a club from Kentucky offered Stengel a contract a contract to play pro ball—so orthodontistry was pushed aside as Casey pursued his dream of playing professional baseball.

Prior to joining the Yankees, Stengel had previous experience managing in the big leagues, if the Boston Braves could be considered major league. During Stengel's six years in Boston the Braves finished fifth once, sixth once, and seventh four times. Hardly the stuff of legends, but Casey left his mark in Boston nonetheless.

"For us, it was more fun losing with Stengel than winning with a hundred other managers," Harold Kaese wrote in the *Boston Globe*. "Unfortunately, the Boston fans did not have the benefit of Stengel's company."

Still, some of Stengel's escapades were witnessed by the Braves faithful. Such as the dismal, rainy day when Stengel appeared at home plate to exchange lineup cards with the umpires while wearing a raincoat and holding an umbrella. Such stunts might have entertained the sparse crowds at Braves Field, but the Yankee Stadium clientele demanded solemnity and excellence from the leader of their club.

Stengel's hiring by the Yankees in October of 1948 was met with surprise and derision throughout much of the baseball world. Dave Egan, a writer known for his sharp criticism and pointed remarks, wrote in the *Boston Record*:

"Well sirs and ladies, the Yankees have now been mathematically eliminated from the 1949 pennant race. They eliminated themselves when they engaged Perfesser Casey Stengel to mismanage them for the next two years, and you may be sure that the perfesser will oblige to the best of his unique abilities."

Over the period of nearly three decades, from 1918 to 1946, the Yankees were a model of stability and excellence. During that span the club employed just three managers, and one of those, Bob Shawkey, led them for just one season. Over that 28-year span, they were the team of Miller Huggins and Joe McCarthy, a distinct and championship organization.

During the brief, turbulent reign of Larry MacPhail, however, a revolving door was installed on the manager's office in the Yankee clubhouse.

Joe McCarthy, a proud man, a manager who stood at the helm of seven championship Yankee teams, could not acclimate to life under the wildly unpredictable MacPhail. The redhead's many tantrums were just too much for McCarthy. In the days leading up to his resignation, McCarthy had been excessively irritable. He'd been suffering from a hard to shake cold, the effects of which made McCarthy more fatigued than usual. Finally, on May 24, he'd had enough and McCarthy sent a telegram to Larry MacPhail informing the Yankee general manager that he was resigning as Yankee manager effective immediately.

"My doctor advises that my health would be seriously jeopardized if I continue."

Bill Dickey came next. The great Yankee catcher was named the first player/manager of the Yankees since Bill Donovan directed the club in 1916. Though Dickey was assured that he would remain the team's manager "through 1947" MacPhail

waffled when Dickey asked for a guarantee that he would return for the following season. On September 13, Dickey decided that working with the volatile MacPhail wasn't worth the
psychic toll.

Next up was Stanley Raymond Harris, or Bucky, as he was
better known.

Nearly a quarter century earlier, Harris was known as "the
Boy Manager" when he led the Washington Senators to back-
to-back American League pennants in '24 and '25. In year one,
Harris did what was expected of a Yankee manager, he won
the 1947 American League pennant and the World Series. As
a follow-up, however, Harris' club finished in third place. On
October 4, the day after the Yankees season-ending loss in
Boston, Harris met with Dan Topping and George Weiss. By
"mutual agreement" a decision was made not to renew Bucky's
contract. A newsman quoted Harris as saying, "It was like being socked in the head with a steel pipe." But in truth Bucky
couldn't have been too shocked by the decision. Despite his
popularity with his players, a rift developed between Harris and
Weiss. Indeed, Harris was a MacPhail guy, which was Bucky's
biggest sin beyond his failure to win a Series every season.

To replace Harris, Weiss wanted his own man. He wanted
a manager who would arrive at the Stadium early, someone
who would work with the kids coming up through the club's
farm system. Another qualification, Weiss wanted a manager he
could reach at all hours. Harris, with his unlisted number, was
impossible to track down once he left the park.

Casey Stengel came to the Yankees with a well-earned reputation of a second-rate manager of second-rate clubs. He
was also recognized throughout the league as something of a

clown. The most oft-repeated Stengel tale related to his playing days when Casey famously tipped his cap to jeering Brooklyn fans. Earlier during the game in question, Stengel had found a bird in the outfield; he took his discovery and placed it beneath his hat and waited for the perfect moment to unleash his find. When Dodger fans began giving him the business, Casey turned to slapstick and released the bird from beneath his cap. The Flatbush catcalls turned into howls of appreciation. Apocryphal or not, the story suits the yarn's main character.

The New York Yankees, however, were not a comedy troupe. A more staid, straitlaced organization could not be found in the major leagues. Indeed, two world championships in as many seasons notwithstanding, Casey remained an imposter of sorts in his own locker room. A portion of Yankee players remained loyal to their old manager, McCarthy, while others maintained their allegiance to Harris. Stengel had numerous idiosyncrasies, such as a habit of referring to his players by their uniform numbers rather than their names. Such quirks did not sit well with many Yankees.

Upon his hiring, a reporter asked Casey what his thoughts were about managing a player of such stature as DiMaggio.

"I can't tell you much about that," Stengel admitted, "being as since I have not been in the American League, so I ain't seen the gentleman play, except once in a very great while."

The quote was pure Stengel, a lot of words adding up to very little said. The press enjoyed the repartee, but DiMaggio found such nonsense undignified. In fact, Joe found little about Stengel impressive. To most observers, Casey Stengel was a poor fit with the Yankees; no one held this belief more deeply than Joe DiMaggio. From the start, the relationship between star player and manager was strained, and a lineup change in the middle of their second season forever ruptured whatever rapport that may have previously existed.

In the summer of 1950, Stengel made the brash decision to move DiMaggio to first base. Casey wanted fresh legs in the outfield, and this change allowed him to keep Joe's bat in the lineup. Prior to implementing his plan, Stengel, appreciating the close relationship Joe had with Dan Topping, approached the Yankees co-owner. Even though Casey was not soliciting council from his boss, he decided that exhibiting deference was prudent. As for Topping, he welcomed being alerted to his manager's strategy, though he offered no opinion on the plan.

Joe, however, learned of the move, not from Stengel, but rather from George Weiss. This galled Joe. Why couldn't Stengel speak to him man-to-man? Why did Weiss have to be brought into the discussion of a lineup change? Besides that, he was a center fielder, Joe believed. He'd never played first base before. For DiMaggio, this move to an unfamiliar position was an affront to him, the perfectionist who was petrified of being embarrassed on the playing field.

The experiment was brief, but not uneventful. During one particular play, Joe stumbled and fell to his knees. Joe's most severe anxiety was fulfilled—looking foolish on the playing field. And also, as he feared, the next day a number of New York papers displayed a photo of DiMaggio scrambling to find his feet.

Stengel shrugged off the criticism that inevitably came with the move. "You're gonna make mistakes," he admitted. "You can't worry about them second guessers."

A leg injury to Hank Bauer paroled Joe from first base following a one-game trial after which DiMaggio returned to the solace of center field. Joe was back on familiar ground, but the simmering feud between player and manager continued. Shortly after the first-base fiasco, Casey again pierced DiMaggio's pride by dropping Joe to fifth in the batting order. And just a few weeks later, in mid-August, the manager informed the press that Joe would be taking a few days off, "for a rest"—without first consulting his player. It was in effect, a benching, and as it was when he was moved out of the cleanup spot in the order. Joe's pride was stung. That he came back from his six-day "rest" rejuvenated did not ease DiMaggio's fury.

DiMaggio practically ignored his manager's existence. Yankee beat writers had no difficulty picking up on the papable tension between the legend and the manager and a few reporters approached Stengel to question him about the volatile situation.

"So what if he doesn't talk to me?" Stengel replied. "I'll get by and so will he. DiMaggio doesn't get paid to talk to me and I don't either. He's getting paid to play ball and I'm getting paid to manage. If what I'm doing is wrong, my bosses will fire me. I've been fired in lots of places before."

Fast forward to the summer of 1951. Prior to the July 7 game at Fenway, Stengel offered writers a peek into his state of mind. The three-day All-Star break would begin at the conclusion of the next afternoon's game, and Casey's club was flagging. And though the Yankees were only one game behind the White Sox, they had lost four of their previous five games. Indeed, his team was fatigued, Casey said. "Four or five of these players are dead tired," he explained. "I'd like to take them out. Good thing they are getting a vacation next week. I hope they come back fresh."

Stengel's diagnosis of his team proved prophetic a couple of hours later as Rizzuto allowed a playable one-hop drive through the infield, which resulted in a double. Rizzuto's misplay was lost in the game summaries however. It was DiMaggio's misplay of a ball in the first inning, a play in which Joe came up short on a shallow fly. That, coupled with a ball hit by Billy Goodman to left-center that DiMag couldn't chase down, prompted Stengel's decision—two plays that a younger version of DiMaggio would have easily made.

At the start of the next inning, Stengel sent Jackie Jensen out to center field. When Jensen reached center he informed DiMaggio that Casey was pulling Joe from the game. With a large Fenway Park crowd looking on, DiMaggio trotted from the field with his head down. Once again, Stengel displayed a complete lack of regard for DiMaggio's stature. At least, that was how Joe perceived events.

Following the 10–4 loss to the Red Sox, DiMaggio's anger was palpable in the Yankee clubhouse. Teammates looked at one another in silence as reporters filed into the room looking for a reaction. Before the final out of the game had been recorded, Red Patterson issued a statement to the press.

"DiMaggio was taken out for a rest," the release read. "He suffered an injury."

Most reporters took Patterson's assertion with a grain of salt. If DiMaggio needed a rest, why wasn't he given the day off? If Joe was injured, why then did he even start the game? To remove a player, a player of Joe's stature in the second inning—and after he had taken his place in center field! There was certainly more to the story than Patterson was revealing.

It was a Boston writer who was the first to reach DiMaggio for comment. Joe was especially biting in his remarks. "There is nothing wrong with my legs or anything else," he said. "I was taken out, and if you want to know more about it, ask Stengel."

The episode conveyed the seemingly absolute dissonance between the manager and the legend. For his part, Casey stuck to his story, the same narrative peddled by Patterson that he was "resting" DiMaggio due to an injury Joe had incurred.

DiMaggio's left leg was ailing, Stengel explained, that's why he removed him from the game.

The Yankees lost again the following afternoon, giving Boston a three-game sweep. The sports pages of New York City's many daily papers did not focus on the Yankees' struggles on the field, however. Instead, readers were given a wide array of opinions on the mini-controversy.

Jimmy Cannon did not hesitate, jumping to DiMaggio's defense, and in his *Post* column, he castigated the Yankees' manager.

"Stengel seemed to deliberately humiliate him [DiMaggio] last Saturday up in Boston," wrote Cannon. "The manager allowed DiMaggio to trot out to center field. Then he chased Jackie Jensen out to inform him that he was out of the game.

"It was a mean little decision. It was a thoughtless act of panic and insensitivity. It was nasty and petty and follows the pattern of cheapness, which has assumed shape since Lonesome George Weiss, the friendless general manager, took change. The prestige of the Yankees diminishes rapidly.

"The abrupt substitution exposed Stengel as a guy who will allow desperation to set ambushes for him."

Running on the opposite side of the same page as Cannon's piece, Milton Gross offered an entirely different point of view.

"DiMag now talks to virtually no one with the ball club," Gross reported. "He never initiates a conversation. On trains, in cabs, and even in the clubhouse, Joe has pulled himself into a shell which is so much worse than this strange moody man had ever worn before. Instead of mellowing in the twilight of his career as so many other stars had done before, Joe sits by himself or walks, silent and unseen by the men with whom he has performed and traveled for so many years."

For his "Speaking Out" column, Gross was able to compel a couple of Yankee players to speak off the record.

"It gives you a creepy feeling to watch the guy," an unnamed player told Gross. "We can't talk to him and he won't talk to us players, just like it's not pleasant for the writers traveling with the team. It's a strained situation all around and what's happened hasn't made it any better."

Another anonymous Yankee was quoted as saying, "Casey doesn't tell me how he feels, but I think he'd like to be rid of the problem. Me? Please don't mention my name but we started winning last year the time Joe was out. I couldn't carry the guy's glove, maybe even now, but I think we'd start winning again if the same thing happened."

Frank Graham weighed in on Stengel's side of the controversy. If there was a problem between the player and the manager, Graham wrote in his syndicated column, the blame fell to Stengel. Joe, Graham reasoned, would always do whatever his manager asked. Graham went back to Joe's rookie season to provided anecdotal evidence of DiMaggio's obsequious nature.

"Do you want to play center field?" Joe McCarthy asked DiMaggio when Joe arrived at the Yanks training camp in 1936.

"I want to play wherever you want me to play," DiMaggio answered.

"How about left field? It's the sun field at the Stadium," McCarthy said.

"I never played in the sun field," DiMaggio replied, "but if you want me to play there, I will."

That Graham's anecdote was back dated 15 years mattered not at all to the columnist. To Graham, DiMaggio remained the same; malleable and reasonable. But the DiMaggio that Graham described wasn't the same fellow so many of Joe's teammates knew. The years had hardened DiMaggio, bitterness and resentment had crept into his being. On the playing field, the calendar was no longer Joe's ally and his ego demanded burnishing from time to time.

In the aftermath of the controversy in Boston, John Drebinger was squarely in Casey's corner. Stengel had made several moves before the start of the second inning and Drebinger believed Casey hadn't had a chance to tell Joe that he was replacing him with Jensen before DiMaggio ran out to his spot in center field. And it was DiMaggio, Drebinger insisted, who blew the incident out of proportion when he snapped at an inquiring Boston reporter to "go ask Stengel" about his being removed the game.

Drebinger wrote in his game account, "[DiMaggio] rarely talks to his teammates or manager let alone anyone remotely associated with the press."

The *New York Times* reporter then recounted a recent train ride from Philadelphia following a night game at Shibe Park.

"DiMaggio, in the Yanks' special diner, sat by himself at a table set for four," Drebinger wrote. "It's a queer set up, but almost everyone traveling with the Bombers is leaving the Clipper severely alone."

"Some of the stuff is pretty brutal," DiMaggio complained of the New York papers. "I'm not sore because they're saying that I'm washed up. They've been saying that for the last five years and I've been proving them wrong. That's something I have some control over. All I have to do is play good ball. But there isn't much defense for some of that other stuff they're writing.

"They're trying to picture me now as a bad influence on the ball club. They say I'm not talking to Casey Stengel and some of my teammates. Now I'm supposed to be a sulker. My batting average may be down, but I'm the same guy I always was. They ought to remember that I sulked a bit when I was hitting .380.

"I was a loner when we were winning all those pennants, too. But now they say I'm giving my teammates the brush. I never did and the ballplayers know it. They're not sore with me, only some of the writers are.

"Not long ago one reporter had the story that I wouldn't sit with anybody on the train leaving Philadelphia. He saw me by himself and jumped to conclusions.

"Sure I asked the Pullman steward for a private table in the diner because I was expecting some friends to join me on the train. They didn't show up.

"Maybe some guys change their personalities overnight but they can't say that about me. If they do it's unfair and below the belt. If there is a ballplayer on the Yankees who thinks I'm disrupting this ball club or am not going out with all I have, I'll fight him."

DiMaggio's was an image carefully cultivated by several influential writers, primarily Jimmy Cannon of the *Post*. More than any other reporter, Cannon propagated the image of the refined DiMaggio. Cannon revealed to his readers an intimate portrait of the star. He wouldn't dare criticize Joe. Cannon's work was designed to portray DiMaggio in only the best light and nothing ever went into Cannon's column that might remotely offend the excessively touchy DiMaggio.

That Cannon often enjoyed the company of DiMaggio away from the park influenced the writer's work in the *Post*. A night at Toots Shor's or "21" with DiMaggio provided Cannon with unprecedented access.

In his July 9 column, Cannon acknowledged his close relationship with Joe. Their friendship, Cannon swore, never seeped into his writing.

"DiMaggio has been my friend since he broke in," Cannon wrote. "It has been more than a relationship of a reporter covering a famous athlete. We are as close as our businesses will allow. We have gone on vacations together, sat around the same restaurants, killed a lot of time together, and know the same Broadway people. It hasn't impaired my job of writing about him."

———

MORE THAN MOST TEAMS, THE YANKEES NEEDED THE BRIEF REST provided by the All-Star break. To onlookers, they had the look of a tired team, and they had limped into the mid-summer respite, both literally and figuratively having lost five of their last six including a three-game sweep in Boston at the hands of the Red Sox. The Yankees emerged from their futile weekend in Boston in third place, behind the first-place White Sox and Red Sox.

"I don't know what to do," Stengel answered deliberately and thoughtfully following the Yankees July 7 game in Boston. "I never know before a game. We're just not making enough runs. Our pitching wasn't great, but it wasn't bad. Our hitting is what hurt us the most."

Lou Miller, a reporter with the *World Telegram*, approached DiMaggio in the clubhouse in the aftermath of the tough 10–4 loss that brought the Yanks and Red Sox into a virtual tie for second place. Miller, a rookie on the beat, was numb to the protocol of the do's and don'ts when speaking with Joe. The aging great stood before a mirror combing his once-rich black hair that was now streaked with a few maverick strains of gray.

"Too bad your drive into the right-field seats in the first inning went foul," Miller commiserated. "A few feet inside, it would've been a two-run homer. What were you doing tonight that was wrong?"

Startled by the commentary wrapped in a question, DiMaggio stared at the young reporter for a moment, and then with a cold stare offered a terse, "No comment."

———

WRITERS FROM AROUND THE COUNTRY GATHERED IN DETROIT FOR the All-Star Game, and, as could be expected, the rift between Stengel and DiMaggio was of great interest. Casey and Joe were each peppered with questions about their feud. Not surprisingly, both played down the dissension and placed the finger of blame for the controversy on the New York press.

Stengel denied that there was any strife between himself and his center fielder.

"In all my years in baseball, I've never known a player who hustled harder or was more insistent on playing for the benefit of the team when handicapped by injury. That's what I think of

Joe. In fact, it's in recognition of his all-time ability that I selected him for the All-Star squad this year."

Al Buck, a reporter with the *Post*, caught DiMaggio at the Madison Hotel just moments before Joe departed for Grand Central Station to catch his train to Detroit. Buck was given an "exclusive" interview by DiMaggio, who was using the newsman as a conduit to respond to his critics.

"Your paper had a couple of columns about me," Joe said. "I want to set the record straight. Jimmy Cannon has been my friend for a long time. I think he stated the case as it should be. Milton Gross joined the ball club last Sunday. I don't know what he was talking about.

"I don't want to get into a controversy. At the same time I don't think it's fair for your newspaper to print what is not true. I have never had any difference of opinion with Casey Stengel. To say that I don't get along with Casey and my teammates just isn't true."

The subject of DiMaggio's availability for the All-Star Game was raised due to Joe aggravating a muscle strain in his left leg while sliding into second base in Boston during Sunday's contest.

"I'll be ready to pinch-hit if Casey Stengel calls on me," DiMaggio said in response to Buck's query. "I'll give it all I've got. That's the way I've played baseball all my life."

Joe had one last thing to add before leaving. "I say the Yankees will win the pennant.... We'll win it all."

Stengel, too, found himself under a barrage of questions when he arrived in Detroit. "They're nonsense," Casey said of the stories stirring up a rift between himself and DiMaggio. "Those stories that DiMag and I don't speak to each other. If I weren't talking to him, would I pick him for the All-Star team and bring him here? Despite the fact the popular poll has not placed him in a leading spot. He's been a great star for many years and a great credit to baseball and the Yankees. Why should I have anything against him?

"Joe, at 36, isn't as great a ballplayer as he used to be. Still he's better than a lot of guys I have now. What happened in Boston was a lot made out of nothing by a Boston writer who went into our dressing room after I had removed DiMaggio from the game Saturday, when he shouldn't have been there, and caught Joe in a heated moment.

"Now that the big guy is not hitting, a lot of people are trying to hurt him through me, I won't let them if I can help it. Up in Boston they've been trying to embarrass DiMaggio through me from the time I've been with the club. Why, I don't know."

Billy Goodman gathered 800,000 more votes than DiMaggio, causing a mild outcry in Boston. St. Louis fans squawked for their Ray Coleman, as did Athletic rooters for Gus Zernial. Stengel argued that DiMaggio was the proper choice.

"How could you leave Joe off that team?" Stengel defiantly asked.

Casey had designated DiMaggio, who had finished fourth at his position in the voting, as the American League's third center fielder. Stengel's selection of DiMaggio to the All-Star squad was done in part to appease the press, but also as a nod to Joe's legacy. DiMaggio certainly hadn't earned a berth on the team by his performance in the season's first three months, but Joe deserved a spot because of who he was and what he had accomplished in the long haul. Still, Casey had no intention of using Joe unless circumstances forced his hand. The aging star could use the rest.

———

"WE WERE TERRIBLE IN ALL DEPARTMENTS," STENGEL SAID OF THE American League squad, "and the less said about it the better." And with that, Stengel put the aggravation of the previous week behind him.

Coming out of the All-Star break, Brooklyn seemed a shoo-in for the National League pennant as the Dodgers held an eight-game lead over their archrivals, Leo Durocher's Giants. The American League remained a muddled mess, with the smart dope declaring the defending champs all but dead in their pursuit to repeat. The pitiful performance by Casey's boys leading into the All-Star sojourn, beginning with their July 4 doubleheader loss to Washington, quickly followed by the fiasco in Boston, had prognosticators looking ahead to the Yankees 1952 prospects.

Casey, however, hadn't given up the ghost. Turning his full attention back to the pennant race, Stengel was confronted with several issues. As his team embarked on another western tour, Casey's first order of business was to plug in Gene Woodling for DiMaggio in center; Joe's knee continued to trouble him and the chances of seeing No. 5 take the field on this trip were slim. Speculation in the press was that the Yanks would be better off if Joe remained on the bench permanently. Such heresy was justified with the speculation that Woodling could hold down center on an everyday basis, flanked by Bauer in left and Mantle in right. Jensen could slip into left against southpaws with Bauer relocating to right. On paper, such maneuvers looked sound, but Casey wasn't dealing with paper moves. In his reality, Stengel could not place a healthy DiMaggio (if Joe would ever come 'round) on the pine. The public wouldn't allow it, his bosses wouldn't hear of it, and the press would make their banner headlines Stengel's own living hell.

From the All-Star break through the latter days of July, Joe spent the better part of three weeks on the bench nursing a variety of injuries. When DiMaggio was deemed well enough to re-enter the lineup, Stengel was less than enthused.

"If he wants to play, I guess that's it," Casey said.

When asked about the possibility of using DiMaggio as a pinch-hitter while Joe was on the mend, Stengel shook his head.

"I did that once before this season and lost him for an extra week," Stengel said. "With the race like it is now, I can't afford to take any more chances."

Notwithstanding their differences, Stengel still catered to DiMaggio's ego. As July came to a close, Casey continued to bat Joe in the cleanup spot, this in spite of DiMaggio's rather anemic performance at the plate.

"No one else has been driving in runs in that spot," Stengel acknowledged. "I've tried Berra, Bauer, and Woodley there. Look it up and see if any of them has done much good."

In other words, Joe D's name would continue to be placed in the four spot. Some members of the Yankee team read the papers and shook their heads upon seeing their manager's rationalization. Stengel's deference to DiMaggio was beginning to cause much antipathy in the clubhouse.

He had always been aloof in the Yankee locker room, but as the season drew deeper into summer, Joe was more detached from his teammates than ever before. DiMaggio's reserved nature had long been known to those who covered the game, but Joe was no longer protected by many New York writers.

Lou Miller of the *World Telegram* reported that DiMaggio

was close to returning to the playing field. Not only would Joe be coming back in short order according to Miller, but the reporter took a different tack than some of his colleagues when examining DiMaggio's relationship with Stengel as well as the press.

"DiMag has been getting along beautifully with manager Casey Stengel and the newspaper boys," Miller wrote. "To put it mildly, he was disturbed when stories first appeared in the papers pointing out the fact that Joe didn't have many heart to heart talks with his manager or the press."

——

THROUGH THE YEARS DIMAGGIO'S LOCKER ROOM ROUTINE HAD varied little. "Cup of coffee, Pete," Joe would tell Pete Sheehy. And Sheehy would dutifully bring DiMaggio a half cup of black coffee. Always half a cup. Joe liked his coffee hot, and a half a cup remained at just the right temperature until he had finished his drink. And there he sat smoking and drinking his coffee. Invariably he sat unaccompanied. Yes, Joe had always been something of a recluse, but he used to enjoy the company of a few teammates. His best friend among Yankee players was Lefty Gomez. Nobody could make Joe laugh like Lefty, and Gomez could poke at DiMaggio in a way no one else was permitted to do.

Though he liked to keep it from the public, Joe loved to read Superman comic books. He enjoyed the adventures of the man from Krypton so much that Joe could barely wait for the new edition of the comic to arrive at the newsstand. The great DiMaggio, however, did not want word to spread of his juvenile reading tastes, and he enlisted his roommate, Gomez, to procure the magazine for him. With Joe standing a discreet distance away, Gomez would approach the newsstand and begin browsing the comic section. While leafing through the available comic periodicals Lefty would holler out to DiMaggio, who was standing inconspicuously in the shadows, "This one, Joe? Is this the one you want?"

Embarrassed, DiMaggio would feebly nod. He would never let anyone else rib him like that, but Joe's affection for Lefty ran deep.

Gomez left the Yankees while Joe was away during the war, following the 1942 season, when Lefty ended up with the Senators. Even with Gomez gone, however, there were still a couple of fellas whose company Joe enjoyed. But those fellas were all gone now. Charlie Keller had been released and picked up by the Tigers, Tommy Henrich was still around, but he was a coach and things just weren't the same, and Joe's closest friend on the Yankees since Gomez left the club, Joe Page, was released by the Yanks early in the season. Henrich and DiMaggio had played side by side for 10 years, a decade of baseball shared. Each man deeply respected and admired the other's skills on the ball field. Truth is, a harsh word never passed between the two. But Henrich could never remember sharing a meal with Joe.

These days Joe's near constant companion wasn't a fellow Yankee, but rather a sycophant.

George Solotaire met the requirements that Joe demanded in a friend, which was for them to ask nothing of him. These conditions were agreeable to Solotaire; the chance to pal around with Joe DiMaggio was too much to pass up.

To call Solotaire Joe's "friend" might be a bit of a stretch, however. In actuality George was little more than DiMaggio's errand boy. Someone to keep Joe's lonely blues at bay. Solotaire was up for this task and then some. He knew when Joe wanted to talk, to laugh, and to be left alone. Solotaire filled all the job obligations. He was obsequious; George regularly pulled Joe's chair out when the two went out to eat. Occasionally Solotaire would even accompany Joe on a date. DiMaggio, the girl, and George. Solotaire knew his job; he'd pull the chair out for DiMaggio while Joe's date got her own chair.

Most importantly, Solotaire knew how to keep his mouth shut.

Solotaire was there sitting by DiMaggio's side following the Yankees July 25 game against Cleveland. Throughout the Yankee clubhouse his teammates excitedly rehashed their dramatic 2–1 win over the Indians. DiMaggio, however, sat apart while in the midst of the revelry. Joe, perched upon a stool in front of his locker, his uniform removed, puffed on a cigarette lost in his thoughts.

With a measure of delicacy, Joe Reichler of the Associated Press approached DiMaggio. Reichler didn't even have the chance to get beyond a salutation before DiMaggio began responding to unasked questions.

"Notice the way we've been winning lately?" Joe asked rhetorically, "1–0, 2–1, 3–2. The pitchers have been carrying nearly all the load. The boys have been in a hitting slump. Maybe I should talk about myself only," he added with a contrite smile. "I haven't been doing anything to help the club. I just can't seem to buy a base hit."

Reichler sensed a chance to interject a question.

"What's the matter, Joe? Can you account for your failure to hit the way you used to?"

A long, silent pause greeted the question. Joe inhaled deeply from his cigarette then discarded the butt on the floor.

"Yes," he finally responded. "I know what's the matter with me. I'm not getting the old snap into my swing."

He then cocked his wrists and demonstrated an imaginary swing. "Right here," he said. "I just don't seem to give it that old follow through."

DiMaggio then drew his right hand from one shoulder to the next. "Up around here, too. I just haven't been able to make the bat come around as quick as I used to.

"It's not that I don't know what's the matter with me. I know what I'm doing wrong. It's just that I can't seem to do anything about it...I'm going to beat it. I'm going to keep swinging until I get the old snap back to me. I know it. I'm going to battle it till I lick it.

"Remember what I said," DiMaggio emphasized calmly. "I'm going to lick it."

7   THE KANSAS CITY BLUES

THE YANKEES KICKED OFF THE SECOND HALF OF THEIR SEASON with an important series in Cleveland without a healthy DiMaggio. Stengel took a look around at his outfield options and wasn't enamored with his choices. Gene Woodling was slated to sit in for DiMag for the time being. Maybe, Casey thought, I should give Jensen a closer look. Jackie's home run at Fenway a few days earlier evidenced the kid's power prospects. Cliff Mapes certainly wasn't a feasible answer; he'd been riding the bench all season for good reason. From Stengel's point of view, the only viable outfielder he had at his disposal was Hank Bauer, who had been hitting with consistency. As for Mantle, his struggles continued, both offensively and defensively.

Coming out of the All-Star break Stengel began a full press on George Weiss. Casey began politicking for Bob Cerv and Bob Wiesler to be called up from Kansas City. Cerv was the power hitting outfielder that Casey craved. Just one year removed from the University of Nebraska, Cerv, Casey told Weiss, would be penciled into left field while Jensen and Woodling shared the center-field duties in Joe's absence. Neither Stengel nor Weiss anticipated DiMaggio to play at all on the upcoming swing through the league's western cities.

Only twenty years old, Wiesler was the hardest throwing Yankee prospect since Lefty Gomez came up a couple of decades earlier. Wiesler would be a much needed boost to the staff, Casey assured Weiss. Despite Stengel's best arguments, George Weiss resisted. In general Weiss opposed using rookies in high pressure situations. Even more, he was reluctant to take two of Kansas City's best players from the club while the Blues were in the midst of a pennant race.

Stengel did get some relief for his pitching corps when the Yankees purchased Art Schallock from the Hollywood Stars on July 12 for $50,000. A small southpaw, Schallock stood 5'7" and barely registered on the scaled at 147 pounds. The 27-year-old Schallock was awarded 11 battle stars as the radio operator aboard the aircraft carrier, U.S.S. *Anzio*. His arrival forced the Yankees to make a roster move. To some, Mantle, given his struggles, was the inevitable choice. A few observers thought Mickey was given short shrift, that Stengel was using his wonder boy as a scapegoat for his team's recent mediocrity.

———

ALLIE REYNOLDS WAS ON THE MOUND FOR THE YANKS AGAINST Cleveland and Bob Feller for the first game following the All-Star break.

Baseball writers had often played up the fact that Reynolds descended from Creek Indians. Allie was often referred to in print as "Wahoo" or "Chief." Reynolds good-natured disposition was on full display during the game as he paid no heed to the time-honored tradition of remaining mum on the subject of an ongoing no-hitter. At the conclusion of the seventh, Allie sat down on the bench next to his roommate, Eddie Lopat, and asked, "Hey pal, do you think I can pitch a no-hitter?"

The following inning, when Berra suggested that Reynolds start off each Cleveland hitter with a fastball, Allie told his catcher that he didn't want to follow that philosophy. "Somebody could guess right and ruin my no-hitter," Reynolds reasoned.

Then, in the ninth, with two outs and two strikes on Bobby Avila, Reynolds barely missed with a pitch a trifle too low.

"Bob," Reynolds yelled in from the mound, "how can you have the nerve to take those kinds of pitches at a time like this?"

With his next delivery, Reynolds stumbled on his follow-through. He rose from the dirt, looked toward the visitors' dugout, and winked. Avila then fouled off Reynolds' next two offerings before swinging and missing to end the game.

The custom of not speaking about what everyone knew was happening made no sense to Reynolds. "What's the sense in kidding anyone?" Reynolds playfully asked afterward. "I could see the outfield lights every inning, and those three big zeroes on the Cleveland side never changed."

No runs, no hits, no errors.

Mixing his fastball with a generous helping of curves and sliders, Reynolds used 119 pitches to toss the first no-hitter by a Yankee pitcher since Monte Pearson accomplished the feat against the Indians in 1938.

Like their opponents, the Yankees had difficulty reaching

base safely. It wasn't until Mantle collected a double off of Feller in the sixth inning that New York had their first hit. The Yankees didn't plate the game's only run until Gene Woodling hit one over the wall in the seventh. Feller went the distance allowing only four hits, but it was Reynolds' brilliance that ruled the day.

The next night Mickey was once again in right, striking out three times in five at-bats. Despite garnering one hit, Mantle was obviously out of sorts at the plate and his play in the field was suffering as a consequence. Shuffling players to and fro was typical of a Stengel's managerial style, but Casey was growing increasingly frustrated with his lack of options in the outfield. He didn't trust Mantle in center, and his center fielder had been hobbled nearly the entire season. Stengel wanted more flexibility with his roster.

By early July, Stengel had amended his early season appraisal of Mantle from, "He's a good ballplayer" to "He's going to be a good ballplayer."

Stengel and Weiss were on opposite sides of the argument in April—Weiss wanted to give the kid some more seasoning, Casey wanted him within arm's reach. The kid was too valuable, too talented, too much of everything to send away and entrust with another manager. The daring, the speed, the power, the youth, most of all Stengel wanted Mantle where he could teach him. But now, three months into the season, he had inched closer to Weiss' stance. The purchase of Schallock forced a roster move and on July 15, Weiss and Stengel agreed that sending Mantle to Kansas City was the best move for the team as well as the kid. Casey called the rookie into his office and broke the news to him.

"We're sending you to Kansas City," Stengel explained to Mantle. "We want you to play every day and break out of your slump. Don't worry, you'll be back here soon."

Mantle heard the words, but didn't believe the sentiment. He thought Stengel was being kind. He was being sent down and he wouldn't be back for a long time, if ever.

The news of his demotion stung Mantle, who unsuccessfully fought back tears as he said his goodbyes in the Yankee clubhouse. Moments later, when reporters began trickling into the clubhouse, Mickey composed himself and valiantly suppressed his emotions as he answered questions prior to the Yankees doubleheader with the Tigers.

"Casey told me about 10:00 this morning," Mickey said, in a hushed voice as his head hung low. "Been kinda expecting it. Guess I've been taking too many pitches."

Someone asked if Mickey had been tutored at the plate.

"No," Mantle said, "Nobody coached me in hitting except once in a while Bill Dickey would tell me a thing or so."

What about in the minor leagues?

"Nope, nobody showed me in the minors, either. They let me hit the way I wanted. It's all right with me," Mantle said. "I'd rather play every day in the minors than sit on the Yankee bench. Nobody has to tell me that I have a lot to learn about outfielding and hitting."

"Shipping Mantle to Kansas City involved a very tough decision," Stengel explained to Dan Daniel. "Mantle is a remarkable player in the making. I do not believe that anybody doubts this…. His greatest weakness with us is his tendency to strike out. In Kansas City he will find the pitching less a strain on his hitting. He will be back. I certainly have not quit on the boy.

He will be a regular on the New York club, to stay, in time."

Speaking with Milton Gross, Casey wanted to emphasize the many positive attributes of Mantle. "If it weren't for the kid, we wouldn't be as high in the race as we are. We didn't get beat many games with the kid in there. He never hurt us in the outfield. There isn't anybody better than him once he gets on base. He fields, he throws, he runs. He makes playing look easy, other guys I got can't reach. It don't make no difference, left or right-handed pitchers against him, like the others I got.

"He's got to learn to bunt better. He's got to get on base more. That's all and then he'll be back and he won't go down any more."

For all his public praise of Mantle, Casey did little to assuage his wunderkind. There was very little nuance to Stengel's managerial style. He did not cater to rookies, or stars for that matter. When Mantle needed a pat on the back, Stengel wasn't there. Nurturing was not Casey's forte.

Weiss placed the blame for the Mantle circumstance on the training school. "We allowed Mickey's spectacular display in Phoenix to manipulate our judgment," Weiss explained. Jaw-dropping home runs of impressive length stirred the imagination of onlookers. Mantle's every move in Arizona seemed effortless, and his potential seemingly unlimited. But these heroics took place in intra-squad games and exhibition contests; Mantle's lack of necessary experience was obvious when confronted with the pressure of a pennant race.

Everything had come too easy, too quickly, for Mantle. The good times were due to slacken, and by the end of May pitchers were learning Mickey's failings and working this knowledge to full effect. Bust him in on the fists; Mantle couldn't handle those pitches. This information spread through the league like wildfire and pitchers were quick to exploit Mantle's weaknesses. As his slump intensified, Mickey was swinging at nearly anything directed toward the plate. The hits dwindled and the strikeouts increased, all the while Mantle struggled to suppress his immaturity and maintain his composure.

As his struggles mounted, Mantle stubbornly resisted adjusting his approach at the plate. A couple of months earlier, Henrich met no resistance when teaching proper outfield technique to Mantle because it was all new to Mickey. But taking tips at the plate? He had learned everything he knew about hitting from his father, and any instructions that varied from Mutt's early teachings were obstinately ignored by Mickey. To accept any batting tips was viewed as a betrayal by Mickey. Loyalty and blood ran deep.

Judged purely by unadorned numbers, Mantle appeared to have earned a deserved place on the Yankees roster. He was third on the club in hits behind Rizzuto and Berra, second in home runs, and first in triples and RBI. But Mickey's 52 strikeouts revealed a lack of discipline and experience at the plate. The strikeouts, combined with his unmistakable immaturity, led him to Kansas City.

During the Memorial Day doubleheader in Boston, Mantle struck out five times. Following the last strikeout, Mickey's frustration boiled over and he broke into tears on the Yankee bench.

Mickey cried out to Stengel following the flood of strikeouts, "Put someone in there who can hit the ball, because I can't."

On another occasion, Indians pitcher Bob Lemon struck out Mantle three times. His futility fueled a tantrum and Mickey recklessly pounded two bats against the dugout wall. Worse than the weeping and fits, Mantle began to allow his struggles at the plate to affect his play in the field.

In the midst of another game Mickey did not get a good jump on an easy fly and the ball fell in for a hit. Following the inning Yankee pitcher Eddie Lopat lit into the rookie.

"You want to play?" Lopat yelled at Mantle, "If not, get your ass the hell out of here. We don't need guys like you. We want to win."

In the course of another game, Mickey failed to run out a ground ball which the second baseman proceeded to bobble. When Mantle reached the dugout he was met by an irate Hank Bauer.

"Don't fuck with my money," Bauer told Mantle.

Mantle remained in Detroit for the Sunday contests at Briggs Stadium. He sat in the Yankee club seats and intently watched as the game played out before him, an elbow on his knee, all the while chewing on his thumbnail absentmindedly. Just a few weeks earlier he'd been the talk of the town, three national publications printed profiles on his sudden rise, he had appeared on TV, and there were endorsements coming at him from every angle.

And now this.

The Tigers' general manager, Billy Evans, took note of the forlorn Mantle sitting in the visitor's dugout before the contest started.

"It's hard on a boy when you ask him to do a man's job," Evans remarked.

Following the game, Mantle retrieved his luggage from the Cadillac Hotel. Red Patterson was there to escort Mickey to the

Detroit airport. Before escaping the lobby of the Cadillac, however, tears once again betrayed Mickey's gallantry. He couldn't
help but wonder if he would ever again return to Yankee Stadium.
He couldn't help but believe he'd been a failure.

———

THE KANSAS CITY BALL CLUB MANTLE JOINED WAS A CONGLOM-
erate of has-beens, disgruntled veterans, and a handful of kids
dreaming of a shot at the big leagues. This band of misfits was
led by their manager George Selkirk.

Selkirk was born January 4, 1908, in Huntsville, Ontario. He
was just four years old when George's father moved the family to Rochester, New York. When he was 19 years old, Selkirk
signed with his hometown Rochester Red Wings, and from
there he bounced around the minor leagues until August 12,
1934, when he made his major league debut with the Yankees.
At the conclusion of that season, Babe Ruth left the Yankees,
and it fell to Selkirk to replace the legendary slugger. The next
spring, Joe McCarthy called upon Selkirk to step into Ruth's
old position, right field. While McCarthy dictated Selkirk's
new position, he gave George the option of not wearing Ruth's
fabled No. 3. Selkirk was just brash enough to believe the number suited him just fine.

"Wearing Babe's number won't make me nervous," Selkirk
said. "I'm going to take his place; I'll take his number too."

Selkirk's 1935 numbers weren't quite Ruthian, but they were
more than respectable with 94 runs batted in, 11 home runs,
and a .312 batting average. Before his days in the big leagues
were over, Selkirk had driven in more than 100 runs twice,

made the All-Star team on two occasions, and batted .300 or better five times during a nine-year career, which was cut short by the war. At the conclusion of the conflict Selkirk returned from serving in the U.S. Navy, his playing days over, but he was far from finished with the game. After the war came Selkirk's second act. Thanks to his habit of running on the balls of his feet, Selkirk was dubbed "Twinkle Toes" by his teammates in Jersey City, years before he joined the Yankees. Now, following the war, Twinkle Toes' days as an active player were behind him. In 1946 he returned to Newark, one of his minor league stops on the way to the Yankees, but this time as a manager. After two years managing Newark of the International League, Selkirk spent three years at the helm of Class A Binghamton before landing in Kansas City.

In the best of circumstances, travel in the minor leagues was a difficult undertaking. For the Blues, as they hopscotched through the Midwest by bus and occasionally train, never staying in one town for more than two or three nights, the summer had been especially arduous. Catching a good night's sleep never proved easy for seemingly at every stop along the way the club shared their sleeping quarters with a convention of one sort or another. There was a conference of young choir singers, the National Barbershop Quartet convention, bowling and golf tournaments.

The barbershop quartet group sang, and sang, and continued singing throughout an early season stay in Toledo. There was singing in the halls, in the bar, in the dining room, and in the streets. The Blues only respite came when they went to Swayne Field. A few players expressed fear that the incessant singing would still being going strong when they next came through Toledo.

The choir singers weren't much into exercising their vocal chords. Instead, this large assembly of teenagers was engaged in noisily destroying the hotel down to the building's foundation.

It was the Indiana State American Legion conference, however, that took convention going to a new level. Theirs was an especially boisterous gathering taking place while the Blues visited Indianapolis in late July. The club arrived at their hotel on the morning of July 28. Even at that early hour, Legionnaires were already patrolling the street in front of the team's hotel. Sirens, firecrackers, whistles, nearly every type of noisemaker known to man were employed to create a cacophony of festivity. One man's symphony is another's garbled racket. For the Blues, there would be no rest before that evening's doubleheader against the Indians.

Following the twin-bill, the club returned to their hotel and found the halls filled with celebrating Legionnaires pounding on doors and inviting hotel guests to join their raucous party. Sleep was fleeting as a drum and bugle corps paraded through the halls at 8:00 Sunday morning. The Blues went to the ballpark bleary eyed, for yet another doubleheader.

And that was on the road. At their home park the Blues had played only a handful of games on a dry home field. Kansas City had seen an abnormally large amount of rain in the spring and early summer, leaving the playing field a virtual swamp at times. On several occasions the natural remedy of the sun's warmth did not dry the field sufficiently and the solution of soaking the playing surface with gasoline and setting it aflame was employed. Dramatic though it was, the scorched-earth plan proved effective.

This world was a far cry from the New York Yankees and the major leagues for Mickey. He caught up with his new team in Milwaukee and in his first game with the Blues, Mantle successfully laid a drag bunt down the first-base line. Following the inning, a pleased Mantle returned to the dugout to retrieve his glove.

"What's the matter with you?" George Selkirk snapped at his newest player.

"Nothing," a perplexed Mantle responded. "Why?"

"I'll tell you why. They didn't send you here to bunt. You're here to get some hits and get your confidence back."

Properly chastened, Mantle humbly replied, "Yes, sir."

The drag bunt would prove to be the high point of Mickey's first week. He became immersed in a terrible batting slump, the strikeouts continued, along with pop-ups and weak ground balls. Mantle wasn't hitting into bad luck, he simply wasn't hitting. To top off his troubles, Mickey was being relentlessly jeered from the stands and the mail criticizing the "draft dodger" continued to arrive via the post office.

The tipping point came after yet another unproductive game. Mickey's hitless streak reached 21 at-bats against the Toledo Mud Hens during his July 22 home debut in Kansas City. Following the contest, Mickey returned to his room at the Aladdin Hotel and phoned his father hoping for a long-distance pat on the back.

"Hello," Mutt answered in a weary voice.

The two hadn't spoken since Mickey's reassignment.

"It's me," Mickey said. "I'm in Kansas City."

"Yeah, I've been reading."

Mickey then erupted with a flow of self-pity. "Well, it looks like I can't play here either. I'm not hitting, Dad. I just can't play anymore."

Mutt had heard enough. He cut off Mickey with a curt, "Where are you staying?"

A few hours later Mutt arrived in Kansas City, bringing along with him the entire family. Riding along in Mutt's truck were Mick's mom, his brother Larry, sister Barbara, and also Merlyn.

If Mickey was expecting a shoulder to cry on, he was terribly mistaken. Mutt chased the rest of the family from the room, and began packing his son's bags all the while scolding the boy in a stern, hard voice.

Living scared was no way to travel through life. Mutt Mantle was ashamed to see his son act this way—a quitter.

"If that's all the man you are, then get your clothes and let's go home. I thought I raised a man," Mutt said. "You ain't nothing but a coward. If you can't play, get a bus and come home. If you want to give up on baseball, well then, you can join me in the mines," Mutt told his weeping son.

His father's harangue came from a place the self-absorbed Mickey couldn't yet understand. The elder Mantle wanted a life for his son beyond the mines of Oklahoma and he was now about to piss away that golden opportunity.

The message was delivered. Mutt looked deep into his boy's eyes. There would be no third chances. It was time to grow up.

All of the Mantles went out for dinner before embarking on the long—and with Mutt behind the wheel—slow, drive back home to Commerce. Mickey was left behind at the Aladdin, alone with his fears and thoughts.

A sleepless night lie ahead.

Mickey's struggles at the plate didn't disappear overnight. A few days after the stern admonition from his father, Mantle was with the Blues in Louisville. Prior to the Blues game against the Colonels, Mantle sat on the dugout steps of Parkway Field and politely answered a few questions from a visiting reporter. The writer, a stringer for the United Press, pestered Mantle with inquiries about the demotion to Kansas City, and what did Mickey believe were his chances of returning to New York this season?

Initially, Mickey skillfully brushed aside the questions. His vague responses of, "We'll have to wait and see," coupled with, "I'll just have to wait and see," weren't good enough for the reporter. The queries continued, and finally Mickey was pushed to an emotional breaking point.

"Of course I hated leaving the Yankees," Mantle blurted out. "Anybody would. But I'm glad I can play every day now."

The United Press writer got what he wanted and so he moved on to George Selkirk.

Mantle had everything, Selkirk acknowledged. "Speed power and all kinds of potential. "I don't know what the devil he's doing down here, but I'm sure not complaining."

That evening in Louisville, Mantle displayed what frustrated the Yankee organization and also what awed them. He struck out three times during the game while swinging wildly on a couple of occasions at ball four out of the strike zone. Mantle also demonstrated his indefinable speed. A single by any other hitter became a double by Mantle, thanks solely to his hustle and unparalleled speed.

During the July 31 contest in Toledo, Mantle stepped to the plate against the Mud Hens. He'd already hit two home runs, a double, and a triple when he came up late in the contest. Manager Selkirk doubling as the Blues third-base coach, flashed Mantle the hit sign. Not certain that he'd understood the signal, Mickey stepped out of the box and looked down the third-base line for verification.

Selkirk gave the hit sign a second time and again Mantle seemed confused.

"Dammit" Selkirk yelled, "that's what the sign is."

On the next pitch Mantle laid down a drag bunt, and easily beat the throw to first.

Unlike his debut game with the Blues, when Mantle returned to the dugout he was not berated by his manager. Rather, Selkirk simply winked at the kid.

———

NEARLY FOUR MONTHS HAD PASSED SINCE MICKEY WAS RE-EXAMINED by his local draft board. Despite two rejections, some skeptics continued to question the validity of the board's decision. The will of these cynics was delivered to the Mantle home on Wednesday, August 1. A letter received that morning by Mrs. Mantle from the Ottawa County draft board solicited yet another examination of Mickey, "at the request of the national director of selective service."

Why was Mantle being asked to undergo a third exam? A controversy arose in the New York papers over the issue. Who forced the government's hand? Was it a rival team? Resentful fans? A grandstanding politician? The White House divulged that it had received three missives protesting Mantle's 4-F status. Several letters were mailed to President Truman, including notes from Mrs. Ivan Hurd and Mrs. Roy Hartman. Mrs. Hurd and Mrs. Hartman each expressed similar complaints. Hurd's husband, Ivan, and Hartman's son Jack, each suffered from osteomyelitis, yet both young men were serving in Korea. Other letters came in to the White House expressing displeasure that any able-bodied athlete be excluded from serving in the armed forces. The letters were handled in a routine manner; they were passed on to the Selective Service.

The Defense Department refused to acknowledge responsibility in the issuing the order. The decision, an administrator for the department said, originated from Mantle's local board. Nonsense, replied an official in Miami, Oklahoma, who insisted that the directive "emanated" from the National Selective Service headquarters before funneling through Colonel Clive Murray, the state Draft Director.

Whereever the order came from mattered not to Mantle. Speaking with his mother by phone in Toledo, Mickey did not protest the decision. "If I have to take another physical, its okay," he said. "And if I have to go into the service, I'll just have to go."

Whatever frustration Mickey may have felt at being singled out for a third examination, he kept these thoughts to himself. Mantle was scheduled to appear for his re-examination August 20, four months to the day since he was last tested.

Life in the bush leagues was not having an ill effect on Mantle. Indeed, since Mutt upbraided him on that night in the Aladdin Hotel, Mickey had completely turned around his attitude, on and off the field. In 40 games with the Blues, Mickey was hitting .364, with 11 home runs and 50 runs batted in. When the call came on August 19 that he was being called back up to the Yankees, Mickey was as surprised as anyone. He thought he might get a chance to join the club in the waning days of the regular season, but he had not expected to be brought back to the club so soon. He was excited by the second chance, certainly.

But the joy he felt at hearing the news was tempered by the impending draft examination.

For Mickey, this was getting to be old hat. He reported to Fort Sill on August 23 and underwent a familiar series of physical examinations, though this time around the tests seemed a bit more strenuous. A small army of physicians conducted the exam, including, ironically, Dr. Charles Grabill, the physician who treated Mantle immediately after Mickey incurred his high school football injury four years earlier.

Following the exam, Army spokesman Lt. E.E. Hamilton met with a handful of reporters who were awaiting the results. The third time was no different than the first two occasions. The team of doctors confirmed the findings of their colleagues who had previously examined Mantle.

Mantle, Lt. Hamilton said, is "unacceptable by present Army standards." Hamilton then admitted that Mantle had underwent an unusually thorough examination so, "there would be no doubt as to his condition, and whether he is eligible to serve."

When Hamilton finished, the reporters were given a few moments with Mantle.

"I'm pretty happy about it," Mickey admitted. "But I'd be just as happy the other way. If a guy's gotta go, that's all there is to it."

How do you think you're going to do with your second chance with the Yanks? He was asked.

"I think the time I spent with the Blues at Kansas City will help a lot, but maybe they're just calling me back to give me a few more pointers."

The brief interview came to a close. Mantle had a flight to catch. He was heading to Cleveland and another chance at the big leagues.

8 A STRAINED SITUATION

WHILE HIS TEAM'S PERFORMANCE ON THE FIELD LEFT MUCH TO BE desired, new St. Louis Browns owner Bill Veeck had cornered the market on entertaining his fans. "Fans" could be a generous term when referencing the hearty few who ventured to Sportsman's Park to take in the terminally bad Brownies. For the July 20 game against the Yankees, the Browns drew a season high 15,212, and Veeck gave those in attendance a thoroughly entertaining pregame show. For starters, Veeck dressed his "usherettes" in fetching beach shorts, which drew the attention of many male attendees. A brief pyrotechnics show was given prior to a vaudeville act and a small circus. The highlight of the festivities, though, was a heart-stopping performance by a young lady who traversed the length of the field on a wire that was strung between two light towers, suspended by only her teeth.

Stengel watched the breathtaking display and saw the act as apropos of his team's recent travails.

"Reminds me of the Yankees trying to hang on in this pennant race," Stengel cracked. "You know, just by the teeth."

The following day, in a stifling 98 degree heat, the Yankees defeated the Browns and moved past Chicago into second place. The White Sox' slide continued, and they now resided in fourth with Cleveland in third, and Boston sitting with the Yankees in the league's top spot. A member of the media was overheard in the press box, referring to the constant shuffling between the circuit's top four clubs, commenting on how "sad" the top clubs were because no one could take control of first place.

Sitting nearby, Veeck chimed in, "If they're sad, how about the losing teams below them?"

JULY 24 STANDINGS

Team	Record	GB
New York	54–34	–
Boston	55–35	–
Cleveland	54–36	1.0
Chicago	53–40	3.5
Detroit	40–46	13.0
Washington	40–50	15.0
Philadelphia	36–56	20.0
St. Louis	27–62	27.5

On July 27, with the White Sox leading 4–3 in the top of the ninth, a torrential downpour came, forcing a delay in the game. Eventually the contest was called due to inclement weather and the score reverted to the score at the end of the eighth, which was 3–1 in favor of New York. The White Sox immediately appealed to league President Will Harridge, who was laid up in

Chicago's St. Luke's Hospital recovering from surgery.

The White Sox were angered at what they believed to be an incompetent decision by the umpire crew as well as the stalling tactics of the Yankees. Chicago's general manager Frank Lane pointed a finger squarely at Stengel, who, Lane charged, "used almost one pitcher for each batter in the ninth." Frank Shea was also guilty according to Lane, because the Yankee reliever "consumed nine minutes coming in from the bullpen."

Following the Chicago--New York series, Paul Richards attacked both Stengel and the umpires, who the White Sox manager believed aided the Yankees.

Stengel, never one to parse his words when he wanted to get a point across, was very deliberate when addressing Richards' charge.

"I suppose Richards is entitled to his opinion about me," Stengel said with a wry smile. "But when he makes cracks about umpires, when he says they are giving the Yankees the pennant, well, he's off track. What a terrible thing that was to say about the umpires needing investigation and being incompetent and favoring the New York club.

"I don't say the umpires are always right, but Richards has no business to say they are throwing games my way. Any games we win, we win ourselves. Nobody has a right to say the umpires are giving us anything. What's the matter with that guy?"

———

THREE DAYS LATER, PRIOR TO THE JULY 30 GAME AGAINST DETROIT, Casey's birthday was celebrated at the Stadium with a large cake at home plate.

"Mrs. Stengel says I am 60," Stengel said. "The records of baseball insist I am 62. Neither Mrs. Stengel nor the book is correct."

A couple hours later, in the bottom of the eighth inning, DiMaggio committed an uncharacteristic mental lapse with the Tigers' George Kell on second base and one out. Joe had returned to the lineup six days earlier against Cleveland, and so whatever rust he may have gathered during the lay-off should have been dusted off when Steve Souchock hit a fly ball to deep center field. DiMaggio easily tracked the ball down, and hauled it in. Thinking it was the third out of the inning, Joe blissfully tossed the ball into Rizzuto at short, and began jogging in toward the Yanks dugout. Kell had advanced from second base, and Detroit third-base coach Dick Bartell began waving Kell home when he realized Joe's mistake. DiMaggio's blunder allowed Kell to score all the way from second, giving Detroit a 4–2 lead. The large crowd of nearly 40,000 greeted Joe's blunder with a chorus of boos, which were met with DiMaggio's usual stoic expression. Minutes later, Joe again heard it from the crowd when he committed the second out in the Yankee half of the frame. All was forgiven by the hometown faithful when Joe awoke from his slumber and his check-swing base hit in the bottom of the ninth brought home Joe Collins, giving the Yankees a 5–4 victory and a two-and-a-half game lead in the standings.

The next morning, George Weiss and Stengel met to discuss the team's roster. A deal had been worked out sending Cliff Mapes to the St. Louis Browns for a handful of players and $10,000. An additional move was made which sent Jackie Jensen to Kansas City. After the roster moves were made,

Stengel spoke with reporters. "I am sorry that Jensen has to go to Kansas City at this rather late stage of the season, and I regret that we had to get rid of Mapes, but that's baseball."

Casey pushed for the blonde Californian to give the mound a fair try in Arizona and he had never completely embraced Jensen as an outfielder. In truth, Jensen hadn't fully regained the faith of his manager after the Yankees broke camp. And though Jensen made the team out of Phoenix as an outfielder and started the season off well, he tailed off after the Yankee's first western trip. Jensen's struggle's at bat, coupled with Stengel's built in antipathy, earned the 24-year-old a ticket to Kansas City.

The Jensen roster maneuver and Mapes trade were both done to make room for Bob Cerv and Bob Wiesler, neither of whom were slated to reach the parent club until 1952. The two Bobs had enjoyed success in Kansas City, Cerv a bit more than Wiesler. The 26-year-old Cerv was only one year removed from the University of Nebraska and he had accumulated 26 home runs and 101 RBI with a slugging percentage of .685 in 98 games.

For his part, Stengel was pleased with the arrival of the two youngsters.

"Lovely, just lovely," Casey commented. He fancied Cerv in particular, and Stengel gave a brief appraisal.

"He's the Yogi Berra type" Stengel explained. "He slides into a base and comes up dirty. Better bring your field glasses because when he hits the ball, it disappears."

Stengel then switched his analysis to Wiesler without a break for breath or mentioning the pitcher's name.

"You'll be amazed," Stengel gushed, "simply amazed. Better have your eyes tested, he'll toss those little peas and on a dark day you won't be able to follow the ball."

As July ended and August began the club was reeling. What the Yanks needed was a visit from the league patsies, and the Browns' arrival at the Stadium was just the remedy Stengel's crew needed.

The Yankees took four out of five games when the Browns came to New York. Though the Yankees didn't see him over this stand, the 45-year-old Browns pitcher Satchel Paige was the focus of Red Sox manager Steve O'Neill's protest to the American League. O'Neill believed that Paige's famous "hesitation" pitch was illegal with men on base. It was a balk, O'Neill insisted.

Stengel was asked his opinion of the mini-controversy and he was more than willing to offer a thought. "That hiccup-type delivery drove our boys crazy in St. Louis," Stengel said, "When he held us hitless for five innings without any ball going out of the infield."

But the pitch itself?

"It must be legal," Casey said, "he's been doing it since I was a boy."

———

DESPITE HIS ANNOYANCE WITH THE PRESS, DIMAGGIO CONSENTED to an interview with Gene Ward of the *Daily News* in early August. Ward waited patiently in DiMaggio's fifth floor suite at the Hotel Elysee for Joe D. to arrive. Joe was running a bit late. A few hours earlier in the afternoon the Yanks had lost to Detroit and all DiMaggio contributed to the defeat was an 0-for-4 day at the plate.

When he finally arrived at his home, Joe was surprised to see the reporter sitting in his drawing room. For a moment Joe forgot the appointment. A weary look came over DiMaggio's handsome face.

"Well, we blew another one," Joe said.

The Great DiMaggio was tired, Ward noted. Dead tired.

A cool gust of air came through the drapery. Joe pulled aside a curtain and let the comfortable breeze wash over him. In recent days Joe had made some concessions to his advancing age. He cut back on his after-hours tour of the city, began allowing himself more sleep, and also reduced his radio and "writing" commitments. His sole focus was baseball.

"We used to play a game in an hour and 40 minutes, crabbing like hell if it ran two hours," DiMaggio said. "I'm really tired."

Ward was curious. "Why are the games running so long?" he asked.

After a thoughtful pause, Joe responded, "Mostly it's the young players, I think. Too many are being dashed into the majors instead of being brought up step by step through the minors."

DiMaggio named no names, but he expressed concern that kids were being pushed to the big leagues, their confidence sorely lacking in trying to maintain the major league pace.

"I used to think I was being held back," DiMaggio said, "but now I'm thankful for those three years on the Coast.

"Now it seems every time a pitcher shows signs of faltering, the manager rushes out for a conference. Or the catchers walk out to the mound and the infielders gather 'round. Too much strategy."

Joe stared out the window and flexed his bum shoulder. "Still gives a twinge every once in a while, but I'm in no position to criticize the way I've been going. I know what I've been doing wrong. Swinging behind the ball. No snap in my swing..." Joe gazed out at Manhattan silently before promising, "I'll bounce back yet."

A brief discussion of the National and American League races ensued before Ward turned the subject to the reserve clause. The issue had been bouncing around the news in recent days.

"All I know is this," Joe replied. "If its continuance means that young ballplayers are to be handled as I once was, then it is wrong. It doesn't affect me now, but in all honesty, I have to tell you that it once caused me a great deal of trouble.

"In 1941, I set that consecutive game hitting streak, yet for 1942 they tried to force the same salary terms on me. Pressure methods were used. An outside smear was attempted and, because of the reserve clause in the contract, I could do little to help myself."

His mental lapse against Detroit withstanding, DiMaggio had returned to the lineup and exhibited flashes of "the Great DiMaggio." But the turnaround was fleeting. Just over a week into August the Yankees had relinquished first place to Cleveland, and Joe's struggles at the plate returned. Speculation was rife in the New York papers that Stengel could be forced to bench the big guy. Such conjecture was absurd, Casey said when asked about the possibility.

Following the Senators 4–1 defeat of the Yankees on August 8 at the Stadium, Stengel snapped at reporters asking him if the time had come to bench DiMaggio.

"I can't take him out now," Casey snapped. "Anyhow, we've got nobody to replace him."

Well, what about the possibility of dropping Joe a spot or two in the batting order? Stengel was asked.

Moving Joe DiMaggio from cleanup? Previously such a thought would have been labeled pure blasphemy. Casey, however, wouldn't dismiss the possibility.

"Don't know myself what I'm going to do," Stengel admitted. "I'm not going to make any decision until I have to give the umpire my batting order. Then you'll know as well as I."

The next afternoon, Casey resisted whatever urges he may have had to move DiMaggio out of the fourth spot, and Joe delivered with a couple of hits, including a triple and his 10th home run of the season.

Relations between DiMaggio and the press had been running hot and cold all year.

Mostly cold.

Joe had been feuding with local writers for much of the summer. Every criticism pricked his thin skin. Yankee beat writers had grown wary of approaching Joe's locker, never knowing what mood the star might be in. Some reporters had taken to avoiding him all together.

He had something to say, however, after he played a big part in lifting the Yankees to a 6–4 victory over Washington in the ninth. The respite from the ravages of time gave Joe something to crow about. He had waited all summer to give it back to the writers who said he was done and buried. Following the game, DiMaggio unleashed a season's worth of pent-up frustration on an unwitting target, Lou Miller of the *World-Telegram*. Sipping a beer while dressed only in a white t-shirt and green undershorts, Joe let loose a diatribe toward Miller, a harangue that was meant for every baseball writer who had written him off.

"What kind of stuff you writing about Bob Porterfield purposely throwing three straight balls to me, then two straight strikes, then a curve to get me out?" DiMaggio asked.

Miller mumbled an answer; the information in question had come from Joe's manager.

The writer's response set Joe off anew.

"Stengel told you that?" he asked Miller. "I'll have to ask him. I'm certainly going to have to ask him when I see him tomorrow.

"The plate is just this wide. If a pitcher could put the ball exactly where he wanted to, the batter would just have to go home. You guys call that good reporting. I'll see if Stengel really said that.

"You're damn right I wanted to make you writers look bad. I'll always try to make you look bad. Just because I have a bad day, you guys want to fire me. Some of you guys are the ones who washed me up in 1946. But here I am, five years later. How are you going to explain these hits I made today?

"Did you ever see me give up on a fly ball in the outfield? Only thing I'm interested in is helping win the pennant again this year."

——

THE PENNSYLVANIA BLUE LAWS DECREED THAT NO NEW INNING could begin after 6:44 PM, and that all action must cease at 6:59 PM. During their August 12 game against the Athletics at Shibe Park, the Yankees batted around in the top of the eighth, scoring five runs and jumping out to a 9–7 lead. Before the Philadelphia half of the frame concluded, however, the witching hour struck, and the score reverted to the 7–4 lead the Athletics had after the seventh.

When questioned afterward, A's manager Jimmy Dykes freely admitted that he stalled so the clock would run out.

"Sure we were killing time," Dykes said. "I have to do what I can to win a game. The only thing they can do is change the rules if they want to prevent stalling."

Unlike the National League, which allowed suspended games to resume at the point of delay, the American League rules decreed that the contest revert to the score of the last completed inning.

Eyeballing the Athletics obvious attempt to slow the game down, Stengel grumbled the A's should have to forfeit the game due to their actions. They made "burlesque out of the game of baseball," he complained. Still, Casey did not formally file a protest with the league office. The whole affair was up to the umpires, Stengel stated.

Casey's words were quickly taken across Shibe Park to Dykes.

"Burlesque? We had no intention of delaying until the Yanks went ahead. But it would have been dishonest of me if I didn't do everything possible to win. That's the main objective."

The next day, as each Philadelphia batter stepped to the plate, Berra issued an indictment.

"You Cleveland lover," Yogi grumbled at every Athletic.

Philadelphia swept a doubleheader the day before, and then handed the Yankees their worst defeat of the year, 16–8.

"What do they think we ought to do," Jimmy Dykes rhetorically asked, "roll over and play dead for them?"

Though he was one of the finest players in the league, Yogi Berra had become something of an afterthought. Yet in this season he had morphed into the single most valuable player on the Yankees. Perhaps realizing that he'd been taking his backstop for granted, Stengel took some time to heap praise on Berra while speaking with columnist Frank Graham while watching his club take batting practice.

"He's the best catcher in the league," Casey said of Berra. "In my opinion he's the best catcher in either league, but a lot of people get mad when you say he is better than the other fellow."

The "other fellow" was Brooklyn's Roy Campanella.

"He knows every hitter in the league except himself," Stengel continued. "He is the only one that don't know what a good hitter he is. But all the pitchers do…. They know that he wants to hit at everything and don't like to take a pitch, even if it's way out here. Ever notice when he gets a 'take' sign? He makes a face like this."

Stengel proceeded to take his comical face and screw it up into an even more comical face.

"They used to pitch him high and low, inside and outside, and he gives them plenty of action. He is the greatest bad-ball hitter I ever saw…. You know what they never do? They never pitch him a strike—they might get killed.

———

ON AUGUST 15, CASEY AND THE REST OF HIS TEAM WERE INVITED to join the Touchdown Club in Washington at the Statler Hotel's Presidential Room for a dinner honoring the Yankee manager. The Touchdown Club was one of the nation's biggest and most influential sportsman groups. Red Patterson introduced each member of the team, who were seated with Stengel at the head table. Before Casey stepped to the microphone, toastmaster Jim Magner asked the band director to strike up some "Yankee" music; the ensemble responding with a rousing rendition of "Dixie."

As the honoree, Stengel was obligated to deliver a short talk. What the Touchdown Club received was vintage Stengel, a 15-minute oration in rapid fire fashion, during which Casey barely paused for a breath.

"We have the best minor league set-up in baseball," Casey informed the audience gathered in the Statler suite. "All of our boys are taught early to play only one way, the right way, the Yankee way. When they come up to us, they're ready."

Every team in the league was out to knock his club off, Casey said, but "that's all right with us. The harder they play, the more mistakes they'll make against the Yankees."

Stengel's club made a clean three-game sweep of the sixth place Senators before heading home for a brief series with Connie Mack's Athletics. The train bringing the team to New York from Washington made a brief stop in Baltimore, where Allie Reynolds joined his teammates for the rest of the journey. Reynolds was in the Maryland city having his right elbow examined by Dr. George Bennett. Five days earlier, in the midst of a 7–4 New York win in Philadelphia, Reynolds felt discomfort in his throwing arm.

"I felt it jerk when pitching to Wally Moses in the ninth," Allie said.

Reynolds told no one of the strange feeling in his elbow at the moment. Instead he focused on registering the last two outs of the game. A home run by the next batter, Eddie Joost, was followed by an Elmer Valo double before Stengel called Bob Kuzava to save the game for the Yankees.

Reynolds stepped aboard the train and was immediately hit with a barrage of questions.

"What did the doc say, Chief?"

"Said my elbow looks better than it did when he kept me out in the spring," Reynolds said. "All I need is some rest and some good thick steaks. Told me to pitch whenever I feel ready."

Stengel received the news privately from Reynolds and came away from the talk pessimistic that the Chief would be ready for the big Cleveland series, just a week off.

"The doc said Reynolds is all right," Stengel said with a bit of uncertainty. "Well, we don't know. Did he see him pitch? Did he make him pitch?"

The Yankees took two of three from the Athletics before embarking on a 14-game road trip that would take them to every American League city with the exception of Boston. As the excursion began, Casey Stengel received some good news from Dr. Gaynor about three of his players who had been laid up with various ailments. Rizzuto, Reynolds, and Morgan were all ready to return to the lineup. Rizzuto had missed the previous five games due to a sore knee. Morgan had been troubled by a sore muscle in his lower right arm. The shortstop would be put to work immediately, but the two pitchers would have to wait a bit, as Casey was holding off on putting the recovered pitchers back into the rotation. Reynolds' enflamed elbow was nearly healed but Stengel wasn't taking any chances coming down the stretch run. Ever cautious, Casey was eyeballing the Yankees trip to Cleveland later in the week as the likely return of Reynolds and Morgan to the rotation. In a season of shuffling chairs atop the standings, the Indians were the current team sitting at the apex, and Stengel couldn't help but be distracted by the looming matchup with the Cleveland club.

"I figure we can go into their backyard and belt the blazes out of them," Casey said as he watched his boys take batting practice prior to their first game in Detroit. "It's the best way to make up lost ground."

Stengel wanted to clarify something; he was taking all the contenders seriously. However, "It's merely that you've got to consider first things first and those Indians are in front of us while the Red Sox still trail us by three games."

Later that afternoon, in the first game of a doubleheader, DiMaggio allowed two balls to go over his head. Both hits turned into triples. In his game piece, Lou Miller referred to DiMaggio as, "the creaking Clipper."

More important than a writer taking cheap shots at a legend, Berra hit his 19th and 20th home runs, one in each end of the twin-bill with the Tigers. However, Yogi suffered an injury in the ninth inning of the nightcap when a foul top hit the third finger of his right hand.

The potential loss of Berra for any extended time frightened Stengel. He alone was the single most vital member of the Yankee club. Thankfully for Casey's wellbeing, Yogi's finger was only bruised and he wouldn't miss any time. But for an instant, Stengel saw the whole season blown to bits had he lost his manager on the field.

The Yankees escaped Detroit with a split of their four games with the lowly Tigers. From the disappointment in Briggs Stadium, they traveled across northern Ohio and arrived in Cleveland on the 23rd for a three-game series at a moment when the hometown team was riding high. The Indians were perched atop the American League standings having won 34 of their previous 45 games, including 15 straight at Municipal Stadium. Practically everyone in the city was feeling brash about the Indians' chances for taking the pennant. The confidence spread among the players, their fans, even the stadium organist who treated the crowd with a tune called, "There's No Place Like First Place and The Indians Are Going to Stay on Top."

Tension and ill humor had plagued the Indians and Yankees rivalry much of the summer. Five weeks earlier Stengel publicly ridiculed the Indians' introduction of a jeep to deliver their relief pitchers to the mound from the bullpen. Yankee pitchers wouldn't ride in such a primitive machine, Stengel cracked, because "They're used to Cadillacs. They won't ride in anything smaller."

The next time the Yanks were in Cleveland for a series starting July 12, Indians general manager Hank Greenberg was ready with his response. A Caddy convertible was placed in the bullpen area prepared to taxi New York's relief pitchers to the hill. The normally good natured Stengel found nothing humorous in Greenberg's gag. If Yankee pitchers needed to make the trek in from the distant reaches of Municipal Stadium, they would walk, not ride, Stengel grumbled.

A rivalry had been born, though the animus had more to do with the first place team confronting their nearest contender than the dispute over transportation to the mound. Prior to the first pitch, the ambience around the ballpark was electric and the lively atmosphere was further engaged when, in the second inning, Gene Woodling came darting toward the infield from his position in left field. Gesticulating wildly toward the scoreboard, Woodling told the second-base umpire that someone was peering out of the scoreboard with binoculars. A brief discussion ensued amongst the team of arbitrators umpiring the game. Their solution was to close the few vents that were open in the scoreboard. After a seven-minute delay in the action, play resumed but the controversy continued well into the night.

"Ridiculous," Greenberg said afterward of the accusation that the Cleveland club was trying to steal signs. "That's old stuff. I've been hearing these same charges year after year. I suppose the Yankees think the only way we can beat them is to resort to underhand stuff. I guess nobody can beat those high and mighty Yankees fair and square."

Indeed, Greenberg had heard very similar charges just one year earlier when Boston manager Steve O'Neill accused the Indians of the exact same crime. O'Neill's allegation was never proven or disproven, though he did receive a pair of binoculars on the Red Sox next trip to Cleveland, a gift from a wiseacre in the press box.

The score was 2–1 in favor of the home team when Gene Woodling again stirred the pot in the seventh inning. A ground ball to short forced Woodling at second, but the Yankee left fielder came in with a ferocious slide, breaking up a possible double play. Indians' second baseman Bobby Avila, victim of Woodling's aggression, rose from the dirt and confronted Gene. Avila took exception to Woodling's slide, and offered the opinion that it was, in fact, a dirty play.

Avila's appraisal set off Woodling's sense of fair play. Even more, taken in the light of what occurred earlier in the game, in which Woodling believed he caught the Indians cheating to gain advantage, the accusation of "dirty play" infuriated the Yankee. Woodling and Avila squared off, both men anxious to settle the dispute with their fists. Before any blows were delivered, though, second-base umpire Bill McKinley stepped between the two would-be combatants. The calm delivered by McKinley's mediation quickly evaporated, though, as players from both teams charged the infield. The scrum was little more than a meet and greet with the exception of Cleveland's starting pitcher, Bob Lemon's attempt to get a swing in on Woodling. Lemon failed to connect and order was restored with no player being ejected.

Cleveland's 2–1 lead held with two out in the top of the ninth when Berra walked, bringing Woodling to the plate. Woodling's starring role as an Indians irritant that day was remembered by the more than 36,000 in attendance. With boos of rabid Cleveland fans ringing in his ears, Woodling lined a single to right field, advancing Berra to third. The belated Yankee rally came to a halt with the next batter, though. Johnny Mize, pinch-hitting for McDougald, hit a looping drive to right-center that Indians right fielder Bob Kennedy flagged down.

Bob Lemon won his 15th while allowing only three hits en route to the complete-game victory. For the Yankees this may have been their toughest loss of the season. In an effort to protect his players, Stengel closed the clubhouse off to reporters following the game, the first time in Casey's three years with the Yankees that he had barred the press from the locker room. The combustible mix of a devastating defeat, the alleged cheating of the Indians, and a rhubarb between the two rivals, compelled Stengel to take such an extraordinary step. Though his public persona was sometimes that of a jester in pinstripes, in reality Stengel was very perceptive. His players needed a break from the meddling questions of the press. The odds that someone would mutter something incendiary were too high for Casey's comfort. He did briefly make himself available to the media. Stengel met with writers outside the clubhouse doors and was anything but himself. His answers were short, and for the most part, uninteresting.

The next afternoon the loquacious Casey returned. Before

the Yankees and Indians took the field Stengel gave beat writers more than the usual allotment of time set aside each day.

Certainly, with Feller, Lemon, Garcia, and Wynn, the Indians had the pitching. But Casey liked his boys, too. Raschi, Reynolds, Lopat—Stengel would take his chances with those fellows against anyone. But he was concerned with the Yanks' lack of punch at the plate.

"Frankly, I figure we got to get a better wallop," Casey said. "If you can hit those long balls, you can make up for any little difference you may find in pitching."

Mantle was due to arrive in Cleveland later that day and Casey had designs on how to utilize the kid.

"Naturally I figure on taking advantage of a fellow like that," Stengel acknowledged. "I don't know what field I'm going to use him in, though. In fact it might be I'll reserve him for use strictly as a pinch-hitter."

———

MANTLE'S FLIGHT LEFT OKLAHOMA CITY AT 8:00 AM AND LANDED at Cleveland's Hopkins Airport seven hours later. Unlike his last arrival in the big leagues, Mickey was not greeted with ballyhoo and fanfare. Instead of being the next sensation, as he had been in the spring, Mantle was now just another farmhand getting the call up. Well, he wasn't just any old minor leaguer, but Mickey's return caused just a ripple of excitement compared to the avalanche of accolades that accompanied him to the Yankees just a few months earlier.

Indeed, things had changed in the few weeks he'd been in Kansas City. There were a couple of new faces in the clubhouse, including Bobby Brown, who had joined the team after being discharged from the Army. Brown was now wearing Mickey's old No. 6, and Mickey found that Pete Sheehy had hung jersey No. 7 in his locker. The jersey had been worn by Cliff Mapes, but was now available following the July 31 trade of Mapes to the St. Louis Browns.

A new number was just a small piece of the change Mantle experienced upon his second arrival in New York. He now had a new place to live, and had also picked up a pair of new roommates, Hank Bauer and Johnny Hopp. The three shared a modest apartment above The Stage Delicatessen, consisting of a bedroom in the rear with enough space for two beds, which is where Hopp and Bauer slept. A second bedroom had barely enough room to accommodate an army cot. This is where Mickey slept. There was also a living room and a small, narrow kitchen. The rookie was assigned to sleep on the cot. He was also the designated gofer, running errands of all sorts for his veteran roommates.

To make room for Mantle on the roster, Bob Cerv and Bob Wiesler had been sent down to Kansas City. In addition to calling up Mickey, Bob Hogue, a pitcher acquired from St. Louis in the Mapes deal, was brought to New York. Though Stengel and Weiss had high hopes, both Cerv and Wiesler disappointed during their shot with the big league squad. The would be potent bat of Cerv, failed to deliver either in average or power—and Wiesler, he of the promising arm, failed to survive the fourth inning in any of his three starts.

Ben Epstein of the *Mirror* questioned Stengel as to where Mantle fit into the Yankees' plans.

"Can't tell until I see him," Casey told Epstein. "But he looks all right, I'm going to play him somewhere in the outfield."

The original intent was for Mantle to provide some punch to an offense that had been struggling of late. Mickey's delayed arrival due to his third army exam was now even more anticipated by Stengel, who suddenly had a shortage of healthy bodies to field. Casey was left with just two healthy outfielders in Bauer and DiMaggio after Gene Woodling aggravated his knee, which was originally injured two weeks earlier in Washington.

———

DIMAGGIO'S BATTING AVERAGE SAT AT .264 AND HE HAD KNOCKED in 58 runs as of August 27. To this point in the season, Joe had been consistently inconsistent. A slump was followed by a streak, which gave way to a slump, and then another streak. Joe was due to break out again at the plate.

Stengel was tiring of the "should you bench DiMaggio?" queries.

"You can't show me one game where DiMaggio has hurt us, and I can show you plenty where he had helped us," Casey said.

"Joe is fielding splendidly, making great catches, and throwing well. He is hitting the ball hard. Unfortunately, a lot of those hits are being caught. Sooner or later, they will start falling safe. When they do, look out."

Maybe Stengel's praise was a diversion. Perhaps he was easing the path to giving Joe a rest.

As Casey spoke, the Yankees were en route to St. Louis from Chicago. Stengel arrived at the Chase Hotel in St. Louis and found a note from Joe McCarthy waiting for him. Since leaving the Yankees in May of 1946, McCarthy had kept whatever thoughts he might have on his old team and their pennant prospects to himself. Even during his brief time managing in Boston, McCarthy stayed mum about the Yanks. So McCarthy's letter written from his farm in Amherst, New York, to Stengel came as a welcome surprise to the current Yankee manager.

"Come back to the Stadium in good shape from this trip, and you'll win the championship," McCarthy advised in his note.

The messaged brought a smile to Stengel's expressive mug. "This is very heartening to me because McCarthy feels the same way I do," Casey explained.

He then rattled off the upcoming road schedule McCarthy referred to in his letter. Two in St. Louis, three in Washington, and a Labor Day doubleheader in Philly. "Our next seven contests are with the three lowest teams in the standings. If we can't beat those clubs, we don't deserve to win, do we?

"Definitely, I intend to play DiMaggio regularly. The guy's running swell and he's doing swell in the field. But if Joe had any aches or pains he hasn't said anything to me about it. And I bet you that unless it's something mighty bad, he won't. I don't mind telling you, I am counting heavily on Joe DiMaggio for the homestretch…. His work in the field, including his throwing, and his batting, too, have been very impressive in the last few days."

He continued, changing his evaluation to a few other players.

"I think Mickey Mantle is a much more confident batter than he was before we shipped him to Kansas City…. I also want to throw a few posies at Gil McDougald."

McDougald's impressive rookie campaign continued to please and surprise Stengel. As of late, McDougald was productively filling in for Jerry Coleman at second base.

Confident as he was in his club, Ol' Case was suffering from a bit of anxiety concerning his moundsmen.

"Of course, when you come down to hard pan, our destinies are tightly tied up with our pitching, and there I am not completely at ease. The fact is, we have four tired arms."

Stengel was referencing Lopat, Reynolds, Raschi, and Morgan.

"They are not sore arms," Casey clarified. "Just tired. But at this stage of the race, what arm isn't a little heavy?"

AUGUST 31 STANDINGS

Team	Record	GB
New York	80–47	–
Cleveland	80–49	1.0
Boston	75–51	4.5
Chicago	70–58	10.5
Detroit	59–69	21.5
Washington	53–72	26.0
Philadelphia	53–77	28.5
St. Louis	39–86	40.0

The Yankees concluded their final western trip of the season in St. Louis on August 29 having won seven of 11 games during the slog. The Yanks were idle on the 30th but still were able to slip into first place by half a game thanks to the Indians 6–2 loss in Philadelphia. Word of their new place in the standings reached the Yankees as they rode the rails heading east to Washington. Stengel felt the need to speak to his players and remind them that there remained a lot of baseball to be played. Nothing had been won yet.

"What you guys have got to do is throw away all those schedules and dope sheets you're using to figure out the future," Stengel began. "Maybe it looks nice on paper when you start to doping how many games the Browns are going to lick the Indians or how many times the Athletics are going to pin back the Red Sox's ears.

"But that ain't the way you win flags," Casey continued. "Hoping or expecting that something will happen to the other fellow don't get you no place. You got to win each one as it comes along yourselves and that's just what I expect to see you do."

Earlier that same day, the Yankees obtained pitcher Johnny Sain from the Braves in an interleague waiver deal for $50,000 and minor league pitcher, Lew Burdette. Filling late season needs was becoming a habit for George Weiss. Two years earlier, Weiss purchased Johnny Mize from the Giants for $40,000, and in '50, the Yankee general manager acquired Johnny Hopp from Pittsburgh at the cost of $40,000. As far as Stengel was concerned the Sain transaction was the last move his team needed to make.

"At the moment there isn't a player we can get, either from our farm organization or from the majors that I'd want. I simply wouldn't know where to play such a guy. I think we got the best club in the league already and there's nobody I'd want to remove from the lineup."

Stengel enjoyed these sessions with reporters. Occasionally he said too much, but rarely did Casey censor himself. The leisurely train rides permitted both the manager and the journalists to relax, while allowing plenty of time to talk about whatever came to mind. Today, Stengel sat with the traveling beat writers at the Yankees' lunch table when a writer mentioned that Indians general manager Hank Greenberg had criticized the Yankees acquisition of Sain. Greenberg had questioned the waiver rules that allowed the transaction, the reporter explained to Casey.

Stengel had no patience to listen to such nonsense. He was fed up with the noise coming from Cleveland, particularly anything emanating from Greenberg.

"When are we going to do something that will suit Greenberg?" an angry Stengel asked. "[Greenberg's] always complaining about something. Just because we pick up a player from the other league when we were fighting his club and a couple of others for the pennant, he wants the rules concerning such things changed. I imagine that, having got waivers on John, the Boston club's chief lookout was not to help us win the pennant, but to make the best deal for Sain.

"What's the matter with him anyhow? Is he trying to claim we put something over on him by buying Sain after the National League had waived the guy? If that's what it is, he certainly is a fine general manager. I'd hate to admit I held a job like that and there was a player on the market but I had to read in the paper what was going on."

Casey then resurrected the charges from the previous month, that the Indians were stealing signs at Municipal Stadium. Where did Greenberg get the gall to complain about the Yankees' accusations?

"All I got to say is, he's a guy who certainly ought to know about signs," Stengel said. "From what they tell me he never was a hitter until they got to telling him what was coming up to the plate to hit."

The arrival of Sain reunited the pitcher with his old manager. Stengel and Sain were together in the same roles with the 1942 Braves. Following that season, Sain went into the service, and when he returned from the war, Stengel had been discharged from the Braves' managerial position. Today, nine years since they were last together, Stengel was a whole lot smarter as manager of the New York Yankees than he was leading the Boston Braves. And the now 33-year-old Sain deserved better than his 5–13 record. In many of his outings this season, the right-handed Sain had received very little support from Boston hitters. Both Weiss and Stengel held out hope that Sain had enough left in his arm to push them over the top.

In Washington, Stengel told a rapt gathering of baseball writers, "We should win the pennant."

This was the first time Casey had made such a brash proclamation.

"My pitching looks good. My starting pitchers are going fine and the relievers have done splendid. I think Sain will help, but even if he doesn't, we've lost nothing. I've got enough good pitchers to win. We have the spirit and the confidence. Our team makes the right plays. We make the double plays, catch the tough fly balls, have power at the plate, and good reserves, We don't lose easy."

———

THERE WAS NO DISGUISING THE FACT THAT DIMAGGIO WAS A shadow of the player he once was. In the 9th inning of the August 25 game against the Indians, the Yankees had a runner on second with two out when Gene Woodling came to the plate. With DiMaggio on deck, Cleveland pitcher Steve Gromek gave

Woodling an intentional pass. That Joe came through with a run-scoring base hit did not overshadow the fact that Gromek preferred to face DiMaggio, rather than Gene Woodling, with the game on the line. This was the first time in his career that an opponent had made such a strategic decision.

A number of Yankee players grumbled amongst themselves. Why wouldn't Stengel put the old man on the bench? As the summer drew on and the pennant race tightened, resentment on the team grew toward DiMaggio.

Milton Gross of the *New York Post* devoted a column to the controversy, speaking to several Yankees about the subject. One anonymous teammate told Gross, "It gives you a creepy feeling to watch the guy. We can't talk to him and he won't talk to us. He just sits there by himself and stews. It's not pleasant for us players, just like it's not pleasant for the writers traveling with the team. It's a strained situation all around."

The rift that had grown between Joe and many of his teammates was epitomized following the September 5 game in Boston. DiMaggio stepped to the plate and the first two pitches to him were each called a ball by plate umpire Cal Hubbard. From the Red Sox dugout, Boston manager Steve O'Neill bellowed his disapproval with Hubbard. The third delivery, another borderline pitch, was also deemed a ball by Hubbard, a decision which set off O'Neill once again. The whole Red Sox bench howled their displeasure as the count reached 3–0. The fourth pitch, though it appeared high and wide, was ruled a strike. The following pitch, even farther outside than the previous, was also called a strike. DiMaggio concluded his at-bat by popping up, but after the game he was seething over the seeming innocuous turn of events.

"Those Boston guys raised the roof when they thought they were getting the worst of it," DiMaggio said to group of reporters. "But when he called those two bad pitches on me, what was our bench doing? Nothing! Not a sound from 'em…. They can all go to hell."

9   NO BREATH TO SPARE

A SEPTEMBER 4 RAINOUT IN BOSTON ALTERED THE SCHEDULE FOR the final week of the season. The change was met with disapproval by members of both the Yankees and Red Sox. The revised schedule now slated Boston and New York to play doubleheaders on both the 28th and 29th, a total of five games in the season's final three days. While his players griped about the revamped schedule, Stengel preferred to see the postponement as a blessing. Eddie Lopat and Allie Reynolds would each get some much needed rest. Besides, if things played out the way Casey planned, those last three days would be superfluous; the Yanks should have the pennant nabbed by then.

Still, things were finally falling into place for the Red Sox. Over the previous couple of weeks, Boston had been suffering with a variety of ills and injuries, but Steve O'Neill's club appeared to be regaining their health in time for the stretch run. Just the previous weekend, Ted Williams had missed a doubleheader when he came down with a temperature of 101 and the grippe. Two days later, Williams was feeling much better and had regained much of his strength. Clyde Vollmer missed several games due to the death of his father, and Bobby Doerr had returned to the lineup after a week's absence owing to lingering back pain.

"They're really in high gear now," Stengel acknowledged. "Getting Doerr back helped them a lot. They didn't lose when Williams was out. You've got to respect them, but I'm certainly not afraid of them. I've said right along, the Yankees were going to win this thing and I have no reason to change my mind. We've got a lot of tough ones coming up with Boston. But we're home right now, and that's where we win."

———

THE RED SOX CAME TO TOWN ON THE 4TH FOR A HIGHLY ANTICI-pated doubleheader at the Stadium. The standings in the morning papers had the Yanks a half game behind the Indians and four-and-a-half ahead of Boston. The team's front office hoped for a turnout of 65,000 for the big game. There were 40,000 in the park with thousands more waiting in their cars, in subway stations, in bars and restaurants. Those outside the Stadium were waiting for the steady downpour to subside before purchasing their tickets. The rain, however, continued, and Yankee management waited an hour and 20 minutes before announcing the postponement of the games over the public address system.

The lineup card Stengel prepared for the game had Johnny Mize moved down to seventh in the order and Berra to sixth. Gil McDougald, the only Yankee with a .300 average, was moved up to third. Stengel was doing what he could to shake some hits out of his dormant lineup.

"Gotta wake 'em up some way," Stengel said explaining his decision. "They're beginning to throw left-handers at us again ever since we beat those Cleveland right-handers."

The seats inside Yankee Stadium were sparsely populated for the start of a rare twi-night doubleheader on September 11 against the visiting Browns. Roughly 5,000 fans were in place for the beginning of the first game. Joe Trimble credited the absence of late arriving patrons to the belief that most people couldn't take the Browns on an empty stomach. Trimble's laugh line aside, the joke was on the Yankees.

As part of their traveling party, the Browns brought Max Patkin to coach third base for them. Patkin barnstormed around the country, performing mostly before minor league crowds entertaining audiences with humorous slapstick antics. This was yet another in a growing list of unorthodox promotions by Bill Veeck. In his brief tenure as Browns owner, Veeck had employed a couple of fans to serve as his team's base coaches. Later in the summer he held a "Grandstand Manager Day," in which fans seated behind the Browns dugout held up placards that provided the answer to tactical moves asked of the crowd by yet another placard. i.e. "Infield back?" The grandstand managers responded with their "Yes" or "No" card. The gimmick allowed St. Louis manager Zack Taylor to sit in a Veeck-provided rocking chair and take the afternoon off.

The Grandstand Manager Day was held on August 24. Five days earlier, Veeck put on his most notorious stunt when he signed 3'7" Eddie Gaedel to a one-day contract. Gaedel came to the plate in the bottom of the first as a pinch-hitter for Browns' lead-off hitter, Frank Saucier. Tigers' pitcher Bob Cain missed the strike zone with four consecutive deliveries, giving Gaedel a base on balls in what turned out to be his only career at-bat. The next day, ill-humored league president Will Harridge voided Gaedel's contract, prompting Veeck to question if the Yankees' diminutive shortstop, Phil Rizzuto, was a tall midget or a short ballplayer.

Patkin's antics at third base paled in comparison with Veeck's recent stunts, but undoubtedly bringing a clown to the vaunted home of the New York Yankees was a not-so-subtle jab at the stodgy pinstripe hierarchy. George Weiss, in particular, was not a favorite of Veeck's and vice-versa. Patkin and Veeck's silly capers were beneath comment for the Yankee brass. What especially galled the home team, though, was the Browns taking both ends of the doubleheader. That the two losses knocked the Yankees from first place was bad enough. But the way the defending champs played during the two games was downright embarrassing. They committed five errors during the day; undoubtedly there was much blame to go around, but DiMaggio's poor performance stood out from the rest. He looked old, and he looked tired. In seven at-bats, Joe accumulated just a bloop double.

In the Yankee locker room following the twin defeats, Stengel was unusually quiet. As he expected, the questions he anticipated came. These queries were met with silence and a wave of the hand. Not tonight. Stengel wasn't responding to any questions on DiMaggio.

Should he sit Joe?

Should he move Joe from the cleanup spot?

He'd heard it all before. He'd been asked all this before. But now, more than any other point of the season, Stengel knew he had to give the question serious consideration. This wasn't the time for a flippant answer, or an endorsement of Joe's vital place on the team. With only 17 games remaining, the season was on the line. To stick it out with DiMaggio—such a decision just might cost the Yanks the pennant. Or, perhaps win it for them. Casey wasn't taking bets on the latter.

Just a year earlier Casey had sat Joe down for a week in mid-August. The break allowed DiMaggio to rest up for the final stretch. Stengel's strategy worked as DiMaggio's average over the final six weeks of the 1950 hovered above .400. This was the decision Stengel wished he had made earlier this season. There was too little time left for such a maneuver now. Yet not even his staunchest defender could deny that DiMaggio's production had plummeted in the preceding three weeks. Over the previous 17 games, DiMaggio was batting only .215 with eight RBI.

What to do? The dilemma kept Casey up much of the night.

Two days and another loss later, Stengel was sitting in his office looking over the league standings.

"We've been fielding badly, and we've been hitting worse," was Stengel's blunt appraisal of his team. "That means something has got to be done. I'm definitely going to shake-up the batting order for today's game. If that doesn't snap us out of the way we've been going, I'll make some more changes tomorrow."

Yes Stengel promised changes were coming, but he wouldn't say just what was going to change.

"All I got to say is we're not hitting with men on base. Anybody can see that."

Without any prompting from the reporters sitting around his office, Stengel began mounting a defense for his center fielder.

"There's no sense in blaming Joe for anything that's happened."

Stengel then recounted Joe's fine outing a day earlier in the Yank's 9–2 loss to Detroit, a performance that included a couple of hits and a walk.

"Why should anybody be making him the goat when a lot of others are far from being anywhere as good?" Casey asked rhetorically.

———

ON THE LAST DAY OF THE 1947 SEASON THE YANKEES HELD A tribute that honored many of the greatest American League players to ever grace a ball diamond. *The Sporting News* dubbed the occasion, "the Festival of the Titans." The event was the brainchild of Red Patterson, who had been inspired by "Lou Gehrig Appreciation Day," which was held on July 4, 1939. On that afternoon, the day Gehrig declared himself to be "the luckiest man on the face of the earth," the Yankees had assembled the 1927 championship team to honor Lou.

For Patterson's revival of the '39 celebration the public relations man brought back all-time Yankees as well as American League greats, and assembled them into two "teams;" "the All-Americans" and "Old-Yankees." Unfortunately, the 1947 event was poorly promoted and drew only 25,000. But those in the Stadium enjoyed every moment of the nostalgic afternoon. A few of the old timers had their uniform pants pulled up a little too high over their hips but the fans loved seeing their favorites wearing the jerseys of their youth: Tris Speaker and Cy Young in their Cleveland Indians togs, and Ty Cobb dressed in his Tiger uniform with the Gothic D sewn over his heart.

The proceeds of the special day were earmarked for the Babe Ruth Foundation. The brief exhibition between the All-Americans and Old-Yankees lasted but two innings, still the "game" wasn't without its memorable moments, such as Ty Cobb's appearance at the plate.

As he came up to bat, Cobb told catcher Wally Schang, "Stand back. I haven't seen a baseball in ages. Let [Waite] Hoyt throw one in so I can see what a ball looks like."

Schang took a step back and Cobb, being Cobb, was always looking for an advantage, even in a meaningless two-inning affair. And so, with Schang sitting a couple feet behind the plate, Waite Hoyt tossed an easy one down the heart of the plate, and Cobb laid down a bunt. Though caught unprepared, Schang was able to recover in time to throw out the 60-year-old Cobb at first.

One invitee did not don his old jersey. Rather than pull on his iconic No. 3, Babe Ruth wore an overcoat as he stepped to a microphone to address the crowd. The sight of the greatest of all Yankees brought a tremendous roar of appreciation. Ruth had hoped to pitch an inning in the contest, but unfortunately his health would not permit. The Babe was gamely fighting cancer which had hoarsened and weakened his once booming voice. As the Babe spoke his thanks to those in attendance, he could barely be heard over the stadium's loudspeakers.

The next year the Yankees celebrated the 25th anniversary of the Stadium's opening on June 13. For the occasion the club brought back the surviving members of the 1923 team. This was the club that started it all when they captured the franchise's first world championship. Like the previous September, a two-inning exhibition would precede the regularly scheduled league contest. But rather than invite a squad of American League stars, the '23 veterans played against a group of Yankee "old timers." The central focus of the silver anniversary celebration was the retiring of Babe Ruth's fabled No. 3. Previously the only number permanently retired by the Yankees was Lou Gehrig's No. 4. But taking the Babe's jersey out of circulation was well past due. Since Ruth left the Yankees following the 1934 season his No. 3 had been worn by George Selkirk, Bud Metheny, and later, Cliff Mapes.

The night before the ceremony, the Ruppert family held a banquet for the retired Yankees at the Ruppert Brewery. Ruth, however, was not feeling up to it. He skipped out on the dinner and many wondered if Babe would be able to make it for the celebration the next afternoon. His health had been deteriorating rapidly in recent months and the forecast called for unseasonable cold and rain.

The day began damp and grey, but the fans overlooked the discomfort that the rain brought. Easily forgotten speeches were given by Mayor O'Dwyer, Dan Topping, and American League president Will Harridge. Wreaths were placed on the memorials of Jacob Ruppert and Lou Gehrig, and then Lucille Mumers sang while a band played the tune of "Auld Lang Syne" as the crowd joined in. But it was the Babe, shuffling out of the visiting Cleveland dugout to a microphone with the aid of Bob Feller's bat to assist him on his journey to the plate that was the highlight of the day. There was nary a dry eye in the House that Ruth Built, as the Babe ambled out to home plate. He no longer resembled the vibrant and strong "Sultan of Swat" of years gone by. No, he seemed much smaller than memory evoked. Ruth's once-sturdy frame now seemed fragile.

He slowly inched toward the microphone placed near home plate. With a coarse voice greatly weakened by the ravages of throat cancer, which Ruth had been valiantly battling for some time, the Babe spoke to the large crowd.

"Ladies and gentlemen, I just want to say one thing. I am proud I hit the first home run here against Boston in 1923. It is marvelous to see these teammates going back 25 years. I'm telling you it makes me proud and happy to be here. Thank you."

While his former teammates took the field for their two-inning chance to recapture past glories, Ruth retreated to the dugout where a camel hair topcoat was placed over his Yankee jersey.

Following the emotional ceremony the game itself was an afterthought. Those in the Stadium walked away with a memory deeply etched, the memory of the Babe wearing his eminently recognizable home jersey. The silver anniversary of Yankee Stadium would also mark the last time anyone wore the Babe's No. 3.

Babe Ruth, the greatest Yankee of them all, succumbed to cancer two months later, on August 16.

Duplicating emotional moments such as Ruth's and Gehrig's farewell speeches would be near impossible. An annual celebration of the Yankees' unparalleled history, however, could still be a unique event. On September 8, the Yankees renewed their now-yearly "Old Timers' Day" prior to their contest against the Senators. A number of Yankee greats came back to the Stadium to celebrate and play in a brief three-inning exhibition game. Tommy Henrich, Charlie Keller, Bill Dickey, Frank Crosetti, Red Ruffing, and Lefty Gomez, among other represented the McCarthy years. Another group, including Bob

Shawkey (who wore his red flannel shirt), Joe Dugan, Home Run Baker, Wally Pipp, Earle Combs, and Roger Peckinpaugh, attended. At least one member from each of the Yankees' 17 pennants were present with Jerry Coleman and Allie Reynolds representing the '49 and '50 championships. Among the honorees present was Lou Gehrig's mother, Christina, and his widow, Eleanor, as well as Ed Barrow, Connie Mack, and Edna Stengel.

A dinner was held for the visiting old timer's at Ruppert's Brewery the evening before the celebration at the Stadium. It was reported to be a "gala affair." Longtime New York sportswriter Tom Meany served as the night's toastmaster. And it fell to Meany to introduce each speaker. Dan Topping, George Weiss, and Allie Reynolds, all addressed the room. Reynolds and Jerry Coleman were the only current members of the team in attendance at the dinner. And when it was The Chief's turn to speak, he let the past Yankee greats know that he and his teammates found their predecessors to be an inspiration.

The highpoint of the evening was Joe McCarthy's turn at the microphone. The evening's honoree gave an emotional and earnest speech. Marse Joe's talk evoked the Yankees glory days. The days of Gehrig and the Babe, of Lazzeri and Lefty, of DiMaggio in his prime. There were so many stories, so many majestic players, Joe couldn't recall every splendid moment. As McCarthy brought it all to a close, he was visibly overcome with emotion.

"This very likely is the last gesture baseball will make toward me," Joe said, while fighting back tears.

The next afternoon, the old timer's and current day Yankees mingled together in the home clubhouse prior to the festivities. As usual, Lefty Gomez commanded the room, not that he craved attention, but eyes and ears just naturally gravitated to the storytelling lefthander.

Tales poured forth from Gomez, each one funnier than the last. He made fun of himself, and also poked at others. No one was spared, not even Joe McCarthy. There was that time that Gehrig would have led the league in homers if it weren't for McCarthy, Gomez said.

Lefty set the scene. Two men were out and Lyn Lary was on second base when Gehrig hit one out of the park. Problem was, Lary didn't realize the ball went over the fence. Thinking the ball had been caught and the third out recorded, Lary hit third base and headed into the Yankee dugout for a drink before returning to his position at short. Gehrig was circling the diamond when he touched the third base bag; Lou was called out for passing Lary on the base paths.

"McCarthy was coaching third," Gomez explained to the crowd gathered around him.

Just then, McCarthy entered the room, the old manager's presence just caused Lefty to raise his voice as he continued his story.

"Joe came back to the dugout steaming. 'Of all the dumb shit, 20 of you sitting on the bench and not one of you had brains enough to tell Lary that the ball was in the stands.'"

Gomez continued, "And [Red] Ruffing said, 'What was the matter with you, Joe? You were closer to him than anybody else.'"

"That," Lefty said to a gale of laughter, "was the last time Joe ever coached at third base...or any base."

Yogi Berra wandered into the room and got caught in Gomez' crosshairs.

"Too bad about you," Lefty said to Yogi.

"What's the matter with me?" a puzzled Berra asked.

"I've often wondered, but that's besides the point," Gomez cracked. "I was just thinking you were born too late. I could have made a great catcher out of you just by throwing my fast-ball past hitters."

Bill Dickey turned the tables on Gomez. Lefty's old catcher brought up the time, it was a Series game, Bill recalled, but he couldn't remember the year, and Gomez hit a rough patch in the midst of the game. There was one man on and two outs with a tough batter waiting in the box. Just then Gomez takes a couple of steps toward the plate and beckons Dickey.

"Have you got any bird dog puppies to sell?" Lefty asked the perplexed Dickey.

"What's the matter with you? Have you lost your mind?" Dickey said.

"No," Gomez replied, "a friend of mine asked me last night if I knew where he could buy a couple of bird dog puppies and I said I thought you might have some and I just thought of it."

The memories and stories continued until the old timers were called out to the field. Before the three-inning exhibition both teams were introduced at home plate by Mel Allen, who also served as the home plate umpire. A special presentation was made by Dan Topping to McCarthy, welcoming the great Yankee manager back home. Topping handed McCarthy a plaque, which Joe took gratefully from the Yankee owner and then spoke a few words to the 35,000 fans gathered in the Stadium.

McCarthy took a moment to single out Barrow, who, Joe said, "made the organization what it is today."

Then, harkening back to the hard fought pennant of the

summer of '49, McCarthy cracked, "Two years ago, when I came into this park with the Red Sox, Casey and the Yankees treated me rotten.

"I feel like I'm at home again," Joe said with a smile.

A three-inning exhibition game pitted the heroes of Joe McCarthy's era against the "Huggins" squad, a group of Yankee greats from the even more distant past. Managing the Huggins team was Clark Griffith. Though he was serving as the president of the Washington Senators, long ago Griffith had managed the Yankees' pre-descendants, the New York Highlanders.

The brief three-inning exhibition provided a cache of memorable moments. In his turn at bat, 65-year-old "Home Run" Baker grounded sharply through the right side of the infield. While running toward first, Baker stumbled and then collapsed on the base line. Though concerns of a heart attack swept through the crowd, Baker thankfully suffered only from a charley horse. After Baker was carried from the field on a stretcher the game resumed. The game was infused with some much needed levity by Lefty Gomez, when he recreated an ancient performance by stepping off the rubber to gaze overhead at a plane passing above. Lefty had pulled the same act years earlier in the midst of a game, causing McCarthy's face to turn three shades of red. It wasn't Lefty's stunt that had people talking, however, it was his bat. Gomez was a notoriously bad hitter who liked to say of his batting aptitude, "I only have one weakness—a pitched ball." But on this day, Lefty knocked a double during the third inning. A big hand from the Ladies Day crowd greeted Gomez when he arrived at second. But he wanted more. Standing on the second-base bag, Lefty motioned to the fans to cheer a little louder, and they responded with a resounding roar.

The next batter, Frank Crosetti, deposited a fat Walter Brown pitch into the left-field stands, giving the McCarthy squad a 2–0 victory.

The official game, which was scheduled to start at 2:25, was delayed by 48 minutes by the old timers festivities. Ed Lopat, in search of his 19th victory, and former Yank Bob Porterfield, faced off in a pitcher's duel. Porterfield had a one-hit shutout when Mantle came up with two out and two on in the bottom of the seventh. In three previous at-bats, he hadn't been able to get the ball out of the infield. Mantle broke the scoreless tie with a three-run homer. The impressive blast traveled high above the Yankee bullpen before landing deep in the right-field bleachers.

———

WERE THE YANKS BEGINNING TO CRACK UNDER THE PENNANT pressure? The subject had been bandied around the press box and the topic had even been broached on a few sports pages. For starters, they'd won only four of eight games during the homestand that many believed would propel the Yankees to the pennant. And then there were three consecutive losses, all against second division teams. That the defending champions committed four errors in the opening game of their series with Detroit, coupled with five miscues in the doubleheader loss to St. Louis, while certainly adding to their mini slump, also gave New York sportswriters fodder to fill column space.

Casey shook his head at the amateur psychology being performed in the New York sports pages. His club's recent performance was proof of sloppy play, not a team choking, Stengel argued.

"Nuts," an irritated Stengel said of the talk that his team was collapsing. "If we cracked so did the Indians when they lost in Washington last night, and when they lost the second game in Philadelphia the other night after they already knew we had lost two to the Browns. If we cracked, then they would say that about the Red Sox when they blew that doubleheader to the A's in Philadelphia on Labor Day.

"It's just one of those things we came off a great road trip and began playing poor baseball. We played badly, losing two to the Browns then again yesterday to Detroit. Four or five of the fellows stopping hittin' and outfieldin' got bad and the pitchin' got shaky.

"The situation hollers for me to do something and maybe I will do it. However, what is there to do, and where are the players to do it?"

Many of the writers in the room had an answer to Casey's open-ended question. The men scribbling Stengel's words into their note pads had one specific cure all move in mind—move DiMaggio out of the clean-up position. And Stengel knew what they were thinking, he'd been through that inquisition before, and he cut his writers off before the question could be asked.

"I want to say Joe is doing his part," Stengel said. "Yesterday he saved us from looking a lot worse against Virgil Trucks."

Johnny Mize, though, well, he was a different story. The veteran Mize came up twice with the bases loaded and failed to deliver on either occasion. Had Mize come through in the third, Stengel argued, they would have pulled Trucks and then all bets were off.

"However," Stengel added, "I am not picking on Mize. The whole situation has bogged down and it had better perk up fast."

The largest crowd to ever witness a regular season contest at Yankee Stadium, 70,040, attended the September 16th game against the Indians. Though the Yanks went into their showdown with Cleveland having lost four out of the last five games against second division teams, the two clubs entered the day in a virtual tie for first place, with New York holding a two-game edge in the loss column.

"We do not look prepared for two important meetings with Cleveland, yet I welcome them," Casey Stengel said just before the series began. "This club of ours has a way of arousing itself for clutch battles. I am confident that when the boys see the Indians out on the field they will muster what it takes to win."

A day before the Indians arrived in town, Stengel approached Berra and asked the catcher his thoughts on moving to clean-up. Yogi demurred. He was too free swinging, not patient enough at the plate for the role, Berra said.

Stengel appreciated the honesty, but he continued to toss the possibility around in his mind. At four o'clock the next morning, Casey made his long-contemplated decision. Berra would bat fourth. DiMaggio would hit fifth.

Finally, after weeks of player grumbling and speculation in the press, sentiment was cast aside. The announcement, perfunctory and official, came from Bob Sheppard, the public address announcer:

Batting first for New York, right fielder, number seven, Mantle

Batting second for New York, first baseman, number forty-one, Collins

Batting third for New York, second baseman, number twelve, McDougald

Batting fourth for New York, catcher, number eight, Berra

Batting fifth for New York, center fielder, number five, DiMaggio

A small murmur emanated from the large crowd, but most spectators failed to recognize the significance of the moment. *The Great DiMaggio batting fifth!*

For his part, Joe swallowed his pride and said nothing. Stengel's lineup shift seemed to pay off in the first when Berra clouted a triple.

In the 5th inning Mantle was on second with the Yankees up 3–1. When Berra stepped to the plate, Indians manager Al Lopez directed Bob Feller to intentionally walk Yogi in order to bring up DiMaggio. Sure, Berra had been on a hitting rampage of late, but that didn't make the slight any less galling to DiMaggio. As Lou Brisse, who had replaced Bob Feller in the fifth inning, delivered the four intentional balls, Joe leaned on his bat in the on deck circle.

"At no other time has this posture of genuflection been significant to me," Jimmy Cannon observed. "Before this multitude a reputation unmatched in baseball was being defaced with contempt."

Cannon's undeniable bias notwithstanding, the moment did not lack in drama. A year earlier, Joe had been bumped out of his customary spot in the lineup and Johnny Mize was slipped into the cleanup position. Nor would this be the first time a batter was intentionally bypassed so an opponent could face DiMaggio. In fact, the Indians had failed in this strategy earlier in the season when Joe delivered a run-scoring single. The Senators, though, successfully compelled DiMaggio to hit into a double play earlier in the year using the same tactic.

Perhaps it was the combination of Stengel's slight alteration to the batting order and the Indians' lack of respect. Whatever it was, this day felt different. This was an afternoon when even the most faithful had to acknowledge that the end was near. Whatever his thoughts, Joe kept them concealed as usual. He stepped to the plate against Brisse calm and focused.

The first pitch was a strike.

The second, a ball.

On the third, DiMaggio checked his swing and foul tipped the ball.

Brisse's fourth delivery was a slider, which DiMaggio struck clean and true. The ball went into deep left-center field, rolling past Indians' center fielder Larry Doby, and coming to rest against the fence, 457 feet away.

"DiMaggio," Cannon wrote, "running with that round-shouldered, long-gaited stride pulled up at third."

DiMaggio's drive brought Mantle home from second and Berra from first, extending the Yankee's lead to 5–1.

Joe's hit prompted a passionate response from the enormous crowd, while DiMaggio's teammates stood in the home dugout clapping their hands together with equal fervor. A stoic DiMaggio stood on third, bathed in applause, vindicated in the moment.

After the game Stengel demurred when asked about dropping DiMaggio in the order. He did, however, explain that Mantle and Collins were at the top because of their speed. McDougald, Berra, and DiMaggio followed because, "they're my regulars."

The first questions directed at Joe, were of course, about the batting order. Did the move bother you, Joe?

"Why, it was logical," DiMaggio replied. "I hadn't been hitting and Yogi had."

Joe was certainly in good spirits. A stack of congratulatory telegrams were waiting on his locker stool following the game.

"When I get a hit now," he said with a bemused smile, "they send me wires."

If Joe felt absolved by his performance so too did Stengel believe his long-delayed decision was the proper move to make. DiMaggio wasn't the only batter shuffled in the order; every hitter in the New York lineup with the exception of the pitcher was placed in a different spot in the order. He had no intention of changing things back the way it was yesterday, Stengel insisted.

"They're my regulars," Casey said. "They play no matter who's pitching. I decided that Joe and Yogi both might deliver better if I swapped their positions and it's a move that's paid off. They'll stay there. McDougald? Why he's earned the job [as the third hitter]. It's September and he's still hitting .300."

Despite the loss, both the Indians' manager and general manager remained fully confident that their club would be representing the American League in October. Al Lopez and Hank Greenberg both believed the Yankees and Red Sox had too many games remaining against one other. Boston and New York would knock the dickens out of each other, opening a path for the Indians, Greenberg and Lopez argued.

Bill Dickey waved away such speculation when told the thoughts of Cleveland brass. "I'm predicting right now that if the Indians even get so far that the pennant depends on their winning the final game of the season with the Tigers, they'll lose it," Dickey said with certitude.

The next afternoon a Yankee fan hung a banner from the Stadium balcony with a message to the Cleveland manager:

Dear Lopez: Walk Berra, pitch to DiMag

The game itself topped even the fabulous theater from the previous day as Eddie Lopat and Bob Lemon hooked up in an enthralling pitcher's duel that concluded with the season's most exciting ending yet.

With the teams knotted at one apiece and one out in the bottom of the ninth, DiMaggio was charitably credited with an infield hit on a ball that Indians' third baseman Al Rosen kicked around. The official scorer's decision made little difference to the men playing, not with the winning run now stationed at first base. Gene Woodling then followed with a sharp single to right, moving DiMaggio over to third. Al Lopez instructed Lemon to issue an intentional pass to Bobby Brown, which brought up Phil Rizzuto.

Before the first pitch, Rizzuto walked down the line for a conference with Yankee third-base coach Frank Crosetti.

"Should I squeeze?" Rizzuto asked.

"You're doggone tootin'," Crosetti replied. But not on the first pitch, Frank advised, "They might be layin' for it then."

Rather than positioning his infielders back hoping for a double-play ball, Lopez pulled them in for the force at the plate. Lemon's first pitch was a called strike on the outside corner. The arbiter's decision was met with vociferous displeasure from Stengel in the Yankee dugout. Casey's colorful critique of the call could be clearly heard around the diamond and in the box seats.

Just before the third pitch Rizzuto signaled DiMaggio that the squeeze was on. This was a play the two had worked to perfection in past seasons, nearly always in a big moment of an important game. And this was arguably the tipping point of the current campaign.

As DiMaggio took his modest lead off of third, Rosen engaged him in some banter.

"I think this man is going to bunt," the Indians' third baseman said to DiMaggio.

With a cold, blank stare, Joe replied, "It wouldn't surprise me."

The tension was palpable as the hard-throwing Cleveland right-hander prepared to present his next delivery. As Lemon reached the apex of his windup, DiMaggio, waiting till the last possible moment to make his break, took off for home. Lemon fired a fastball inside, a near impossible placement for Rizzuto to successfully execute a bunt, yet The Scooter expertly placed the ball along the first-base side of the mound. DiMaggio, who was 30 feet from home when bat touched ball, set his right foot on the plate before Lemon could even pick up the ball.

In the jubilant Yankee clubhouse Rizzuto replayed the key moment of the game over and over, a new telling for each reporter who approached.

The pitch was so far inside, Rizzuto exclaimed, "The ball was right at my gut. It would have hit me if I hadn't bunted it!"

Twelve games remained in the season. Cleveland trailed the Yanks by one, and the Red Sox still remained viable at two-and-a-half back. Stengel, though, thought the pennant was as good as won.

"I'm not claiming anything, mind you," Casey said from his Stadium office. "And don't nobody try to quote me as claiming anything. But I got to admit a club can't forever be losing big ones as those Indians have been doing and still stay in the midst of the fight unless they get a quick reprieve."

THE YANKS HAD JUST DEFEATED THE WHITE SOX 5–4 ON THE 20ᵀᴴ, and Berra had gone 1–4 at the plate, but Stengel decided to shuffle DiMaggio, who had gone hitless, back to clean-up. The Yankees had won four of five since Casey made his headline-making decision, but this fact did not play a part in his thinking.

"There's no sense in denying that we're not hitting," Stengel said, repeating a mantra he'd been chanting for weeks. "We're not punching in the pinches like we ought to be doing and we're not blasting enough long balls.

"So I've got to take some measures before it's too late."

Though he wouldn't reveal exactly who offered the advice, Stengel mentioned that one of his coaches believed sitting Mantle might be the answer. As he always did when his coaches offered their thoughts, Casey listened, but he quickly dismissed the suggestion. Regardless of whether a right hander or left hander was on the mound, Mantle would remain in right field.

"The kid has hit 13 homers for me," Casey explained to reporters, "and has driven in 64 runs."

The next day several anonymous Yankees spoke to writers and revealed to reporters that they were pleased to be playing the Red Sox with the pennant on the line. The team from the Hub lacked heart; that was the belief throughout much of the New York clubhouse. Boston had started a slide at the beginning of the month, a skid that showed no sign of letting up.

"When these guys up here start slipping under pressure they go all the way, and it's almost certain they're in such a skid now," a Yankee player told Hugh Bradley of the *Journal American*.

The Yankees defeat of the Red Sox, coupled with the Indians

loss to Detroit put New York a game-and-a-half in front of Cleveland. Still Stengel felt it necessary to address his team. Inside the cramped visitors' clubhouse inside Fenway Park, Stengel stressed to his players the need to continue to apply pressure.

Waiting for Cleveland to lose was no way to win a pennant, Stengel said. "We can't guess ninety-five wins is going to do it," Stengel told his club. "What we got to do is figure on winning every one we've got to play."

Everything seemed to be falling into place for the Yankees. Everything, that is, with the exception of their catcher's batting slump. Yogi had been fretting over the impending birth of his second child. Berra had been the team's most consistent hitter all season, but Yogi was hitless in his last 15 at-bats as the Red Sox series concluded. Carmen Berra gave birth to Tim hours after the Boston series came to a close. Following the delivery, both mother and son were doing fine. Now that Yogi was assured that his wife and newborn son were both in good health, the hope was that the old Berra bat would return for the stretch.

———

TO SAY STENGEL OPERATED DIFFERENTLY THAN HIS CONTEMPORARIES would be an understatement. Just as he had a few days earlier when decided to shift flip DiMaggio and Berra in the order, Casey often made his biggest and most difficult decisions in the dead of night, at three or four o'clock in the morning. It was common for him to contemplate the upcoming game's batting order for hours before finally determining just the right sequence. No other manager shared his decision making process with the press as Stengel did. It was a rare day when Casey didn't open up and disclose to reporters what he was thinking and just why he was thinking it.

He was also quick to acknowledge his own blunders if a move backfired. Usually these confessions were given before reporters even asked their questions.

"I know, I know, it was a stupid move. In letting Bauer try to steal I broke up what should have been a big inning. Ol' Case ain't infallible, is he?"

This day, hours before the Yankees could possibly clinch their third consecutive pennant, was very typical.

"We came to life in our hitting against the Red Sox," Stengel acknowledged, "but we were in a long slump before that, and I got to be frank about the fact it's been quite a while since I've been fully satisfied with the way we've been socking with men on the sacks, or the way we've been delivering the long ball."

"From day to day, until everything is over, or until we show we can slug consistently. I'm pretty apt to keep changing.

Casey then offered several different scenarios, lineups he might, or might not, use.

Who knows, "It all depends on the way I figure things on any given day."

He certainly liked his club's chances to put this thing away, probably even this weekend, but Stengel wasn't declaring it over just yet.

"I ain't saying we're in and don't you go quoting me on anything like that," Stengel said before the Yanks' three-game series with Philadelphia. "But I'm willing to admit we didn't come all this way in front to flop."

About an hour before game time Friday night, the Athletics

mischievous manager Jimmy Dykes sent a note across the diamond to Stengel.

"Well, you're about in," Dykes wrote. "The pressure is off and you can stop worrying."

A victory against the sixth place Athletics would clinch no less than a tie for New York, but the diminutive Philadelphia lefthander Bobby Shantz spoiled the day for the home team. Shantz allowed just six hits en-route to a 4–1 Athletics win. This was Shantz's fourth victory of the season over New York, a dominance not lost on Stengel. Two other men had defeated the Yankees four times during the '51 campaign, Mel Parnell and Virgil Trucks. Indeed, Parnell, Trucks, and even Shantz were allowed to successfully ply their trade. Stengel did not deny this entitlement.

"After all, they're grown men," Casey acknowledged. "They have a right to beat any club once in a while or maybe more often than not. But this Shantz is smaller than a minute. He's a little boy."

Stengel then referenced the Eddie Gaedel episode that took place a month earlier. If memory served, American League president Will Harridge was not amused by Veeck's shenanigans. Harridge immediately banned short people from the league. How short, however, Harridge did not clarify. Perhaps, Casey hoped, Shantz would not meet the new league height requirements.

"If he was any smaller we'd have a chance. We could call attention to the new American League rule banning midgets."

Stengel let out a sigh, before adding, "Well, I guess we'll stagger right up to October with no breath to spare."

His team's offensive deficiencies had been the bane of Stengel for much of the season. Shantz had pitched well, certainly. And the Athletics' fine left-hander certainly seemed to have the

Yankees' number, but Casey was pointing the finger at his hitters rather than praise Shantz.

The Yankees' scheduled day off before the Red Sox came to the city was canceled. Stengel ordered his team to report to the Stadium for some much-needed hitting drills. He was there the next morning waiting for his players to arrive. Once they were all assembled and ready to head out to the field, Casey had one thing to say to them. Uncharacteristically, he kept the message short. In a firm voice, Stengel addressed the room.

"I want this thing settled tomorrow."

———

ALLIE REYNOLDS WAS ON THE MOUND FOR THE YANKS IN THE FIRST game of the September 28 doubleheader against the Red Sox. Just hours earlier, Allie's wife Earlene had collapsed. Though it was later determined that Mrs. Reynolds had an inner ear infection, at the time she was felled Allie had no idea what the cause of her illness was when he departed for the Stadium. He arrived at the ballpark with a knot in his stomach, and to add to Reynolds' anxiety it was American Indian Day and special homage was being paid to him at the Stadium. Still, the Chief pitched magnificently, allowing only one hard hit ball all day, which came in the seventh when Ted Williams smacked a sizzling ground ball directly at Jerry Coleman.

With two outs in the top of the ninth, Reynolds and the Yankees had a comfortable 8–0 lead when Williams stepped to the plate for the fourth time. The first delivery was an off-speed pitch that Williams took for a strike. Williams fouled the next pitch high in the air, about 15 feet behind the plate. Berra jumped up, tossed his mask aside, and tried to locate the ball. He seemingly had settled under the ball, but then Berra staggered. Yogi had slightly misjudged the flight of the pop-up, and he stumbled to his left while reaching out in desperation to catch the ball. The catcher lay sprawled in the dirt as the ball caromed off his mitt and fell safely to the ground.

The crowd let out an audible groan, but Reynolds exhibited no distress over Berra's foible. Reynolds had run in from the mound while the ball was still ascending, and he was standing a few feet from Berra as Yogi fell to the ground. Without any display of disappointment, the Chief helped Yogi to his feet, patted his catcher on the back and threw his arm reassuringly around the backstop's shoulder.

Williams later admitted that he was pulling for Berra to catch the foul, but once the ball fell safely, "I became more eager to break up the no-hitter."

Catcher and pitcher returned to their positions, and with the next pitch a near perfect repetition of the preceding play was acted out. This time Williams' foul traveled high up toward the Yankee bench. As the ball made its way downward, Berra, sturdy on his feet, was ready. He squeezed the final out of the Yankees' 94th victory tightly in his mitt and immediately both Berra and Reynolds were surrounded by teammates who had flooded out of the dugout.

The celebration continued in the clubhouse as every Yankee player pounded the Chief on the back or gave him a hug. Stengel offered his best wishes, and then told Allie, "You can have the rest of the season off."

After each teammate had a chance to congratulate him, Reynolds spoke with reporters for a few moments.

"This one was different from the Cleveland one," Allie admitted. "I didn't kid around today during the game...you fellows wrote about that and I received a lot of letters bawling me out for breaking baseball tradition. You'd be surprised how many people were sore about it. So, this time, I never said a word."

Reynolds' achievement was unique. He had just become the first American Leaguer to throw two no hitters in one season. Lost in the merriment of the victory was the fact that the Yankees had clinched at least a tie for the pennant. News of this wasn't mentioned in the clubhouse, though. There was still another game to be played.

The payoff for the long, hard slog came in the second game of the doubleheader. A season that saw the Yankees chasing the White Sox and catching them, the Red Sox and catching them, and finally, the Indians and catching them, was inching to a culmination. Stengel and his team had been in and out of first place countless times during the summer. And now, in the shadow of Reynolds' masterpiece, the pennant-clinching game was a bit anticlimactic. The Yankees' third consecutive pennant was delivered when New York built up a big lead early and never looked back. It was DiMaggio's three-run homer in the sixth that pushed them over the top. The final out of the game, the pennant winning out, came when Joe's little brother Dominic hit a lazy fly ball to Gene Woodling. As they trotted in from the outfield, Woodling handed the ball to Joe.

Minutes later, DiMaggio sat in front of his locker fondling the gift he had just received from Woodling.

"This is one I'm going to keep," DiMaggio said with a smile.

In the subdued New York clubhouse much of the attention

was focused on Joe. A reporter asked him the inevitable question. Was this your last pennant race?

"I don't know," DiMaggio answered quietly. "This isn't the time to talk about it. The work isn't finished. I really don't want to say anything about it now."

On entering the clubhouse, Stengel immediately made his way to his center fielder. Whatever rancor existed between the two vanished for the moment.

"Joe," Casey said, "I wanna thank you for everything you did."

The atmosphere in the Yankee clubhouse varied little from any other regular season victory. Certainly, smiles were plentiful as were backslaps. Players made their way around the locker room to offer congratulatory handshakes with their teammates.

Jim Brideweser sat with Jerry Coleman, and the visiting Whitey Ford. Their conversation centered not the Yankee pennant, but rather Boston's season-ending tailspin. The three men were in agreement, the Red Sox were a team that had to be torn down and rebuilt, or next season they would surely finish among the league's second-tier clubs.

Sitting at his locker stall, Mickey Mantle looked around the room in wonder. He had spent the previous month performing adequately under the radar of the press. The media's spring fascination with Mickey had faded following Mantle's brief detention in Kansas City. The kid had done some growing up in the minors and since being called up, Mickey had contributed down the stretch. And now, here in the pennant-winning Yankees' locker room, the atmosphere was so business-like. Why wasn't everyone jumping around and hollering? Mickey wondered. Why weren't they pouring beer on one another just like the pictures he'd seen in the papers back home when teams had won championships?

For the Yankee's though, they hadn't won the championship just yet, only the American League flag. There was such little overt excitement that print photographers found themselves prompting various Yankees to feign merriment so they had something to turn in to their editors.

There was champagne, but not until everyone had dressed and shuffled into the Stadium club. There the players gathered with their wives and girlfriends. The bubbly at this party was not used for dousing, but instead it was properly consumed. The invitations even extended to team employees and to the writers who covered the club. This certainly wasn't the most exclusive invitation in town, as a total of 200 reveled until midnight.

The next morning, reporters sat with Stengel. Over the course of an hour, Casey ruminated about the American League season. He recalled the pennants won in the past two seasons, and the difficulties endured during each of those campaigns. This year was no easier, Casey admitted. Cleveland with their big-four pitching staff gave the Yanks everything they could handle. Boston, they suffered the tough break of losing Bobby Doerr and Vern Stephens. Maybe with those fellows the Red Sox would be celebrating right now.

"I made some mistakes during the season," Stengel admitted, "but I called the turn in some cases."

As an example, Stengel mentioned Gil McDougald. "I saw what McDougald could do for us after I had inspected him during the training season. He is the best new player in the American League.

"One of my big mistakes was shipping Mickey Mantle to Kansas City for the middle third of the season. He should have been with us all through the campaign. I figured back in April that we would win the pennant with 96 games. We needed 95. My mistake, and a happy one."

FINAL AMERICAN LEAGUE STANDINGS

Team	Record	GB
New York	98–56	–
Cleveland	93–61	5.0
Boston	87–67	11.0
Chicago	81–73	17.0
Detroit	73–81	25.0
Philadelphia	70–84	28.0
Washington	62–92	36.0
St. Louis	52–102	46.0

10   GOD IS IN HIS HEAVEN

ON AUGUST 11, THE NEW YORK GIANTS WERE A DISTANT 13 GAMES
behind the Brooklyn Dodgers in the National League pennant
race. Then, in what was the greatest turnaround in baseball history, over the course of the season's final six weeks the Giants
won 37 of their last 44 games. This most improbable comeback
miraculously propelled Leo Durocher's club into a tie with the
Dodgers. The flat-footed tie forced a best-of-three playoff between the two rivals, the winner of which would represent the
National League in the World Series.

The Yankees would be forced to sit idly by for several days,
thanks to the Dodger-Giant playoff. Some experts believed
the break would benefit the champs, especially for the veteran
players on the Yanks who could use a few days' rest. Stengel,
however, was wary that his boys might be a bit overconfident.

"The idea that both the Giants and Dodgers are pooped from
their race to the wire and will be even worse after they finish
the playoff is natural," Stengel said "The boys might get the
idea they're playing the St. Louis Browns again."

He always loved an attentive audience. And now, with the eve of the Series at hand, Stengel was center stage. The opportunity presented Casey with the occasion to wax whimsical on his stratagems and philosophies, whatever came to mind. And Casey being Casey, he couldn't resist telling his writers about the deluge of ticket requests he'd been inundated with.

"Some of my friends seem to think I own Yankee Stadium," Stengel moaned. "I keep tellin' them that I only work there."

At the same time the Giants and Dodgers were meeting for their first game, Stengel gathered his players for a session of batting practice. Bill Dickey was the only member of the Yankee family to attend the National League playoff at Ebbets Field. Following the hour-long hitting session, Yankee players retreated to their dressing room and listened to the last few innings of the Giants' 3–1 win.

The next afternoon nearly every member of Stengel's team watched in person as the Dodgers evened the playoff series with a lopsided 10–0 whitewashing of the Giants. Stengel did some spectating and a little bit of scouting, but mostly he socialized during the contest. For some time, Casey held court beneath the Polo Grounds' stands in the concessionaire's cash room where the nickels, dimes, and quarters procured from an afternoon's worth of hot dogs, peanuts, and soft drinks were separated by machines. A long succession of old friends and rivals offered their congratulations to Stengel. Mrs. McGraw always took the time to seek out Casey and this day was no different. Mrs. Topping came by, too. Even Hank Greenberg, exhibiting great sportsmanship, offered his hand to Casey.

Jimmy Powers happened upon the scene and was surprised to find Stengel in such an odd locale. The sound of rattling coins seemed to Powers to be a fitting backdrop for Stengel to receive visitors, given the wealth Casey had supposedly accumulated through various intuitive investments. Thanks to a tip he received from one of his players while managing in Brooklyn, Stengel hit it big when an oil well he invested in came in. Stengel also took the advice of a Dodger stockholder and invested in a company that produced a new wonder drug—penicillin. Yes, everyone around the game believed Ol' Case was rollin' in it.

Stengel grimaced at Powers' suggestion.

"Every time I pick up the paper I got a whole new oil field, I own half the state of Texas and my income tax on California real estate is greater than my gross salary as manager. It's a plot to soften me up for the big bite," Stengel replied.

"I hear you just signed to manage the Yanks in 1952," Powers said, perhaps shooting for a scoop.

This was a touchy subject for Casey. Talk of him coming back for another year has been knocked around for several weeks. The sticking point wasn't the Yankees willingness to have Casey back or Stengel's desire to return, rather it was Mrs. Stengel who was the fly in the ointment. Edna had made her feelings known on this topic to her Casey, certainly, but also to a select few reporters. In fact, during the Yankees' pennant-clinching celebration Edna said to Dan Daniel, "Maybe we should let well enough alone and go home."

Casey was 61 years old, it was time for the two of them to return to Glendale and enjoy the good life for a while, Edna believed.

Stengel hesitated before responding to Powers' question. He looked at the writer in silence as the words were carefully formed before being offered for interpretation.

"What did that other rich man always say coming down the gangplank when the reporters asked him questions? You know, J.P. Morgan. He started that 'No comment' stuff. That's me, the no-comment kid."

Powers took the discussion to safer ground. Well what about the Series?

"It's not going to be easy. Both these clubs have pitchers and hitters. They can cause you trouble. We look for a hard wrestle. Always expect to get your brains beaten out. Then if you have a rough time you're more or less ready for it."

Dodgers or Giants, Powers asked, who would you prefer?

Stengel rubbed his chin thoughtfully before providing Powers with a closing nugget.

"I always say, if you can play a team with a one-legged catcher you got a big edge. What do you always say?"

———

A NUMBER OF YANKEE PLAYERS WERE SEATED BEHIND THE THIRD-base dugout with their family and friends for Game 3 of the National League playoff, including Mickey and Mutt. Practically every member of the team was pulling for the Giants because the Polo Grounds had a much greater seating capacity than Ebbets Field and World Series checks were calculated by the click of the turnstile.

The Dodgers held a seemingly secure 4–1 lead in the ninth, and the Yankee players present seemed certain that Brooklyn would be their opponent in the Series. Yogi Berra decided to beat the traffic. Yogi was fast on his way to his Montclair home when news of Bobby Thomson's dramatic game-winning home run for the Giants came through his car radio.

A brief breather would have been appreciated by the Giants. A day off or perhaps two would have served Durocher and his charges well before jumping into the Series following the dramatic conclusion to the National League season. The Giants were preoccupied with chasing down the Dodgers all summer and a little break would allow an opportunity to refocus on the new task at hand. The schedule showed no mercy, however. The Series would begin the very next day at the Stadium.

The heart-stopping National League finale left Stengel nonplussed. Bobby Thomson's heroics aside, the Giants hadn't won anything yet.

"They still got to play us for the championship of the world, which my men and I are very much looking forward to, competing against them all, Mr. Durocher and his very excellent players, who'll give us a fine contest, I am sure, when we play the Series games, which no matter what Mr. Thomson has done, remains as yet, if you catch the drift. My men are ready."

Given what appeared to be an insurmountable Dodger lead just weeks earlier, the Yankees hadn't bothered to scout the Giants until late September. Leo Durocher's club, a confident bunch, had Carl Hubbell and Tom Sheehan camped out at the Stadium since September 11, when the Yanks began their final homestand against the league's western teams. Hubbell and Sheehan spent the better part of two weeks scrutinizing the Yankees' strengths and weak spots. It would be their hated rivals, however, that provided the most revealing report. The Brooklyns, as Casey Stengel referred to the Dodgers, generously gave the Giants their scouting report on the Yankees. Brooklyn scout Andy High offered detailed insight on each member of the Yankee club.

Mantle—*"Has a very good arm, but is not a sure outfielder. Keep running on all fly balls."*

Berra—*"Does not have a real good arm when pushed, but his pitchers hold you pretty close at first base and you have to break to run on him a lot."*

McDougald—*"Runs well and will run. He will take the extra base."*

The evaluations continued covering every member of the Yankee roster, but it was High's evaluation of DiMaggio that cut the deepest

"He can't stop quickly and throw hard...You can take the extra base on him...He can't run and won't bunt...His reflexes are very slow and he can't pull a good fastball at all."

——

AFTER THE YANKEES CLINCHED THE PENNANT, MICKEY'S DAD AND two of his pals from home, Trucky Compton and Turk Miller, made the long drive to New York to see Mutt's boy play in the Series. Mickey was taken aback by Mutt's appearance. When Mick had last seen his father in late July he was noticeably thinner, but now it seemed as if another 30 pounds had evaporated from his father's once-sturdy frame. He was concerned, but Mickey said nothing as he hugged his father, whose clothes were draped over his diminishing body.

Turk and Trucky, too, certainly noticed Mutt's deteriorating health, but they were determined to make this trip one of celebration. The three Okies were shown the town by Mickey, including a stop at Rockefeller Plaza. Mutt, standing before the statue of Atlas in front of the building, wondered aloud, "Shoot, the Statue of Liberty's smaller than I thought." When Mickey was preoccupied with his duties as a Yankee, Turk, Trucky, and Mutt were left to their own devices in the big city. They wandered the streets, took in the sights, and had a few drinks. A long afternoon in a tavern resulted in Trucky throwing up in a stranger's hat. For the trip to Yankee Stadium, navigating the subway system proved too challenging, so the trio walked three miles instead.

One evening during the visit, Mickey introduced his father to Holly Burke as his "very good friend."

Brooke and Mantle had continued their relationship throughout the summer. Even Mantle's demotion to Kansas City failed to end their liaisons. On several occasions, Brooke met up with Mickey in various International League cities for a tryst.

Mutt sized up Brooke in an instant, and he didn't like what he saw. Later in the night he pulled his son aside.

"Mickey, you do the right thing and marry your own kind."

"It's not what you think," Mickey stammered.

Mutt reminded his son of Merlyn; she was a good gal and she loved him.

"After the Series you better get home and marry her."

Mickey could do little but nod in assent.

———

THE BANNER HEADLINE OF THE OCTOBER 4 *DAILY NEWS* EXCLAIMED "The Shot Heard 'Round the Baseball World," in reference to Thompson's blast off the Dodgers' Ralph Branca. But that was yesterday's news. The battle for the championship of the world was beginning in the Bronx.

Leo Durocher popped out of the Giants' dugout and was immediately engulfed by reporters. Journalists and photographers swarmed the Stadium's playing field before the first game. Baseball writers from nearly every major paper were present looking for any angle they could find on the upcoming series. And there were shutterbugs looking to snap shots of all the major participants. For the camera men, Durocher refused to pose for any staged photos.

"I haven't done it all season, why now?"

Despite laying down the law, Durocher made an exception. He stopped long enough to embrace Stengel for a group of photographers.

As for the men with notebooks, Durocher gave them plenty of humorous asides, though little of substance.

"I hear Horace Stoneham has purchased the Waldorf Astoria," Leo cracked. "He's taken over the hotel for the Giants and chased out General MacArthur."

With "No-Hit" Allie Reynolds on the mound for Game 1, the Yankees were optimistic about their chances against the Giants. The Chief's 40 appearances were tops on the team. Reynolds, though, didn't tally as many innings as either Lopat or Raschi because Allie was used in relief on 14 occasions during the season, racking up seven saves in the process. His opponent was the rather unremarkable Dave Koslo, he of the 10–9 record. Still, Stengel feared his club would suffer from a bout of overconfidence.

That morning before departing his apartment for the ballpark, Mantle was experiencing a case of the nervous jitters. The ride down Fifth Avenue with his father eased his butterflies a bit, however. During the journey to the Stadium a sense of calm came over Mickey as he gazed out of the cab at the grand buildings along the route.

Under a dark, grey sky, the new commissioner of baseball, Ford Frick, tossed out the first pitch. The gloomy weather prompted the Stadium lights to be flipped on at 3:09. Through a haze of smoke wafting above the stands, Al Dark knocked a three-run homer in the sixth, but it was Monte Irvin who was the game's star. The Giants left fielder hit safely four times, however it was Irvin's clean steal of home in the first inning that stole the show. Reynolds was aware of Irvin's proclivity to swipe home, which he had successfully accomplished five times during the season.

"I was watching him," the Chief explained. "But he got a good jump and I threw wild to the plate."

Irvin, along with Hank Thompson and Willie Mays, formed the first all-black outfield in Series history. This small piece of social history was lost in the hubbub as the Yankees went down for the first time in a Series opener since Carl Hubbell beat them 6–1 in 1936.

Mantle drew two walks, but did not hit safely in any of his five trips to the plate. Meanwhile DiMaggio, who flew out four times in four at-bats, expressed no concern over the 5–1 loss. "It may be a little unusual to be a game behind for us," Joe said afterward, "but they tell me this is a best-four-out-of-seven affair."

The next day the Yankees held a 2–0 lead through four innings when Willie Mays stepped to the plate, leading off for the Giants in the top of the fifth. Mays, the Giants' heralded rookie, had turned his season around after a slow start and played an instrumental part in the Giants miraculous comeback in August and September.

Standing in right field, Mantle had the craggly voice of his manager running though his head. Prior to the start of the Series, Stengel pulled Mantle to the side. "Take everything you can get over in center," he ordered Mantle. "The Dago's heel is hurting pretty bad."

Heeding Casey's directive, Mantle was shaded a couple of steps toward center and he was off at the crack of the bat as Mays lofted a high fly to right-center. Mantle was running at full speed when he heard DiMaggio call him off the ball.

"I got it," Joe shouted above the din of the crowd.

It was Mickey's ball for certain, but protocol said he should defer to the great DiMaggio. Mantle, at full flight when he heard Joe's call, pulled up to give way when his spikes were caught in a rubber drain cover. Mickey's legs went out from under him and he crumpled to the turf as if taken out by a sniper's bullet.

DiMaggio easily hauled in the fly ball before quickly turning and attending to the stricken Mantle. Kneeling before Mick, DiMaggio placed his hand on Mantle's shoulder. "They're coming out with the stretcher, kid," Joe told him.

Stillness came over the large Stadium crowd. Those familiar with the Stadium's terrain all had the same thought. He'd stumbled over a sprinkler located in that very spot of the field. The reaction turned from apprehension to fear; more than one spectator's mind turned to Mantle's osteomyelitis infected left limb. The disease, as so many had learned through the papers, could be fatal.

For moments, for what seemed like eternity, Mickey lay completely motionless.

The team's trainer, Gus Mauch, rushed out and Frank Crosetti brought a towel to put under Mantle's head. Yankee players anxiously shuffled around the field as Mauch looked Mickey over.

Mutt was seated with his pals a few rows up behind the Yankee dugout. He quickly rushed down from his seat, and was now nervously watching the frightening scene play out on the field. Mickey was taken off the field on a stretcher carried by five teammates. They took him through the Yankee dugout, past Mutt, and into the clubhouse.

Between innings DiMaggio came back to check on Mantle, as did a number of other teammates. The severity of Mickey's injury took the luster off the Yanks' win. The postgame celebration was subdued. When he would be right again no one knew for certain, but there was no doubt that Mantle would be lost for the rest of the Series.

"That'll hurt us, sure," Stengel acknowledged. "That boy has knocked in around 60 runs for us. Hank Bauer will replace him."

Uncharacteristically, the Yankees allowed a photographer into the normally "off-limits" trainer's room. Despite his discomfort, Mantle played along with the intrusion. With a towel placed across his midriff, Mickey sat up on his elbow and posed for a few photos while wanly staring at his injured limb.

Reporters were also permitted in to question Mantle about what had happened in the fifth inning. Despite the trepidation he felt for his baseball future, not to mention the pain coursing through his knee, Mickey took a few moments to answer questions.

"I didn't try to stop short or anything," Mickey explained in a calm voice. "I simply was running for the ball and my knee pops. I wish I knew what happened. There was no hole in the ground, either. I fell and I stayed on the ground. I was really thinking about a broken leg. When I tried to get up, I found I couldn't stand, it was so painful. I dropped and didn't move because I was scared.

"I have a lot of baseball ahead of me and it would be terrible for me if this knee handicapped me badly from here out."

To another reporter Mickey slightly revised his story, saying the knee "buckled when I stepped in a hole or something. Frankly, I don't know...I didn't pass out. I was just frightened.

Mantle then retreated to the trainer's room where Dr. Gaynor wrapped his knee in ice and placed splints on each side of the leg.

The 3–1 Yankee victory took a backseat to the concern and curiosity over Mantle's injury. As the crowd filed out of the Stadium, exiting the park through the center-field gates, a few fans stopped and examined the area where Mantle collapsed.

———

HIS TEAM HAD JUST WON TO EVEN THE SERIES AT ONE GAME APIECE, but Joe was disgusted with his performance. He had yet to get a hit in the Series, and though he was in no mood to rehash the afternoon, DiMaggio sat at his locker and politely responded the all questions. Mantle, of course, was on everyone's mind.

"He could have stepped in that hole," DiMaggio acknowledged. "I thought of that right away.... I was scared, he was so still."

Yes, the Giants' starter Larry Jansen had Joe's number. "He threw me nothing but out balls all game," Joe admitted. He wrapped up the interview with an optimistic, "Tomorrow's another day."

By the time Mickey returned to his father's hotel room a couple hours later the leg had swollen to such an extent that he felt compelled to remove the bandages. The next morning the knee was so inflamed Mickey couldn't place any weight on the injured leg. With the aid of crutches, Mickey hobbled down to the street with Mutt, where they hailed a cab for Lenox Hill Hospital. Their taxi pulled up in front of the hospital's 77th Street entrance. Mickey stepped out onto the curb and reached out to his father for support. As he placed his full weight on his dad, Mutt collapsed in a heap onto the sidewalk.

Father and son were both admitted to the hospital, where Mickey's knee was examined and an array of tests were conducted to ascertain Mutt's sudden frailty.

———

THE SCENE SWITCHED TO THE OTHER SIDE OF THE HARLEM RIVER for Game Three.

"The Ol' Joint hasn't changed too much," Casey said as he took a long look around the vast confines of the Polo Grounds. "They've double-decked the grandstands since I played for the Giants and they've moved the press box off the ground, but outside of that, it looks just about the same."

Stengel couldn't help but take a jab at Giants management and their ticket snafu. Inexplicably, the Giants waited until after they won the playoff to print tickets for Games 3, 4, and 5. The delay coupled with poor distribution led to thousands of fans being shut out and countless tickets fell into the hands of scalpers. Ducats with a $6 face value were going for $50 a pair on the secondary market.

"All the trouble with the tickets came because they [the Giants] were afraid to print 'em in advance. We weren't. We printed ours way in advance. We had no trouble.

"You can tell the Giants did a rush job," Casey said. "Their tickets have the new commissioner's name on 'em, our tickets haven't."

The National League champs were taking batting practice as Casey cracked wise.

"They ain't foolin' me," he said, nodding to the other side of the diamond. "They're a good ball club. Still, there must be some pitcher besides Clem Labine that can stop them.

"Reynolds couldn't stop them. Not the way he was going. But they didn't do much hitting against Hogue and Morgan did they? They kind of stopped them. And if they could do it, maybe we got a couple other pitchers around here that can. They might see Reynolds again one of these days, too. I might send him in there to fog that ball past them."

The new commissioner couldn't have asked for a more perfect October day to put on a baseball show. A record crowd poured into the Polo Grounds dressed in shirt sleeves. The ambience of ideal weather coupled with a 6–2 Giants win made for a spectacular afternoon for the home crowd. A close game shifted on a dime in the bottom of the fifth thanks to the pugnacious Eddie Stanky who worked a walk from Vic Raschi to reach first base.

Stanky was pure metal and spunk. He was also an all-around pain in the ass. He would do whatever it took to gain an edge or get under his opponent's skin. In the first game of the Series the Yankees cried foul when Stanky (as the Yankee bench saw it) interfered with Berra as Yogi was trying to throw out a runner. Guilty or not of this perceived infraction, this would have been absolute Stanky. He occasionally took a step over the line, whatever it took to win.

With Stanky leading off first, Leo Durocher called for a hit and run, but Berra was thinking right in time with the Giants manager. Berra called for a pitchout. Al Dark futilely threw his bat at the ball, and Berra fired down to second. Yogi's throw reached Rizzuto with plenty of time to spare; Stanky was out by a good six feet, on that everyone could agree. But Stanky's aggressive slide kicked the ball from Rizzuto's glove as the Yankee shortstop applied the tag. Stanky rose from the dirt and continued on to third as the ball rolled into center field.

A rhubarb broke out on the field as Rizzuto and McDougald engulfed second-base ump Bill Summers in protest.

Stanky should be out. He never touched second base!

He should be out! Rizzuto tagged him and held the ball plenty long enough.

Stengel emerged from the dugout and joined in with his players in complaint. The Yankees' objection fell on deaf ears. Instead of two out and nobody on, the floodgates to a five-run inning opened when Dark brought Stanky home with a single.

The Yankee dressing room was unusually quiet following the game. As expected, Casey sat patiently and answered the questions posed by the multitude of reporters surrounding him.

"We lost on a field goal," Stengel said with a forced smile, referring to the Stanky play. Even in defeat Casey could crack a joke. "It was such a good kick that they gave Stanky five points instead of three.... I couldn't see from the bench myself, but both Rizzuto and McDougald insist he missed the bag and they are honest kids. That's why I argued.

"That play," Stengel added, "made the difference."

As could be expected, sitting across the park in the Giants' dressing room, Leo Durocher viewed the controversial play differently.

"He came to the park to play ball," Durocher said of Stanky. "And he did. You have to hold the ball tight when Stanky is around you."

———

THROUGH THREE SERIES GAMES DIMAGGIO WAS 0–11 AT THE PLATE and had left 10 runners stranded on base.

"I've just been lousy," Joe admitted after the third game. "That's all. I'm not looking for sympathy. I don't want any. Everybody has to chip in to win these things. I haven't helped a bit."

By coincidence, Joe received a call later that evening from Lefty O'Doul, who phoned to discuss a planned postseason exhibition tour of Japan. After talking business for a few moments, Joe asked his mentor, "What am I doing wrong?"

O'Doul, who managed DiMaggio in 1935, asked Joe what type of bat he was using.

"Thirty-four ounces," DiMaggio responded. "I used it yesterday for the first time. Before that, and early in the season, 37 ounces."

"Thirty-four is light enough," O'Doul replied. "It seems to me you're getting your body too far out in front of your arms, and therefore you're pushing the ball. You're swinging too hard."

—

CASEY STAYED UP LATE IN THE EVENING VACILLATING ON WHO TO send to the mound for the fourth game. Reynolds needed at least one more day of rest before he could go again, so that left Casey with the option of the old guy, Sain, or the young guy, Morgan. He wasn't enthralled with either choice, not with his team down two games to one. The inner debate raged back and forth and finally, as the clock inched toward midnight, Casey made his decision. It would be the kid. He'd try and get seven innings out of Morgan and have Sain ready to go in the bullpen. With that decided Stengel then sat down and scribbled out a new batting order, something different to add punch to an anemic offense. Starting pitcher selected, an altered batting lineup made out, Stengel then hit the sack for a few hours of sleep before heading to the ball yard.

And then the rains came.

When Stengel arrived at the Polo Grounds Sunday morning rain showers had already begun to fall. Taken in tandem with gusty winds howling through the park, the steady downpour made for a blustery October day. Casey would periodically shuffle over to the window and peer out to see if the abysmal conditions continued.

Finally, Commissioner Frick recognized the futility of waiting any longer. Out of consideration for ticket holders, Frick called off the game before too many fans started commuting to the park. At 11:30 AM Frick announced that the game would be postponed until the next afternoon.

"Quite a break, quite a break," Stengel murmured with a great deal of relief. "Things are looking up. I had a new lineup worked out for us, but I'm not sure it'll be that way when we start playing tomorrow."

What he did know was his starting pitcher would now be Allie Reynolds.

Given the three-game playoff they endured against Brooklyn while Stengel and his players sat in the stands eating popcorn, it would seem likely that the extra day's rest would help the Giants more than the Yankees. But Durocher already had his rotation set with Sal Maglie ready to go, and now, thanks to an assist from Mother Nature, Stengel could match Leo with his Chief.

Before his team took the field for the fourth game of the Series, Stengel offered them a few words. His brief address was neither a pat on the back, nor a biting critique. It also wasn't one of his patented sprawling soliloquies. No, today, Casey was short and to the point.

"None of us have been doing anything worth a damn," Stengel told his club, "including me. So let's go."

———

"GOD IS IN HIS HEAVEN AND ALL'S RIGHT WITH THE WORLD," wrote Bill Corum to begin his October 9 column in the *Journal American*. "Galloping Charlie the Mercury-footed messenger arrived right on time to get this copy of the paper. The subways are hitting on all rails and the buttons. Times Square is breaking out all over with smiles, courteous policemen are leading pleasant old ladies across the streets, every cab driver from here to Hoboken is telling his fares how it happened. Everybody's happy.

"Ol' Joe hit one."

The game could have been termed a tale of two center fielders.

On the Giants' side, their rookie center fielder endured what was perhaps his worst day since reaching the big-league club in late May. Willie Mays came up to bat on four occasions with men on base. He flew out once, and grounded into a double play three times.

In the other dugout there was a slump just waiting to be snapped.

DiMaggio's hitless streak reached 12 before he came to bat in the third with two outs. He rapped a hard hit ball through the left side of the infield, and though the single had no impact on the game, the crowd recognized the significance. Even Giant fans didn't want to see Joe continue to struggle. A loud cheer came from the Polo Grounds' stands as Joe safely reached first base. More noteworthy though was Joe's fifth-inning home run. DiMaggio's bat was enlivened and so too were his teammates'.

Sitting in his locker stall inside the visitors' clubhouse moments after being the catalyst for the Yankees' Series-tying 6–2 victory, DiMaggio was sporting a wide grin when reporters came a calling. Gone for the moment was the embittered star who begrudgingly answered questions during the season; his responses more often than not pointed and clipped. But not today. On this afternoon, in the afterglow of World Series success, DiMaggio was more than happy to spill the secret of his success.

"I did some things differently today," Joe explained. "I got my timing back by shortening my swing.

Joe referenced the conversation with Lefty O'Doul regarding the lighter bat, and said he'd also been given a batting tip by Lew Fonseca. Fonseca had been filming the Series for years, and prior to Game 4 he intently watched as Joe took batting practice. He'd filmed that famous swing on hundreds of occasions, and something was definitely amiss, Fonseca surmised. When DiMaggio stepped out of the cage, Fonseca approached and respectfully informed Joe of the slight variation he'd noticed in the swing. Joe listened politely. "I hope I don't forget," he said with a laugh before leaving the field.

"Did Fonseca's tip help?" DiMaggio was asked.

Joe just smiled. He was soaking up the moment. He accepted countless congratulatory handshakes, and enjoyed recapping every aspect of the game.

In the first, Joe whacked a monstrous blast off the left-field façade, just outside the foul line.

"My best shot," Joe recounted.

The fifth-inning round-tripper with Berra on base was "my eighth World Series homer," DiMaggio told reporters.

He was relevant again, vital to his team's success. Joe didn't want to let the moment go.

"This is a good club," Stengel said of his team in the postgame press scrum, "and it is awake on good days. We could feel it, as soon as they went out on the field. We were alive and ready and finally played a good ball game. Looks like we're gonna be all right. Joe came out of it, and that helped. I told you if the big guy started hitting, nothing could stop us, and I mean it."

Stengel concluded the postgame interview and headed toward the showers. After taking a few steps, Casey looked back over his shoulder at the pack of writers, winked, and added one final thing.

"And DiMaggio will bat fourth again tomorrow."

———

DOCTORS AT LENOX HILL COULD DO LITTLE FOR MICKEY'S IMPAIRED leg, the swelling made it difficult to determine the extent and precise damage done to the knee. For Mutt, the diagnosis was worse than a bum knee. The *New York Times* reported that Mutt was admitted to Lenox Hill, "Because [he] became so upset when his son slipped that he too required hospitalization."

The truth was far worse. Mickey certainly feared something terrible, given his dad's dramatic weight loss, but tried not to entertain such thoughts.

One of Mutt's doctors entered Mickey's room and removed any delusions of hope, however.

"It's bad news," he said. "Your father has cancer."

"Where?" Mickey inquired.

"It's Hodgkins' Disease. I'm afraid there's not much we can do."

"Is there a chance?" Mickey asked.

The doctor's grim look was all the response needed.

Robert Williams of the *Post* joined Mickey and Mutt as they viewed the Series' fifth game on a primitive television set. The severity of Mutt's illness was not overtly discussed, not between the two Mantles and certainly not with a probing reporter. Baseball, as usual, was the topic between father and son.

The Longines clock located in the deeper reaches of the Polo Ground displayed 1:48 when Gil McDougald capped his phenomenal rookie season with a third-inning grand slam, breaking a 1–1 tie. Viewing his fellow rookie's heroics elicited a smile from Mickey, but Mantle would offer no other display of emotion.

"Don't you ever get excited?" Williams asked.

"Sure, I get excited," Mick responded.

"Well, how do you act?"

"I don't know," Mantle answered. "Don't guess I'd notice it if I got excited."

"I brought him up to be a ballplayer," the elder Mantle explained to Williams. "I named him Mickey after Mickey Cochrane."

Were you always a Yankee fan, Williams asked?

Mickey, by now well immersed in Red Patterson's lessons, replied, "Yeah, always."

Who was your childhood hero?

Stan who?

"Joe DiMaggio," Mickey answered by rote.

Mutt then interrupted. "We had a little trouble getting him to bat left-handed. He always wanted to bat right-handed but we kept him at it."

Just then DiMaggio appeared on the television screen. It was now Joe's turn at bat.

"I hope Joe tags it," Mutt murmured, "for his sake. He's a great one."

"So do I," Mickey quietly added.

His boy, Mutt said, had "lots of years" ahead of him in baseball, before adding an ominous caveat: "if his legs hold out."

The Mantles' game commentary continued, but the conversation drifted toward the personal, also.

"What will you do this off-season?" Mickey was asked.

"Hunt, fish."

What about work? Do you have any plans on getting a job this winter?

Nah, Mickey answered, "Maybe a little work around the house,"

Mantle then mentioned Commerce and his girl back home, Merlyn. He planned on marrying her this coming off-season, Mick revealed.

"I'm getting out of here tomorrow or the next day," Mickey told the reporter.

Mutt, however, couldn't conceal a look of anxiety when he interjected, "They didn't tell me when I'm getting out."

Mickey smiled and then told his dad, "Well I'll write letters to you."

Father and son shared a laugh over that line.

The outcome of the Series' fifth game had been decided for some time as the Yankees ran up an insurmountable lead on the way to a 13–1 victory. Eddie Lopat started off well and continued to get better as the game progressed. He kept Giant batters off balance all day with a perplexing mix of pitches, each as effective as the next. It was Giants first baseman Whitey Lockman who officially concluded the long afternoon for Leo Durocher's men when he grounded out to Phil Rizzuto. The game's final out also brought the afternoon to an end for the Mantles. Mutt needed some rest, and Mickey had to return to his 9th floor room.

Mickey gingerly lifted himself out of the hospital bed and slipped into a wheelchair for the commute upstairs. Before being led out, Mickey reached out and softly placed his hand on his father's arm. Their eyes locked, and a wordless moment later Mickey was wheeled toward the hospital elevator.

———

JUST A FEW DAYS EARLIER THE GIANTS SEEMED TO HAVE THE Yankees down and the referee's count had reached seven. Then the rains of Sunday morning came breathing new life into a previously moribund Yankee outfit. And here they were, one game away from their third consecutive championship with their 21-game winning ace on the mound.

"We've got the best of it," Casey said in a boisterous Yankee clubhouse following the fifth game. "It's a short series, and we've got to win only one. They need two."

At the end of five-and-a-half innings, the game was knotted at one when Hank Bauer cleared the bases with a three-run triple.

The Giants started their half of the seventh with back-to-back singles, which prompted a Stengel visit to the mound. Casey went to the bullpen and brought in Johnny Sain to relieve Raschi. Sain stifled the Giants' rally without allowing a run. In the next frame, Sain seemingly had the Giants bending to his will when, with two outs, the situation went awry. A single was sandwiched between two walks when Ray Noble, representing the go-ahead run, stepped in as a pinch-hitter. With Yankee fans holding their breath and Giant rooters sitting on the edge of their seats, Noble took a called third strike with the bat sitting on his shoulder.

The 4–1 Yankee lead held as the game headed to the bottom of the eighth. Leading off their half of the frame was Joe D. As DiMaggio stepped into the batter's box, the large crowd recognized that history was being played out before them. In all probability this would be Joe DiMaggio's final major league at-bat.

Joe rose to the occasion. He connected with a Larry Jansen delivery; in an instant of clarity the acrimony of a long, aching season vanished. The swing, so unique, so graceful; the stride toward the mound with his left leg, while his right drove into the pitch; the beautiful follow through as the bat wound its way around Joe's torso, the bold No. 5 prominently displayed on his broad, pinstriped back. The vision is etched in memory. DiMaggio drove Jansen's pitch to right-center field for a double.

The fans responded with a rousing ovation. Moments later DiMaggio was thrown out at third when Gil McDougald attempted to sacrifice him over with a bunt. Joe rose from the infield dirt, slapped the dust from his pants, and began trotting off the field. The Stadium crowd again stood in unison, their cheers escorting Joe all the way to the Yankee dugout. The tribute began anew when DiMaggio jogged out to his center-field position to begin the ninth inning, the applause sounding in symphony with Joe's loping strides.

NOTHING IN THIS SEASON CAME EASY FOR STENGEL AND HIS YANKEE team, and so it seemed fitting that the final three outs should not be effortless either. As they had in the eighth, the visiting club loaded the bases, this time with three consecutive singles by Stanky, Dark, and Lockman. Stengel had seen enough of Sain. Johnny had gotten out of a couple of jams already, but Casey wasn't taking any chances at this late date. Bob Kuzava got the call to bring the season to a close. The 28-year-old left-hander induced the next two Giant batters to fly out, but each out brought a run home, inching Durocher's team to within one. Leo then went to the bench once again for a pinch-hitter.

Sal Yvars came within a whisper of being a Series hero rather than a footnote.

Yvars hit a whistling line drive to right. Surely the ball would drop in, but Hank Bauer was playing shallow for the right-handed pull hitter. The game, Series, and season came to a close when Bauer made a spectacular, sliding catch on the seat of his pants.

As the celebration made its way into the locker room, the hard-bitten Bauer couldn't suppress the wide grin that spread across his face.

"First I saw it, then I didn't," Bauer said of the final out. "I saw it again, just in time. I was damn lucky."

This victory marked the 14th Series victory for the Yankees, and by the measurement of most experts, many of whom had witnessed every championship edition, this '51 club was the least of an exemplary group. Such an appraisal was merely extending credit to Stengel's masterly handling of the too-frail, too-young, too-old lineup.

Casey entered the locker room and made his way to DiMaggio's stall.

"We couldn't have done it without you," Stengel said to Joe while patting him on the arm. After speaking with DiMaggio, Casey made his way around the clubhouse thanking each player individually.

In the locker room, in the midst of back slapping, hugs, and beer, Phil Rizzuto marveled at his manager's knack for pushing the right buttons.

"I never met a man who could fool you so much," the Yanks' shortstop said. "You figure he's kind of talking around a circle, but in the end, he's right on the ball. Either he knows more baseball than anybody I've ever met or he's got a sixth sense or something for figuring what's going to happen. No matter how strange a move looks when Case makes it, it turns out just the way he wants it."

On the other side of the dressing room, Stengel was swarmed by writers. Casey made no attempt to disguise his jubilance. "We did it! We did it! We did it!" he yelled above the din

Dozens of reporters descended on New York to cover the Series for their local papers, and understandably a number of them wanted the scoop from the triumphant and always quotable Yankee manager.

He talked strategy for a few moments, then tipped his hat to Durocher and the Giants for a fine season and tough Series.

Were you scared at all? Casey was asked.

Pointing toward Bauer, himself surrounded by writers, "He caught the ball," Stengel said, "and I caught my breath."

In the celebratory clubhouse DiMaggio greeted the reporters who visited his locker with a smile. His mood was markedly different, more amiable, than it had been all season. If this wasn't the toughest championship, it certainly did feel as if it were. He took a sip of beer and softly said to himself, "We won. We won. We won."

Unlike his manager, who was shouting the victorious declaration for all in the room to hear, DiMaggio's words could barely be heard by reporters standing five feet away. Joe was happy. He was a champion once again. And certainly his increased production in the Series' final games aided in improving Joe's temperament. For the moment, Joe wanted to bask in the glow. He brushed aside questions of retirement. Now wasn't the time to discuss that, Joe explained. He just wanted to savor the moment.

Stengel slipped away from the media crush and retreated to his office. A couple a Yankee beat writers followed closely behind. Casey collapsed into a chair, leaned back, and propped his feet up on the desk. He took a drag on his cigarette, and the put a cap on a tough, trying season.

"The Yankees are still the Yankees. You can put that in at the end."

11   BANZAI DIMAGGIO

GUY LOMBARDO AND HIS ROYAL CANADIANS PROVIDED THE TUNES.
Tonight was an evening of celebration, of dancing and drink, some good food, and more drink. The Yankees and their extended family gathered at the Biltmore Hotel immediately following the postgame merriment in the team's clubhouse. The party began at eight in the evening and did not wrap up until four the next morning. Unlike 1950s' post-Series celebration following the Yanks' sweep of the Phillies, there was no hint of bitterness attached to the night. Tonight the microphone was turned off. There were no speeches, not like last year when George Weiss made a few unpleasant remarks to the room, pointed comments directed at players who wanted to discuss their contracts in the midst of the celebratory festivities.

On this evening, 1952 was in the far distance. The question of Mickey's knee being healthy by spring wasn't asked. Nor did anyone overhear a discussion of whether Joe would be back for one more year. Contracts? Not tonight. Not after the trying season this bunch had endured.

Just one night of drink and dance, a few hours to revel in it all.

———

THE OCTOBER 22 ISSUE OF *LIFE* MAGAZINE CONTAINED AN ARTICLE which provided excerpts from Andy High's scouting report on the Yankees.

Stengel had made his way back across the country to his home in Glendale when *Life* published the piece. Though Stengel was far away, a New York reporter reached out for Casey's thoughts on High's much-discussed critique.

"I don't think I ought to say whether it was a good report or a bad report," Casey said. "Maybe it was, and maybe it wasn't. I didn't see anything in there about us going on to win the last three games of the Series. Somebody must have slipped up on that one.

"We had some scouts, too, you know. Only we concentrated on Brooklyn because we figured the Dodgers had such a substantial lead they wouldn't be able to blow it.

"But if something had happened to prevent us from winning the American League pennant, I doubt we would have done anything with our report besides turn it over to the Bronx paper drive."

Though readers found High's evaluations and observations to be fascinating, the publication of this information would prove embarrassing to DiMaggio. When the magazine hit the newsstands, however, Joe was in Japan. Three days after the Series victory, Joe left New York for San Francisco before departing his hometown for an All-Star barnstorming trip of Japan. Prior to leaving New York, DiMaggio had one stop to make. He'd made his decision. The Series was his last hurrah and Joe wanted Dan Topping to be the first to know that he was going to announce his retirement. At 11:00 AM on the morning of the 13th, Joe stopped by the Stadium and paid a visit to Topping in the Yankee owner's office. The two men met behind closed doors for more than two hours, during which time Topping persuaded Joe to give the matter of retirement a little more deliberation.

"You might feel differently a month from now," Topping told Joe. "Why don't you make your trip to Japan and give this matter a little more thought? When you get back to the States in about a month from now, I'll be waiting right here for you. Then we'll talk it over some more."

Out of respect and deference to his friend, DiMaggio agreed to give the subject "a little more thought, and a little more time."

But the decision had already been made; mentally and physically Joe was done. This upcoming Japanese tour was simply a favor for Lefty O'Doul.

He bade Topping goodbye, and along with his teammates Billy Martin and Eddie Lopat, DiMaggio was off to LaGuardia, where the trio would catch a flight to the West Coast.

———

JAPANESE BASEBALL DIDN'T BEGIN WITH LEFTY O'DOUL. THE GAME certainly did prosper in Japan thanks to Lefty's generosity and perseverance, however. O'Doul first visited Japan during an exhibition trip of major league players following the 1931 season that also included stops in the Philippines and China. He continued to visit the Far East at the conclusion of the big-league season every year, culminating in 1934, when O'Doul was charged with the responsibility of putting together a squad of players, a group that wouldn't embarrass.

He started his career on the mound, but Lefty proved to be nothing more than an average pitcher. The switch was made in the middle of his career: from the mound O'Doul was moved to the outfield. At the plate O'Doul shined. He twice led the National League in hitting and in 1929 while with the Phillies, Lefty set a senior circuit record with 254 hits. He finished his sterling 11-year major league career with a .349 batting average. As respected as O'Doul was on the field, he was equally admired off the diamond. O'Doul was highly intelligent, personable, and indefatigable.

The Japanese were reluctant to accept professionals in baseball. A certain distain was held for those who accepted payment for playing the game. The 1934 American touring group, with their good-natured charm and professional behavior, altered the Japanese mindset. With O'Doul's encouragement and assistance, the Tokyo Giants embarked on a 110-game barnstorming tour of the states the following year.

The war put a stop to these goodwill tours. O'Doul, however, believed in the amity that could be fostered through such endeavors, and in 1949 he returned to Japan with his San Francisco Seals. O'Doul thought baseball could provide a form of diplomacy, and this faith was proven out. The Seals' visit was met with great acclaim; hundreds of thousands came out to greet the team when they landed in Tokyo, and at each stop along the tour the ballparks were filled to capacity. O'Doul was even received by Emperor Hirohito at the Imperial Residence during this trip.

"It is a great honor to meet the greatest manager in baseball," the Emperor told O'Doul. "It is by means of sport that our countries can be brought closer together. I want to thank you personally."

Deeply touched by the sentiment expressed by the Emperor, O'Doul responded modestly. "I've waited a long time for this day."

During the pregame ceremonies prior to each contest, the flags of Japan and the United States were raised simultaneously, a major gesture considering this was only slightly more than four years after the conclusion of the war.

The following fall, O'Doul once again made a goodwill excursion to Japan, on this occasion his only companion was Joe DiMaggio. Lefty and Joe's three-week trip encompassed a number of clinics in which the two San Franciscans taught Japanese ballplayers the finer points of the game. These "instructional schools" were held before standing-room-only crowds. At one stop, DiMaggio engaged in a home run hitting contest with "Japan's Babe Ruth," Makoto Kozuru. Before 50,000 fans. Kozuru hit four out of the park while Joe, with his two homers, handled the defeat with good nature.

Prior to arriving in Japan, DiMaggio and O'Doul stopped in Korea and made a number of visits to American troops recovering from battle wounds. One of these stops was to a mobile surgical hospital in Pukchong, the farthest North American front in Korea. These front-line stays, however brief they were, did much to boost the morale of the wounded soldiers touched by the two baseball stars. These visits also bolstered the friendship between O'Doul and DiMaggio. Months later, when Lefty broached the possibility of bringing a groups of players back to Japan in the fall of '51, DiMaggio did not hesitate to sign up for the trip.

For this latest excursion, O'Doul assembled an array of ballplayers from around the Major Leagues and a handful from the Pacific Coast League. In addition to DiMaggio's teammates Martin and Lopat, along for the ride were Joe's brother Dom, Bill Werle and George Strickland of the Pirates, Boston's Mel Parnell, as well as Bobby Shantz, Ferris Fain, and Joe Tipton of the Athletics.

The tour got off to an auspicious start. The chartered flight taking the O'Doul All-Stars from San Francisco to Honolulu was delayed over an hour. Then, once airborne, the plane was in flight for two hours before returning to San Francisco for some mechanical "tinkering." Patiently waiting in Honolulu was a stadium full of fans itching for the start of a scheduled 7:00 PM exhibition between O'Doul's Stars and a pick-up team of Hawaiian semi-pros and U.S. servicemen.

The airplane carrying the All-Stars finally reached Hawaii at 9:45 pm. Behind a police motorcycle escort, the Stars were rushed to the ballpark. Despite the lengthy delay, the 15,000 spectators in attendance remained enthusiastic when the first pitch was tossed at 11:00 PM. They were treated to just one at-bat by DiMaggio, who was struck out on three pitches by semi-pro Tuck Correa. Given the long day of sitting on an airplane and then dashing to the stadium with no chance to catch their breath, it came as little surprise that All-Stars fell to the rag-tag collection of islanders and servicemen, 8–6.

O'Doul's team didn't have much of a chance to recuperate from the long day of air flight and the late night of baseball. At 4:30 the next afternoon the group's Pan American flight touched down at Tokyo's Haneda Airport to a rapturous greeting. Japanese authorities estimated 1 million fans were on hand to meet the All-Stars. A caravan of cars brought the players into the city. The route, which traveled along the Ginza, was flooded with people of all stripes. Men and women, students and laborers, children and the elderly, magnesium flares were fired skyward to announce the arrival of the American baseball delegation. The leading vehicle bearing O'Doul and DiMaggio inched slowly along. What little movement the procession made was due to the diligence of American military police as well as Japanese police. As their car moved slowly along the boulevard, the manager and star player heard the exuberant cries from the crowd, "Banzai O'Doul!" and "Banzai DiMaggio!"

Thousands more looked down from above, from office towers and department store windows. They created a thunderous din and rained down on the parade of cars a cascade of shredded paper. Three blocks off the Ginza another large gathering of fans waited in front of the building that housed the newspaper *Yomiuri Shimbun*. The initial agenda had the American ballplayers stopping at the paper to make a brief appearance with the sponsors of the tour before checking in at their hotel. The local police, however, questioned their ability to control the boisterous crowd and requested that the visit to the *Yomiuri Shimbun* be canceled.

Loudspeakers set up in front of the paper's building announced to the large gathering,

"We thank you for this enthusiastic turnout to welcome the baseball stars, but the authorities concerned thought it better for the players to go direct to their hotel so they are not coming here. Please breakup and go home."

Bypassing the newspaper, the motorcade proceeded directly to the hotel. Before DiMaggio reached his room, a Japanese reporter had finagled his way to the front of the pack and asked Joe if he would return to the Yankees.

"I haven't made my mind up yet," Joe replied with a smile.

Fresh off their four games to two victory over the Nankai Hawks in the Japanese World Series, the Yomiuri Giants were the first team on the tour schedule. The 50,000 fans overflowing Korakuen Stadium saved their loudest cheers for Joe, who had one hit and a walk in three at-bats. It was the younger

DiMaggio, though, who starred. The Boston center fielder scored three times while collecting a double and single.

The following day, the DiMaggio brothers each shared in the spotlight. General Mathew Ridgeway and his wife sat in a light drizzle as Joe and Dom each hit a home run en-route to leading the touring Americans to an 11–0 victory over the Mainichi Orions. Afterward, the elder DiMaggio gave an interview that was aired over the Armed Forces Radio Network. The first question posed was hardly original, nor was Joe's response.

"Well, I feel the same way about that as I did when I talked to Dan Topping in New York right after the World Series. I haven't changed my mind about quitting."

The tour continued from Tokyo to Toyama, Osaka, and Shizuka, before returning to Tokyo on November 10. Fifty thousand fans, including 5,000 American soldiers and occupation personnel, had already found their seats in Meiji Park on a very cold November afternoon when 5,000 wounded Korean War veterans were brought onto the playing field. The servicemen received a rousing ovation as they were led to their auxiliary seats located just below the first-base bleachers. Anticipation was high and the crowd's expectations were met as Japan's Central League All-Stars held a 1–0 lead over the barnstorming Americans when DiMaggio came to bat in the top of the eighth. On the first pitch Joe hit a lengthy foul ball, a blow that only built the suspense. DiMaggio sent Shigeru Sugishita's next delivery deep into the left-field bleachers.

The crowd erupted as Joe rounded the bases, his head down in his usual home run trot. The words that greeted him upon his arrival in Tokyo now serenaded him once again as Joe made his way home.

"Banzai DiMaggio!" they shouted. "Banzai DiMaggio!" Ten thousand years of life....

When he reached the dugout following his home run, DiMaggio said to his traveling teammates, "That's it gentlemen. That's my farewell."

Following the game, Joe announced to the press that he was flying back to the United States immediately. He was headed home for business reasons which "have nothing to do with my contract" with the Yankees, Joe insisted as he spoke with reporters after the game.

"I've certainly enjoyed Japan, but I simply have to get back to the States."

He had barely set foot on California soil when the question began anew.

"I'll make up my mind when I'm good and ready," Joe snapped at reporters. "I'll make up my mind and then do as I please."

When will you meet with Dan Topping?

"I'd rather not talk about it," DiMaggio responded.

He then excused himself. Joe wanted to go see his son. Nine-year-old Joe Jr. was attending the nearby Black-Foxe Military Institute.

———

THE END CAME OFFICIALLY ON TUESDAY, DECEMBER 11. THE Yankees called a press conference at their 5th Avenue suite in the Squibb Tower and every newsman understood the reason behind the gathering; Joe was finally hanging them up. A few moments before two o'clock, Red Patterson made his way through the room jammed full of media. The Yankees P.R. man handed out a release to the reporters. The statement was brief. "Joe DiMaggio today announced his retirement as an active player." The press release continued on, reciting Joe's career statistics and highlights.

There were turkey sandwiches set up for the media, cheesecake, too. And though baseball writers liked nothing better than a free meal, it was Joe D., seated beneath a large wall mural that highlighted his playing career, who garnered the attention of the room. "Why are you quitting?" DiMaggio was asked.

In a voice barely audible in the crowded room, Joe responded, "I no longer have it."

"I know I was beginning to slip as far back as three years ago," DiMaggio continued. "The old timing was beginning to leave me and my reflexes were beginning to slow up.

"I began to think seriously of retiring last spring," DiMaggio admitted to the room packed with photographers, writers, and newsreel men. "By the end of the season I had made up my mind definitely. I told Dan Topping of my decision to quit. He asked me to think it over for a couple of months. Out of deference to Dan, I did as he asked. It had become a chore for me to play. I found it difficult getting out of bed after a night game.

"Right now I feel wonderful," Joe said with a grin. "But I can't forget those torturous days and nights of agony. No. I've played my last game of ball and I have no regrets. I feel that I have reached the stage where I can no longer produce for my club, my manager, my teammates, and my fans.

"When baseball is no longer fun, it's no longer a game."

A writer asked Joe if he thought Mantle could make the switch from short to center.

"Why not?" DiMaggio replied. "I made the jump from

shortstop to center field." DiMaggio then told the gathering that he, in fact, broke in with the Seals at short in the final days of the 1932 season. The following spring Joe remained at the position, playing every exhibition game at shortstop until the final two days of training camp.

"Then I went in to pinch-hit for the right fielder and when the inning was over I started for the clubhouse, figuring I was through for the day. [Seals manager Jimmy] Caveny intercepted me and yelled, 'Get back there in the outfield.'"

"It can't be done overnight," DiMaggio added, "Mickey has the speed, the arm, and the aptitude; he can do it in time."

"Joe, did you spend any time counseling Mantle?"

"No. It was never necessary. Nobody knows more about outfielding than Tommy Henrich and besides, Mickey was not ready for center field a year ago."

For the better part of an hour Joe stood by, patiently posing for photographs and answering questions. Standing on each side of DiMaggio were Yankee co-owners, Dan Topping and Del Webb. Webb appeared to be on the verge of tears when he spoke to reporters.

"We did everything we possibly could to get him to stay," Webb said, "but we couldn't force him."

Like his partner Webb, Topping was also having difficulty accepting DiMaggio's decision.

"I was hopeful until late yesterday that Joe would change his mind," Topping said. "I don't know why he had to quit, sick as he was last season he did better than most of the players hanging around."

Despite their friendship, Topping failed to grasp the driving force behind DiMaggio's greatness, how he carried himself on and off the field, exactly what it was that made him exceptional. Joe was not just "another player." If he couldn't be *Joe DiMaggio* any longer, then the time had come to step away from the game.

Casey Stengel was there too, posing for photos with the retiring legend and saying all the right things.

"He was more than just a player," Casey said of DiMaggio. "He was our silent leader. Without him we couldn't have won the pennant last season. He always gave everything he had, no matter how badly he felt. He served as an inspiration to the rest of the club. He was more than just a player. He was an institution. It was a privilege to serve as his manager.

"Naturally this changed my plans. Of all the players I ever had, DiMaggio was the greatest and to get a man to replace him I'd have to go pretty far. There isn't an outfielder in the American League as good as he was."

But there was no sense in being maudlin; Stengel was already planning for next spring. His new center fielder, Casey declared, would be Mantle.

"He is very young, but he has a lot of promise," Stengel explained "The kid deserved a shot. Sure he's green. He can throw good and hit both ways. He developed faster than any ballplayer I've ever seen last season. It was amazing in view of the fact he had been a shortstop. He may continue to pick up just as fast, but if he can't make it we have others."

Word reached Commerce, Oklahoma, that the torch had been passed. Mantle had just come in from an afternoon of rabbit hunting when a reporter informed him of Stengel's declaration.

"I've been hearing that for a long time from a lot of people," Mantle said. "I was expecting it. It won't be the same without

Joe, though. It will be impossible for anyone to take his place—
he's that great.... They can count on me doing the best I can. I
promise that much.

"All I can do is my best, and I'll sure give that," Mickey emphasized. "It's a great break for me. Anybody would be crazy if
he didn't want to play with the Yankees. But I sure hate to see
old Joe leave the game."

Mickey was still recovering from the devastating knee injury he incurred during the second game of the Series. In the
weeks following Game 6, Dr. Gaynor changed his diagnosis;
a torn muscle, torn ligaments, torn tendons...exactly what the
damage was Gaynor couldn't pinpoint with certainty. The bottom line was, the leg would never be the same. Mantle would
never again run with the same blazing speed that left on-look-
ers speechless.

The Yankees wanted a second opinion and on October 22
Mantle was sent to Johns Hopkins Hospital. Specialists at
Johns Hopkins concurred with Mantle's New York physi-
cians. The catastrophic injury didn't require surgery, only rest.
For six weeks in the aftermath of the calamity, Mantle wore a
full leg brace that locked at the knee. During the first week of
December, the Yankees asked Mickey to come to New York so
Dr. Gaynor could check his knee.

"Examination reveals the cartilage was not damaged, and
that the torn ligament on the inner side of his right leg has completely healed," Gaynor reported.

Mickey was outfitted with a brace to wear for a couple of
weeks, a "knee cage" as it was known. Once he discarded the
brace, Gaynor prescribed a series of exercises and also gave
Mickey a weighted boot to strengthen Mantle's weakened leg

muscles. The Yankee physician assured reporters that Mickey would be completely healed and ready for spring training.

Ready for spring training?

Mickey took the doc's word for it, but Florida and the start of spring training was less than three months off and he could barely walk at that moment.

With little else to do while recovering, Mickey had time to think—far too much time to think.

It seemed as if he'd lived a lifetime in the last 12 months. There was the storybook beginning, those weeks when it seemed as if the whole city of New York was behind him. That was followed by the overwhelming feeling of failure and rejection that came with the demotion to Kansas City. He hit the bottom and almost quit, but instead he refocused and did some growing up. The Yankees called him back and he contributed down the stretch for the pennant. What should have been the pinnacle of the season, the World Series, was shattered when his knee was decimated.

Yes, he was a world champion now, but it didn't quite feel like he'd always dreamed it would.

Right now all he could do is wonder.

Would his father live to see him play another game?

Would his knee recover for him to once again play with natural abandon?

Could he possibly live up to the expectations that came with replacing Joe DiMaggio in center field?

He was filled with anxiety and apprehension.

The one certainly Mickey Mantle could count on? Life as he once was knew it would never be quite the same.

ACKNOWLEDGMENTS

MY PRIMARY RESOURCE FOR THIS PROJECT WAS THE WORK OF numerous sportswriters who were there and watched the 1951 New York Yankees baseball season unfold. The beat writers provided expert game coverage and behind-the-scenes material, while the columnists supplied their unique opinions on the events and people that are covered in this book.

No book of this nature is written without the assistance and cooperation of others.

I would like to thank Charley Feeney, Bob Wiesler, Jerry Coleman, Bill Skowron, and Stan Isaacs.

James Zobel of the MacArthur Foundation

David Clark of the Truman Library and Museum

Bill Dean, I appreciate all your help with this project.

Special thanks to Yankee historian and all-around good guy Marty Appel. Marty was always there to answer my questions and to steer me in the proper direction.

And finally, my bride, Mickie. Thanks always for your love and encouragement.

You and me… it's a beautiful thing, this life we have.

BIBLIOGRAPHY

National Baseball Hall of Fame and Research Library—Subject files: Mickey Mantle, Joe DiMaggio, Casey Stengel
Society for American Baseball Research—Oral History Project
Joyce Sports Research Collection—University of Notre Dame
Eugene C. Murdock Baseball Collection—Cleveland Public Library
Joe DiMaggio—FBI file
Mickey Mantle—FBI file
Harry S. Truman Library and Museum
General Douglas MacArthur Foundation
www.baseball-reference.com

BOOKS

Allen, Maury—*Where Have You Gone Joe DiMaggio: The Story of America's Last Hero* Dutton, 1975

Appel, Marty—*Pinstripe Empire: The New York Yankees From Before the Babe to After the Boss* Bloomsbury, 2012

Cramer, Richard Ben—*Joe DiMaggio: The Hero's Life* Simon and Schuster, 2000

Golenbock, Peter—*Dynasty: The New York Yankees 1949–1954* Prentice Hall, 1975

Kennedy, Kostya—*56: Joe DiMaggio and the Last Magic Number in Sports* Sports Illustrated Books, 2011

Leavy, Jane—*The Last Boy: Mickey Mantle and the End of America's Childhood* Harper: 2010

Mantle, Mickey with Herb Gluck—*The Mick* Doubleday, 1985

Mantle, Mickey and Ford, Whitey with Joseph Durso—*Whitey and Mickey: A Joint Biography of the Yankee Years* Viking Press, 1977

Whittingham, Richard—*The DiMaggio Albums* Putnam, 1989

NEWSPAPERS

Arizona Republic
Boston Globe
Chicago Daily News
Chicago Defender
Chicago Tribune
Christian Science Monitor
Cleveland Plain Dealer
Hartford Courant
Los Angeles Herald
Los Angeles Times
Newsday
New York Daily Compass
New York Daily Mirror
New York Daily News
New York Herald Tribune
New York Journal American
New York Post

New York Times
New York World Telegram
St. Louis Globe Democrat
San Francisco Chronicle
San Francisco Examiner
The Sporting News
Washington Post

MAGAZINES

Baseball Digest
Baseball Magazine
Colliers
Confidential
Life
Look
Sport Magazine
Time